Tara Medley

Start Where They Are

Differentiating for Success with the Young Adolescent

Karen Hume

PEARSON

Education
Canada

Toronto

Library and Archives Canada Cataloguing in Publication

Hume, Karen
        Start where they are : differentiating for success with the young adolescent / Karen Hume.
Includes bibliographical references and index.
ISBN 978-0-13-206913-7
1. Individualized instruction. 2. Middle school teaching. 3. High school teaching. I. Title.
LB1031.H86 2008   373.139'4   C2007-903870-0

ISBN-13: 978-0-13-206913-7
ISBN-10: 0-13-206913-X

Vice-President, Publishing and Marketing, School Division: Mark Cobham

Vice-President, Marketing and Professional Field Services: Anne-Marie Scullion

Publisher, Pearson Professional Learning: Debbie Davidson

Research and Communications Manager: Chris Allen

Director, Pearson Professional Learning: Terry (Theresa) Nikkel

Project Co-ordinator, Pearson Professional Learning: Joanne Close

Developmental Editor: Elizabeth Salomons

Senior Production Editor: Jennifer Handel

Copy Editor: Laurel Sparrow

Proofreader: Karen Alliston

Production Coordinator: Sharlene Ross

Composition: David Cheung

Permissions and Photo Research: Christina Beamish

Art Director: Alex Li

Art Coordination: Carolyn E. Sebestyen

Cover and Interior Design: Alex Li

Illustrators: David Cheung, Kevin Cheng

Cover Image Credit: Ellen Schuster/ The Image Bank/Getty Images

e-Learning Team

Publisher, e-Learning: Sandra Nagy

Managing Editor, e-Learning: Kelly Ronan

Production Coordinator, e-Learning: Shonelle Ramserran

Manager, Integrated Media Solutions: David Jolliffe

Supervisor e-Learning Resources: Laura Canning

Senior e-Learning Resources Developer: Robin Blair

Videographer: The Shooting Eye

6 7 8   11 10 09

Printed and bound in Canada.

Contents

CHAPTER 1

The What, Why, Who, When, and Where of Differentiated Instruction 1

CHAPTER 2

Start Where You Are: Teacher Beliefs and Knowledge 18

CHAPTER 3

Start Where They Are: Characteristics of Young Adolescents 36

Contents (continued)

Contents (continued)

About the Author

In the tradition of the quizzes that begin each chapter, find the one lie about the author in Four Truths and a Lie, below. Unlike the quizzes, the answer is not provided, but if you meet Karen during one of her many presentations, she will be happy to tell you which one is the lie.

Four Truths and a Lie

1) Karen won two provincial awards for a year-long integrated and differentiated program developed for her grade 7/8 class.

2) The largest of Karen's three St. Bernard dogs wears a 40" collar. His name is Goliath.

3) Karen has written and published on adolescent literacy and action research.

4) Karen loves to drive long distances.

5) Karen is currently on leave from her role as Education Officer at the Durham District School Board, a large board in southern Ontario.

For more information about Karen's professional activities, go to **www.pearsonprofessionallearning.ca**.

Acknowledgments

Fingerprints are the perfect symbol of differentiation. No two prints are exactly alike, even in identical twins. They are the most notable indicators of our uniqueness. And they are consistent; fingerprints remain the same throughout our lives, making them, in ancient times, as valid as signatures on legal documents.

Fingerprints are also a perfect symbol for acknowledgments because this is a place where authors want to thank those individuals who have offered the unique and consistent support that only they can provide.

Thank you to the wonderful team in the Pearson Professional Learning Division—Vice President, Anne-Marie Scullion; Publisher, Debbie Davidson; Project Co-ordinator, Joanne Close; and Research and Communications Manager, Chris Allen. They all demonstrated huge commitment from long before the first word was written, and they continue to do so to this day. Thanks to Alex Li at Pearson for the great cover and interior design, to Craig Featherstone for his help with the Success for Every Student model, and to Jen Handel and the production team for tolerating an author with a not-so-hidden desire to dabble in layout and production.

When we decided to produce an e-book, Pearson's E-Learning Publisher, Sandra Nagy, and Managing Editor, Kelly Ronan, made that process fun and fairly effortless on my end—no small feat given the huge amount of effort required on their parts. My concern about where we would get video footage from a variety of grade levels and subject areas lasted for about a millisecond, then my friend Deb Cummings stepped in and recruited a wonderful group of teachers. You will read their words in this book and see their images in the e-book. Thank you to Janice De Fazio, Donna Moreau, Nancy Porteous, Kelly Porter, Shauna Power, Bill Ray, Kathy VanDewark, Bob Harrison, and, willingly drummed into service at the eleventh hour, Cathy Correll and Melissa David. Thanks also to the many consultants and administrators involved in this project.

I am so lucky to have people in my life who provide unwavering encouragement and support. Just as we leave our fingerprints behind on everything we touch, the following people have made a significant and positive difference to me in this year of many "firsts." Forever thanks go to my parents, Gerri Hume and Ross Hume, and to my friends, Kim Airdrie, Roberta Dick, Brad Ledgerwood, Demetra Saldaris, and Eileen Sheppard. It is a pleasure to be able to acknowledge and thank you for your many kindnesses through the tough days and the exhilarating ones.

The careful reading by reviewers from across the country is gratefully acknowledged. A second reading will show you the many places where your insightful comments have made this a better book.

Review Team

Rey Sandre, Teacher
Toronto Catholic District School Board

Lisa Rinke, Teacher
School Distrct 43, Coquitlam

Laurie Gatzke, Vice Principal
Regina Board of Education

Dr. Michael R. Muise, Principal
Algonquin and Lakeshore Catholic
District School Board (Kingston)

Denise Calvert, Co-ordinator of
Special Education
Simcoe Muskoka Catholic District
School Board

Carol Hryniuk-Adamov,
Reading Clinician
Winnipeg School Division

George Clulow, Co-ordinator,
Instructional Services Dept.,
AVID District Director
Langley School District #35

Diane Gagley, Consultant, Special
Needs
Calgary Catholic District School Board

Deidre McConnell, Assistant Principal
Calgary Board of Education

Lynn Landry, Literacy Leader
Halifax Regional School Board

Introduction

There are thirty-two books about differentiated instruction on my bookshelf, along with five videotapes, three audiocassettes, and two collections of articles. A number of these resources are by Carol Ann Tomlinson, the educator and author who defined the field a dozen years ago and whose work informs and deepens our understanding of how to recognize and teach the individuals in our classrooms—without individualizing our instruction. In the arena of authors writing about differentiated instruction, Tomlinson is first among equals; we walk in her footsteps and are in her debt.

If Tomlinson's work is as foundational as I claim, and if you've read anything by her or by anyone else writing about differentiated instruction, why read *Start Where They Are*?

Four Good Reasons to Read This Book

1. Differentiated instruction is situated in the context of an effective classroom.

I have worked with many excellent, confident, knowledgeable teachers. Without exception, they tell me they're not sure they really understand differentiated instruction. Is it what they have always been doing, but with a different name? Is it simply a matter of giving students choice in how they demonstrate their learning? Surely there must be more to it. If so, what are they missing?

At the root of these questions is a concern all teachers share. There are just over 1000 hours of instruction available in the typical school year. Some of those hours are lost to non-instructional activities and various disruptions. In fact, some researchers (cited by Marzano, 2003, p. 25) suggest that the number of instructional hours actually available is closer to 696 per year, *at best*. With so much to do and so little time to do it, we have to make every moment count. How can we be sure differentiated instruction is worth our energy and our students' time if we don't know whether we're doing it correctly?

It is a legitimate concern. A cornerstone of differentiated instruction is that you have to be effective first and differentiated second. Every example in this book is therefore of a practice known to enhance student achievement. Where differentiation is appropriate, the practice is then varied to meet the needs of individual learners. If you do not differentiate the activities, you can be confident that any of the activities you try will enhance your students' achievement. If you do differentiate, and I sincerely hope you will, you can take your time learning how to do so appropriately, all the while knowing that you are delivering an effective program.

2. *Start Where They Are* is written exclusively for teachers of grades 6–9.

Young adolescents are at a unique point in their development. They're not simply a little bit older than a grade 5 student and a little bit younger than a grade 10 student. They have developmental needs that we, as their teachers, have both the ability and the responsibility to address.

Authors such as M. Lee Manning and Rick Wormeli, along with organizations such as the National Middle School Association, seek to redress the imbalance between the dearth of professional books for teachers of this age group and the plethora of those for teachers of younger students. This book joins that chorus, but also sings a solo by talking about effective differentiated instruction exclusively for grade 6–9 students. All the examples are for this specific age group; no modifications are necessary.

3. This book is written so that you can *start where you are.*

Imagine you had access to a work coach—someone totally dedicated to helping you achieve your goals as a teacher without requiring that you work at it 27 hours a day. Or fast-forward into the future where you can key a few details into a computer and print a professional book or burn a DVD with a multimedia program developed just for you, including exactly what you want to know and presented in the style most helpful to your learning preferences and needs.

If you had access to a coach or to an intelligent, responsive computer, how would your teaching life be different? For starters, your work would be more focused because you'd be able to zero in on exactly what you need, and when and how you need it. If you wanted to, you would get closer to working synergistically in ways that are deep and meaningful. If you chose to keep doing what you've always done, your coach or the computer would help you polish your current practice or articulate to yourself and others how what you are doing is beneficial to your students. If someone worked with you in ways that recognized your individuality, it is reasonable to think that your work life would become considerably more satisfying, less frustrating, and more manageable in terms of time and energy.

It does not make sense to learn about differentiated instruction in an undifferentiated, one-size-fits-all manner. This book must meet your needs—whether you're about to start your teaching career next week or to retire from teaching next year; whether you have never heard of differentiated instruction or know so much that you should be writing your own book; and whether you're a learner who just wants a few new practical ideas or one who wants lists of further readings so that you can immerse yourself in theory as well as practice. This book is structured to meet the needs of every learner so that you can start where you are and progress at your own pace.

4. Assessment and instruction are interwoven.

Because I know nothing about you—not your working environment, your background, or even your expectations of this book—I have to count on your knowing your needs and learning preferences well enough to meet me halfway and choose what works for you from the options provided in this book. All the chapters have self-assessments to assist you in determining where you are now in your understanding and use of various differentiated instruction concepts, and what might be logical, manageable next steps.

Similarly, information about assessment before, during, and after learning is embedded throughout the book in the places where you'll be thinking about how to assess your students.

Blackline Master **Study Group**

How To Use This Book

Start Where They Are is designed to meet your needs. There are more than 70 blackline masters on the CD accompanying this book. Some are intended for your use, either on your own or in a study group or professional learning community; others are intended for use with your students.

You will see other icons, marked "Classroom," "Author Talk," "Reflect," and "Student Talk." If you have the e-book version of *Start Where They Are*, these icons will be "live," giving you access to video footage of Canadian teachers at work in their classrooms. It is so much easier to think about differentiated instruction when we can see it in action.

I encourage you to read Chapters 1 and 2 in their entirety. Chapter 1 explores my model of differentiated instruction, giving you the organizational framework you need when making choices about how to read the rest of the book. Chapter 2 provides an opportunity for you to clarify your beliefs and to chart your reading and learning plan.

At that point, you may want to zero in on one particular area. Say, for example, you are most interested in powerful instructional strategies. You can do the self-assessment for that topic, and then read just those pages in the book. On the other hand, you could do all the self-assessments together, create a plan, and focus on a different topic each term. Or maybe you just want to read the book from start to finish. As you make decisions about how to use this book and as you read, I encourage you to be aware of your preferences as a learner. The deeper and more thoughtful your understanding of your own learning needs and preferences, the easier it is for you to recognize them in your students.

Human beings differ with their gifts and talents.
To teach them, you have to start where they are.

—Yuezheng in 4th century B.C. Chinese Treatise, Xue J

The What, Why, Who, When, and Where of Differentiated Instruction

What Is Differentiated Instruction?

Differentiated instruction is effective instruction that is responsive to the diverse learning needs and preferences of individual learners. It is a comprehensive framework or organizing structure for how we understand and enact the teaching and learning in our classrooms—all the teaching and learning, not just the instruction we differentiate.

Definitions often aren't particularly helpful, and this one is no exception. When teachers ask, "What *is* differentiated instruction?" the question really means, "Tell me how this is different from what I'm already doing. What does it look like? What's involved in differentiated or responsive teaching? What does it mean for me, with my students, in my classroom?" We want personalized answers, not generic ones. So I hope you will allow me to be personal and to try to speak to *you* in this book. Although using the term "we" is more inviting and inclusive—and I hope you're planning to read and discuss this book with colleagues; that you're not working alone—the fact is that *you* are making the choices and taking the actions; all I am doing is providing suggestions and cheering you on. Therefore, I will use "you" throughout the book, with apologies in advance for times when it may feel directive.

If you remember only one word of my formal definition of differentiated instruction, I hope you'll remember the word "framework." Differentiated instruction will feel unnecessarily complicated and difficult if it is added to the many "top priority" initiatives you are expected to incorporate into your classroom in a single school year. But if you view differentiated instruction as a framework, it will help your teaching life make more sense and be more coherent. You won't need to juggle competing priorities, trying desperately to keep each ball in the air. You will see where each priority—whether voluntarily adopted or centrally mandated—fits into the overall framework and you will be in a better position to work synergistically.

AUTHOR TALK

A Framework

Panel 1: WELL, I DID WHAT THEY RECOMMENDED FOR STRESS:

Panel 2: I STUDIED ALL OF THE THINGS I HAD TO DO,

Panel 3: AND I ASSIGNED EACH ONE AN A, B, OR C PRIORITY.

Panel 4: HERE'S THE LIST -- 182 As, 2 Bs, AND 1 C. NOW WHAT?

Copyright Grantland Enterprises; www.grantland.net.

"Completely Unsettled, phrasal *noun*: that emotional state that usually follows an Incident in which you Completely Misunderstand what is happening and then Completely Become Confused. Similar to Anxiety*, but without the running away bit."
—*The Pooh Dictionary*

Here is a specific example. Bullying was a big problem at Dan's school, especially among the older students. At the end of the previous school year, the staff had voted to implement a schoolwide, year-long focus on character education the following September. Dan, a grade 7 teacher, had voted in favour of the proposal.

Dan returned to school a few days before the students in September to find the character education initiative in full swing. Posters for September's focus—respect—were everywhere, Dan was asked to volunteer his class to do a skit at the second week's assembly, and there was a teaching kit the size of a small armchair sitting in the middle of Dan's desk.

Dan had been reading about differentiated instruction and was interested in trying some strategies that would help him be more responsive to individual needs, but now, faced with all this extra work, he decided, "I'll keep everything else I do the same, and I'll make this the year for character education. I'll leave differentiated instruction for when I have more time, maybe next year."

Dan's reaction is completely understandable, but he doesn't have to choose. The framework for differentiated instruction that you are going to be introduced to in this chapter will help you think about and organize what you do in your classroom. It's a framework that, quite simply, makes the best possible use of your energy and your students' time and should keep you from feeling overwhelmed.

Differentiated instruction involves multiple points of entry to important, essential work. You must be an effective teacher before you can think about being an effective differentiating teacher.

An effective teacher is one who has a powerful, impressive effect on student achievement. Before you crumble under the pressure of that sentence, recognize that—whether talking about teachers, learning environments, or instruction—effectiveness is measured along a continuum. As long as you are at least halfway along the continuum between highly ineffective and highly effective, you can have a powerful impact on your students' achievement (Marzano, 2003, p. 75).

> "Many things which cannot be overcome when they are together, yield themselves up when taken little by little."
>
> —*Plutarch*

The differentiated instruction framework therefore reflects both an unequivocal focus on what matters—effective teaching that results in high levels of achievement for every student—and great flexibility in how this goal is achieved. The components of this comprehensive framework form the outline for this book. By guaranteeing that the examples presented are effective practices that are then differentiated, you can comfortably *start where you are* with the framework component of your choice, increasing the overall effectiveness of your classroom program, and taking the time you need to gradually incorporate differentiation into your regular practice.

Learn More About Effectiveness

Robert Marzano's factors of teacher effectiveness will be referred to often throughout this resource. If you are looking for an overview of his research results and an explanation of the statistical processes he used to obtain them, begin with *What Works in Schools: Translating Research into Action* (2003, ASCD).

Success for Every Student: The Model

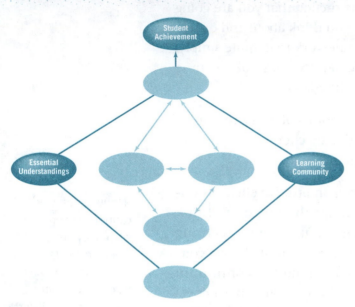

Figure 1.1
Components of the Framework: Essential Understandings and Learning Community

The ovals in the outer diamond represent the conditions of effectiveness that are the preconditions for differentiation. In the left and right corners of the outer diamond in Figure 1.1 are Essential Understandings and Learning Community. The former is what is taught; the latter the context in which teaching and learning take place. Both are required for effectiveness; both hold constant in a differentiated classroom. For instance, Essential Understandings are essential for all students: all students work to the same high standards on the same essential outcomes. Differentiation is in *how* students learn, not in *what* they learn. Similarly, your focus when building a smooth-running classroom Learning Community is on the overall needs of the entire class, not the particular needs of an individual. A classroom managed one individual at a time would be chaotic and ineffective. Chapter 5 explores the Learning Community in further detail and Chapter 6 deals with Essential Understandings.

At the bottom corner of the outer diamond is Teacher Beliefs and Knowledge, as shown in Figure 1.2. Your beliefs about teaching and learning and about the students you teach influence your actions. These beliefs, along with your knowledge of the essential understandings of the subjects you teach, support your effectiveness. Chapter 2 explores the relationship between your beliefs, knowledge, and actions and your students' achievement, in addition to the specific beliefs of a differentiating teacher.

At the top corner of the outer diamond, also in Figure 1.2, is Appropriate Challenge. This is the art of teaching: our ability to hold expectations constant, but to pitch our instruction, based on evidence, to the right degree of challenge and the right amount and kind of support for each individual. This takes us into the territory of the individual student and, therefore, into differentiation. In fact, whenever you see a reference to the individual, you should read it as code for "opportunity to differentiate."

Given the book's title, it should come as no surprise that I believe true effectiveness in helping students achieve educational success requires recognizing and responding to individual differences;

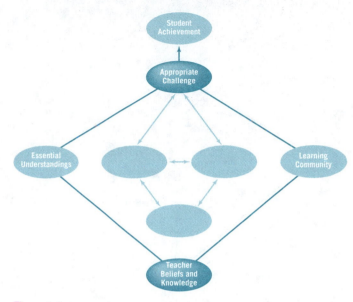

Figure 1.2
Components of the Framework: Teacher Beliefs and Knowledge, and Appropriate Challenge

that you start where they are. Certain teacher beliefs, including a belief in appropriate challenge, are simultaneously conditions of effective classrooms and of effective differentiated classrooms. Chapter 10 deals with Appropriate Challenge.

The components shown in the outer diamond provide the context for effective differentiation; those in the inner diamond are the nuts and bolts of how to do it. Note the arrows that extend in both directions. These reflect the dynamic nature of differentiated instruction; all actions are based on multiple points of reference. This, incidentally, is why teachers sometimes find the concept of differentiation difficult at first.

At the bottom corner of the inner diamond, and central to any discussion of differentiation, is Knowledge of Students, shown in Figure 1.3. Teachers who believe that learning should be student-centred develop an extensive knowledge of their students, and continue to build and act on that knowledge throughout the year. If you are familiar with Tomlinson's model (1999, p. 15), Knowledge of Students encompasses the three aspects of students she says should be paid attention to when

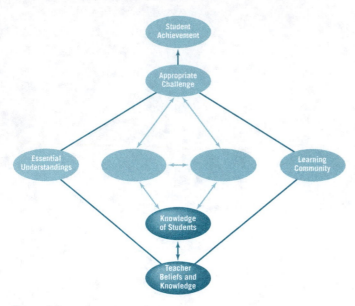

Figure 1.3
Components of the Framework: Knowledge of Students

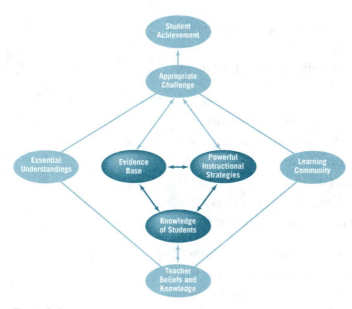

Figure 1.4
Components of the Framework: Knowledge of Students, Evidence Base, and Powerful Instructional Strategies

differentiating: interests, learning preferences, and readiness to learn a particular concept.

You will explore students' learning preferences and interests in Chapter 4; Chapter 7 deals with students' readiness to learn. Since this book is specifically for teachers of grades 6–9, Chapter 3 is included to deal with the particular developmental needs of young adolescents.

Knowledge of Students both informs and is informed by the last two components of the model: Evidence Base and Powerful Instructional Strategies, as shown in Figure 1.4. Using the term *evidence base* rather than the more common term *assessment* emphasizes the wide variety of evidence that a differentiating teacher takes into account, including self-evaluations, teacher reflections, and an ever-increasing knowledge of individual students, along with the full range of formal and informal assessments for, as, and of learning. Because effective differentiation demands that many different kinds of evidence be collected, analyzed, and acted upon throughout the year, references to evidence and examples of useful evidence are found throughout this book. For specific and in-depth discussions divided according to the common categories of diagnostic, formative, and summative, please refer to Chapters 7, 10, and 11, respectively.

All the evidence you gather about your students informs and deepens your knowledge of those students, allowing you to refine the next round of evidence collection so that you have an increasingly rich understanding of what your students know and can do. And, of course, the more you know about your students, the more precisely you can gather evidence of their understanding. For example, if you know that a student is stronger with images than with words, you might provide test questions that allow students to draw rather than write their answers.

Powerful Instructional Strategies should be read as an assertion and a reminder that not all instructional strategies are created equal. Your vision of success for every individual necessitates that you be smart in devoting your energy, creativity, and time to differentiating those strategies proven to have a significant, positive, and demonstrable impact on student achievement. Chapter 8 examines how to design units and lessons to make use of powerful strategies, and Chapter 9 focuses on the strategies themselves.

Notice in Figure 1.4 that these components are connected by a double-headed arrow to demonstrate the inseparable nature of evidence and instruction, and that both are linked to Knowledge of Students. Knowledge of your students naturally influences which instructional strategies you use. For example, if you know that many of your students learn better when working in groups, you are more likely to make extensive use of cooperative learning strategies.

To review the Success for Every Student model, which is just about complete, you can trace the inside diamond for the key elements of differentiated instruction. To ensure you have the appropriate context to access the power of differentiated instruction, trace the outside diamond. Teacher Beliefs and Knowledge, a focus on Essential Understandings, the development of a strong classroom Learning Community, and Appropriate Challenge are all necessary conditions of an effective classroom and necessary preconditions of differentiated instruction.

Success for Every Student Model

To complete the model, as shown in Figure 1.5 on page 9, two more double-headed arrows are needed: one between Essential Understandings and Evidence Base, and one between Learning

Community and Powerful Instructional Strategies. Focusing on essential understandings determines what you gather in evidence of those understandings and how you gather that evidence. The evidence of student understanding, in turn, determines what you do next to enhance that understanding.

Likewise, the strength of your learning community affects the powerful instructional strategies you are able to use, as anyone who has attempted advanced cooperative learning structures too early in the year will attest! At the same time, the instructional strategies you use influence the development of your classroom community. This is often evident early in the school year when, for example, your class works together to produce something to share at a parents' night or open house, or when your use of a strategy uncovers a strength in one of your students and the whole community reconfigures their understanding of that individual.

If you are familiar with Tomlinson's model (1999, p. 15), the centre line in Figure 1.5 is where her three categories of what can be differentiated in the classroom—content, process, and product—could be placed, recognizing that each of her categories requires all three of Essential Understandings, Evidence Base, and Powerful Instructional Strategies.

To test the model, we can take Dan's schoolwide, year-long initiative of character education and do a think-aloud to determine if the framework of an effective differentiated classroom supports the school's character education initiative.

→ I **believe** that young adolescents need to feel safe and comfortable, and be willing to take risks if they are going to **achieve**.

→ Therefore, I will devote a lot of time this fall to building a strong classroom **learning community**. The character education work we are doing will help with that community development.

→ I'm glad we are beginning with respect because my general **knowledge of these students** from other teachers and from my observations of who got into trouble and spent time in the office last year tells me that lack of respect for self and others is an issue.

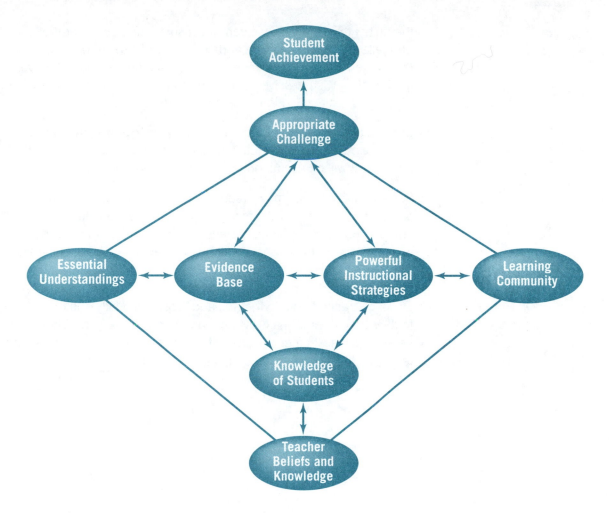

Figure 1.5
Success for Every Student

→ Since differentiation requires that my students be comfortable working at different levels of **appropriate challenge**, I really need to work on the principle of mutual respect. I want my students to see that fairness means everyone getting the support they need to be successful, and that there are many equally valid paths to the same destination.

→ There are **essential understandings** that all my students need to arrive at, but not through isolated and decontextualized character education lessons that have nothing to do with my curriculum expectations. Instead, I can be creative in incorporating these understandings into the units I teach. Maybe we can begin social studies under the umbrella theme of challenge and conflict, and explore how those conflicts were resolved. In science or math, students can use whatever method they wish to solve a problem, and we can compare the variety of approaches that led to the same conclusion.

→ Speaking of comparing, that's one of the **powerful instructional strategies,** so I know that teaching students how to do it at a sophisticated level will be useful throughout their lives.

→ Some of my students may already be quite good at basic comparison, and I'll want to move them more quickly to the advanced forms of comparison, namely, metaphor and analogy. To determine who is where and who needs what, I will build an **evidence base** beginning with a pre-assessment of their ability to compare as well as of the essential understandings of our unit of study. I'll continue collecting evidence, related both to the unit and, observationally and anecdotally, to their behaviour in the classroom and in the schoolyard. Then I will be able to see whether our character education focus is making a difference. I'll use the evidence I gather to determine what I am going to do next, both in our schoolwide focus and in my classroom curriculum.

Planning Your Reading

Use this chart to plan your approach for reading this book. Place checkmarks in the appropriate columns to record your thoughts about your current practice, then prioritize the chapters you intend to read.

"Better go home and make a net, rather than dive for fish at random."
—*Chinese proverb*

	1 This is an area I would like to know more about	2 I'm comfortable with my work in this area	3 This is an area of strength
Essential Understandings (Chapter 6)			
Learning Community (Chapter 5)			
Teacher Beliefs and Knowledge (Chapter 2)			
Appropriate Challenge (Chapter 10)			
Knowledge of Students (Chapters 3, 4, and 7)			
Evidence Base (Chapters 7, 10, and 11)			
Powerful Instructional Strategies (Chapters 8 and 9)			

Review your reading order, thinking about the following questions:

→ Are you planning to read all the chapters or only selected ones?

→ If you intend to read all the chapters, are you going to read them in the order presented in this book?

→ If you intend to read selected chapters only, are all your selections from the first column, or are there some from the second and third columns?

→ Are you going to start with the topic you know the least about, or with an area of strength?

You will find more information about the meaning of your choices in Chapter 2 on page 34. For now, just record your thoughts. Whether your record takes the form of a "well-documented journal" or a few hastily scribbled notes, knowing what and how you think is important to differentiated instruction and makes for fascinating reading down the road.

"What characterizes mind changing under ordinary circumstances is that it occurs largely beneath the surface; unless one has a keen memory or a well-documented journal, one may be surprised to discover that one ever held a contrary point of view."
—*Howard Gardner*

Why Differentiate?

REFLECT

Challenges and Benefits of Differentiated Instruction

Whether you are an experienced differentiating teacher or a novice, some aspects of differentiated instruction are bound to be a significant departure from your current practice, and perhaps a threat to parents' or colleagues' understanding of a "typical" grade 6–9 classroom. Your students' responses will give you plenty of confirmation of the value of differentiation, but in early days you may need to make frequent reference to the following list.

When students...

➔ find out about themselves as learners, they become more independent

➔ start where they are, progress in learning is genuine and lasting

➔ work on tasks at the appropriate level of challenge, they are neither frustrated nor bored, but motivated

➔ study essential content, learning is richer and deeper

➔ learn to appreciate differences, they work more collaboratively with their peers

When teachers...

➔ provide the appropriate level of challenge for each individual, they spend much less time motivating students to work

➔ work to build a classroom community of mutual respect and support, discipline problems decrease

➔ invite students to participate in making decisions, the classroom atmosphere becomes one of teacher and students as supportive co-learners

➔ meet individual needs, their repertoire of instructional strategies grows

➔ become clear about a subject's essential content and don't have to worry as much about covering the curriculum, creativity and pleasure in teaching returns or is enhanced

IN YOUR ROLE

The lists of benefits are not in any particular order. Take a minute to prioritize them for your own classroom.

You will refer to your prioritized list in Chapter 2.

Who Needs Differentiated Instruction?

Robert Sylwester (1995) tells us that we have "designer brains." Scientists at the Salk Institute for Biological Studies (2005) claim that "Brains are marvels of diversity; no two are the same, not even those of otherwise identical twins." John Mazziotta (as cited in Lin-Eftekhar, 2002), who along with fellow UCLA director Arthur Toga led the nine-year project involving more than 7000 participants that created a comprehensive, high-tech brain atlas, says, "No two brains are the same. Their shape. Their size. The way they are organized."

With brains as unique and individual as fingerprints, everyone benefits from having instruction differentiated some of the time. Adults have a fair degree of control over their world, and so can readily self-differentiate without even realizing they're doing it. We choose careers that fit our learning styles: working alone or with others, with words or images, with deadlines or open-ended assignments. We choose courses according to our preferred learning format: online or face-to-face, theoretical or practical, or various combinations of both. Students, however, don't have these opportunities; they need your assistance.

When you anticipate differentiating for individual students in your classroom, the number of possible variations and permutations can be overwhelming. Teachers fear that differentiated instruction is simply special education writ large: an individual education plan for *every* student instead of just for identified students. While it is true that differentiated instruction is responsive to the needs of individual learners, it does not involve individual plans. Rather, it is understanding that there are many ways to learn, recognizing that some students learn differently than others, and providing those students with opportunities to learn in ways that work best for them. This may mean that you offer individuals choice from a limited range of options. It may mean that you cluster students according to their learning preferences and provide a few different ways to process new material. Either way, differentiated instruction means "limited range" and "a few different ways," not 30 individual lesson plans.

> "What should I be but just what I am?"
> —*Edna St. Vincent Millay*

> "Nobody can be exactly like me. Even I have trouble doing it."
> —*Tallulah Bankhead*

Some educators suggest that differentiation should take place when regular instruction isn't meeting a student's needs. I call that *reactive differentiation* and question the advisability and value of waiting until there is a problem before acting. It is so much more difficult to differentiate "in the moment" than it is to be proactive and plan for it. I think of reactive differentiation as a game of volleyball, with the teacher on one side of the net and 30 students on the other. The teacher serves the ball then scrambles madly, trying to volley with 30 individual respondents. It is the stuff of nightmares.

Proactive differentiation, on the other hand, is like a game of chess and the effective teacher is the chess master. Chess players recognize from the outset that the playing pieces on the board are not all alike. They understand the strengths and limitations of each piece, and they are knowledgeable about hundreds of different moves that result in success. Chess-playing teachers make extensive use of proactive differentiation. They think of a way to address the varied learning needs and preferences in their classroom and develop their idea before the instruction is needed. That is not to suggest, however, that everything a student does should be differentiated. There are many, many times when whole-class instruction is appropriate and preferable.

IN YOUR ROLE

List as many instances as you can where you are confident that whole-class instruction is doing a reasonable job of meeting all students' learning needs.

Then make a second list, listing as many instances as you can where differentiation either made a difference or would have if it had been used.

And remember, when you do decide to differentiate, you provide students with a limited range of choices that can broaden as they discover more about what works for them as learners.

Where Is Differentiated Instruction Appropriate?

The short answer is that differentiated instruction is appropriate in every class of academically diverse learners. The shorter answer, then, is *everywhere*. When assessment and instruction are appropriate to a learner's preferences and needs, success is an inevitable byproduct for all learners, including students who are gifted, identified as having learning difficulties, or new Canadians.

Differentiated instruction is appropriate in schools that rely on standardized test scores, in portable classrooms, in impoverished communities, in combined classes, and in situations where you meet with a different group of students every 40–70 minutes. That is not to say that it is not more difficult to differentiate instruction in some environments than in others. It is. Some of the barriers to differentiation might include:

- The physical environment—Your classroom space is too small for the number of students you have, even when they sit still.

- Resources—You have one computer, one set of textbooks, and no budget for the varied resources that you know would enhance differentiation.

- Scheduling—You share your classroom with other teachers and it is a problem to be constantly moving desks.

- Classroom management—You find it a challenge to keep students working and are afraid that choice and varied tasks would result in chaos.

- Time—You feel that your head is barely above water now. You cannot imagine ever having enough time to even think about differentiating, never mind actually doing it.

- Support—You are interested in differentiated instruction but know that your colleagues/administrator/parents would not be supportive.

"Thou hast only to follow the wall far enough and there will be a door in it."
—*Marguerite de Angeli*

You may find that none of these issues are barriers for you, that some or all of them are, or perhaps that you can add another six to the list. There is certainly no point in pretending that barriers do not exist. However, there is also no value in deciding that we are going to be defeated by the obstacles that are in our path. In Chapter 2 we will talk about ways to diminish the obstacles, and in the remaining chapters of this book we will explore a great many practical and not at all time-consuming ways to completely remove them.

IN YOUR ROLE

Identify the barriers you anticipate facing or that you have faced in implementing differentiated instruction in your classroom. When you can clearly define the problem, you are more than halfway toward the solution. Keep your list of barriers for future reference.

Understanding is enhanced when you process new information a number of times and in a variety of ways, and when it is connected to previous knowledge or experiences. To reinforce your understanding of the Success for Every Student model before leaving this chapter, you may wish to:

→ Complete the blank organizer of the model (Blackline Master 1.1), either independently or with the support of the list of components.

→ List each component on a separate sticky note, decide whether any components are missing or unnecessary, and then move the components around until they're in an arrangement that makes sense to you.

→ If you are an experienced differentiated instruction teacher, compare this model to the model you are currently using, noting any similarities and differences.

→ Compare a recent lesson or activity to each component of the Success for Every Student model. Was your lesson or activity an example of differentiated instruction? Which component(s) were the deciding factor in determining whether or not you differentiated?

 Discuss with others how the Success for Every Student model supports the implementation of initiatives your school is working on this year.

Choose a clip about differentiated instruction from the e-book version of *Start Where They Are* or from any other source. Watch for instances of differentiation and places where it might have been helpful. What advice would you give to the teacher in the video clip to help them take an appropriate next step in differentiating their instruction?

Talk about the situations in your life where instruction was differentiated to meet your specific learning needs. What difference did differentiation make to your success in learning new concepts or skills and/or to your belief in yourself as a learner?

Start Where You Are: Teacher Beliefs and Knowledge

QUIZ

Teacher Beliefs and Knowledge

Read each pair of statements. Check the one that most consistently represents your beliefs or actions. Ignore the voice that tells you to check the "correct" answers.

The upside down answers are most representative of the key principles of differentiated classrooms for young adolescents. Compare your responses to the chart you filled out in Chapter 1. You may want to revise your reading plan for this book.

1A There should be little, if any, difference between teaching a grade 8 or a grade 10 student.

1B There should be a significant difference between teaching a grade 8 or a grade 10 student.

2A If some students already know some of the material they are about to learn, I don't take them through it a second time.

2B If some students already know some of the material they are about to learn, they can help the ones who struggle.

3A My students look to me to solve classroom problems such as excessive noise or group disputes.

3B My students and I solve classroom problems together.

4A I tend to use the textbook to sequence my lessons and make sure I'm covering the content.

4B I tend to use the textbook only when it seems appropriate and base my teaching on key questions and principles.

5A You often see different students doing different things in my classroom.

5B You rarely see different students doing different things in my classroom.

6A I believe that my struggling students need consistency, repetition, and practice.

6B I believe that my struggling students need interesting and engaging work.

1B ▶ **Young Adolescents, Chapter 3**

2A ▶ **Evidence Base, Chapter 7**

3B ▶ **Learning Community, Chapter 5**

4B ▶ **Essential Understandings, Chapter 6**

5A ▶ **Instructional Strategies, Chapter 9**

6B ▶ **Appropriate Challenge, Chapter 10**

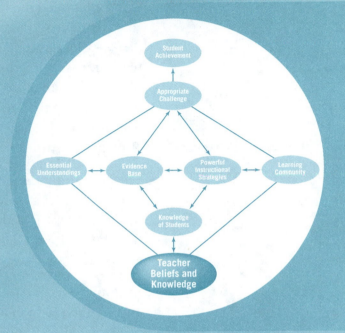

7A When I need to assign marks for report cards, I allow my students many different ways to demonstrate their learning.

7B When I need to assign marks for report cards, I need one consistent way to measure learning.

8A I make use of beginning-of-year diagnostics to establish long-term ability groups.

8B I make use of flexible, short-term learning groups.

9A I am doing my job if I focus on remediating and eradicating student weaknesses.

9B I am doing my job if I focus on developing student strengths.

Mental Models

AUTHOR TALK

Misconceptions Limit Learning

Do you remember any of the misconceptions you had about the world when you were young? I used to believe that whatever direction I happened to be facing was north. My geography teacher wasn't impressed when he learned of this belief just a couple of weeks before presenting me with the high school geography award, but I maintain that my confusion was understandable. I clearly remember my grade 1 teacher physically turning me to face north and saying, "North is the direction you are facing."

Teachers and parents help us uncover and challenge many misconceptions, particularly scientific ones. We learn that north is independent of our egocentric little world, that the moon doesn't follow us, and that the earth isn't flat. We learn to understand the phenomena we've always seen, in a new way.

As adults, we like to believe that we grow out of our limited views and see the world in all its complexity. We don't. Our misconceptions of childhood are supplanted by the mental models of adulthood. Senge et al. (1994, p. 235) describe mental models as "the images, assumptions, and stories which we carry in our minds of ourselves, other people, institutions, and every aspect of the world. Like a pane of glass framing and subtly distorting our vision, mental models determine what we see."

Often mental models serve us well. Believing we understand a new teaching strategy we've been taught allows us to feel comfortable implementing the strategy in our classrooms. If our mental model were that we didn't feel we could try a new strategy until we had an expert, nuanced understanding of it, we'd never try anything new. Duffy (2003, p. 34) calls these mental models "functional" because they "provide relatively effective guidance."

However, there may be times when our models are dysfunctional, incomplete, or just plain wrong. Overriding the distinctions among these three model types is a single similarity: they all produce negative outcomes. Sometimes negative outcomes are limited to the model holders, as the following story by Jane Kise (2006) reveals.

There's a pair of long underwear hanging in the Mission House Museum in Lahaina, Hawaii, where the year-round temperature averages a balmy 30°C. This underwear, and presumably many other pairs just like it, came to Hawaii in the early 1800s with a group of missionaries from New England. Back home, they always donned woolen long underwear on the first day of October and wore it every day until April. It's not surprising that the missionaries packed the underwear. When you're charting new territory, it helps to plan for every contingency. It is surprising, however, that they *wore* the underwear when in Hawaii, every day from October until April.

The story seems unbelievable, doesn't it? It's hard to imagine anyone today being so attached to their long underwear. But, as Kise reminds us (2006, p. 70), "Long underwear beliefs come from sources or influences you aren't aware of or erroneous assumptions that what worked for you, or what worked in another place, will work for others or in a new situation." The New England missionaries felt uncomfortable in a new and stressful situation. Long underwear was a tradition to which they could and did cling.

We all have long underwear beliefs—unconscious, unchallenged beliefs and assumptions formed by our history, our experiences, and our personality. They are often evident when we have a problem to solve; that's when we tend to lock in on something that worked for us before, to interpret a situation through the lens of past experience.

"The world we have created is a product of our thinking. It cannot be changed without changing our thinking."
—*Albert Einstein*

For example, the first time you saw the classic nine dot problem, you may have been stymied.

Connect the nine dots with four straight lines, without lifting your pencil from the paper.

Then you realized, or were told, that you were seeing the nine dots as if they were a box and were assuming that the lines couldn't extend beyond that box. With that information, you might have solved the problem.

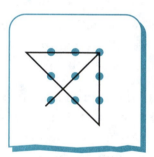

A solution to the nine dot problem

IN YOUR ROLE

For many of us, that's the beginning and end of the nine dot problem. It's a neat party trick, something we can share with our students as a cautionary tale about the problem with assumptions. What if I invite you, however, to identify *six other* erroneous assumptions and successfully solve the problem in six different ways?

Give it a try, and think about the power of our assumptions and our beliefs in controlling what we see. (Hint: Think of the paper as flexible.)

Try the nine dot activity with your students. It is a great way to see who can creatively think beyond their assumptions.

Models of Teaching and Learning

All teachers have mental models about how students learn, what teachers do, our responsibility for a student's success or failure, the behaviours that are indicative of a "good student," et cetera. Consider, for example, how *you* would interpret the question asked by seven-year-old Donald Zinkoff on his first day in grade 2 (Spinelli, 2002, p. 50):

Second grade is no more than a minute old when Zinkoff gets off on the wrong foot with his teacher.

He asks her how many days of school are left. Not in this year but in all remaining eleven years. The teacher, whose name is Mrs. Biswell, thinks it is the most annoying, untimely question she has ever heard. Here she is, all bright and shiny for first day, and this kid in the front row can't wait till he graduates from high school. It's insulting and disrespectful. She comes closer than she ever has before to saying, "That's a dumb question." Instead she says, "Don't worry about it. You'll be out of school soon enough."

Months later, Mrs. Biswell's beliefs about Zinkoff are still being confirmed. He is always laughing, always volunteering answers, most of which are wrong. Mrs. Biswell can't imagine that such a mediocre student could possibly like school; his "reckless enthusiasms" must therefore be "ploys to annoy her."

Mrs. Biswell's interpretation isn't surprising. All of us, whether our models are functional or dysfunctional, do our best to maintain our cognitive equilibrium. We try to make new information work with what we already know. If it's an easy fit, we have no problem accepting new information. Sometimes new information will even expand and enrich our model. But if the information doesn't fit with what we believe, we have to choose either to reject the new information or to reject our model. Which choice do you think most people tend to make?

> "Faced with having to change our views or prove that there is no need to do so, most of us immediately get busy on the proof."
> —*John Kenneth Galbraith*

Depending on our own prior experiences, some of us may have had as much difficulty imagining other reasons for Zinkoff's first-day question as we had uncovering multiple assumptions about the nine dot problem. Mrs. Biswell certainly did, and her early perceptions likely influenced what she noticed about Zinkoff throughout the year. What she didn't know is that Zinkoff's grade 1 teacher began the year telling her students that they had before them two thousand one hundred and sixty days of adventure, of opportunity to learn, to become whatever they want to become. Here is the paragraph after Mrs. Biswell has told Zinkoff not to worry, that he'll be out of school soon (Spinelli, 2002, pp. 50–51):

> *Zinkoff has no intention of worrying about it. And he certainly doesn't want to be out of school. He simply wants to hear her say a really big number in the thousands, so he can feel that his days in school will never come to an end.*

> *He has thought every teacher starts out the school year like Miss Meeks, but now he guesses he was wrong.*

Mental models that limit students unfortunately aren't just found in children's novels like Spinelli's *Loser*. MaryEllen Vogt's research revealed how teachers' perceptions of high and low achievers altered those students' classroom experiences (Vogt, 2000). She found that teachers, when working with perceived

high achievers	low achievers
• encourage student interaction and creative approaches to learning	• prepare structured lessons with few opportunities for creativity
• have warm and personal relationships with students	• emphasize discipline and spend little time on relationships
• offer extensions to learning, including independent learning	• cover less content and acknowledge students for trying hard, but not for the quality of their thinking

Myths and Truths of Differentiated Instruction

"Beliefs and assumptions about teaching, whether in a school or in any other context, are a direct reflection of the beliefs and assumptions the teacher holds about the learner."

—*Jerome Bruner*

Examining Your Models

Mental models are difficult to change because they are invisible. We don't notice them until there's a failure of some sort, and then we tend to attribute the failure to someone or something outside of ourselves.

Here is a model I held on to for quite a long time: I was in high school when the movie *The Paper Chase* was released. It's about a group of students going through law school under the tutelage of the strict and incredibly demanding Professor Charles W. Kingsfield, played by John Houseman. Kingsfield is either going to turn those students into razor-sharp lawyers or he is going to force them to recognize their own inadequacies and quit law school. In scene after scene, we have evidence that our hero (Timothy Bottoms) is rising to the occasion. The light in his dorm room burns late into the night; close-ups show our bleary-eyed hero over a mound of books and papers. We feel the injustice when Kingsfield decimates his arguments, and cheer when he is so well prepared that the professor has nothing to condemn and is forced to extend admiration and respect.

The conclusion I drew from this movie, at the impressionable age of 14, was that intellectuals behaved in a certain way. I wanted to be an intellectual, or at least be seen as one, so I carried around stacks of books, worked late into the night, argued my ideas in every class and, for a while at least, thought I preferred and learned more from sarcastic and insanely demanding teachers.

I started my teaching career in a grade 1 and 2 combined class, and my entrenched mental model of academic rigour clearly wasn't going to work with six- and seven-year-olds. My first teaching experience allowed me to alter my beliefs, fortunately, or my work with young adolescents a few years later would have been very different. I can easily imagine that I might have modelled my role as teacher after Professor Kingsfield (although without the caustic attitude, since that never really did sit well with me), and that I might have viewed a student's inability to meet my academic demands as a failing of either the student or society.

Examining our mental models, and challenging the ones that aren't working for us or our students, is not fun. The alternative, however, as Duffy (2003, p. 36) reminds us, is worse:

> *Left unexamined and unchallenged, mental models influence people to see what they have always seen, do what they have always done, be what they have always been, and therefore produce the same results.*

Implications for the Classroom

It is important to remember that your beliefs can and do have significant implications for how you work with students. Review your responses to the quiz at the beginning of this chapter. Choose one belief that is supportive of differentiated instruction and, if there are any, one that is not. For each belief, consider the implications for classroom practice. Blackline Master 2.1 provides an organizer for this purpose. You will need two copies of the organizer, one for each belief. Note that this organizer is in student-friendly language so that it can also be used by your students as you work with them to develop a classroom learning community. (See Chapter 5.)

IN YOUR ROLE

Are there movies, books, or experiences that influenced your decision to become a teacher? If so, what was it about their portrayal of teaching or learning that captivated you? Are vestiges of those actions evident in your teaching?

 Think about why you became a teacher. Use your memories of the hopes and dreams that called you to our profession to prepare a five-minute presentation for your group. Depending on your interests and strengths, you may want to:

→ create a collage of words and/or images

→ write a narrative about a significant, influential event or person

→ draw a life map charting the steps in your journey

Stages in the Change Process

What do you do if you decide you need to change your mental models? Begin with congratulating yourself. By recognizing the limits of your model and that there may be other ways of thinking about your situation, you have brought your beliefs to the surface where they can be examined. At this point, there are a couple of options. Which one you use depends on your circumstances and on how well you know your own mind.

Option 1

You can act your way into a new way of thinking. Be willing to try a strategy or a technique you don't believe will work. Consider your trial an "experiment" to remove the pressure of succeeding or failing as you are learning something new. Enlist someone to provide you with feedback and support as you practise the new action. If you try to provide yourself with feedback, it is likely that you will resort to your old beliefs.

"Nothing ventured, something lost."
—*Roland Barth*

REFLECT

Taking a Risk

> I LIKE HOMEWORK. HOMEWORK MAKES ME HAPPY.
>
> I DON'T WANT TO GO OUTSIDE. I WANT TO DO MATH PROBLEMS.
>
> BLEHHH
>
> MY BRAIN ALWAYS REJECTS ATTITUDE TRANSPLANTS.

If you are a hands-on learner and like to jump in and "give it a go," you will likely find this option very effective. It is also worth a try if you have recently attended a one-time professional development inservice. Guskey (2000) suggests that if we try new actions after an inservice and see an improvement in student achievement, a change of belief will follow.

"What we have to learn to do, we learn by doing."
—*Aristotle*

Option 2

You can engage in mental "surgery." Gardner (2006, p 145) suggests that you "define [your entrenched view], understand the reasons for its provenance, point out its weaknesses, and then develop multiple ways of undermining that view and bolstering a more constructive one."

This option works if you are a reflective individual with a good understanding of how you learn. "A person who knows her own mind—how it learns best—is most likely to be able to change her mind effectively" (Gardner, 2006, p. 148). It also works for logical mathematical learners who enjoy using reason to find the strengths and weaknesses of various situations.

Reflection

The most valuable time spent teaching . . .
Is not spent teaching.
How can that be?

The most valuable time teaching,
Is the time spent reflecting.
Thinking.
Questioning yourself.

What went well?
What flopped?
What has promise?
What caught the interest of the learner?
What lost the interest of the learner?
Who needs my attention the most?
Why can't I get Robert engaged?
Why does Kim seem to fade into the woodwork?
How can I break through Michael's anger?
Who seems interested enough to explore on their own?

It's strange,
Almost eerie,
How,
In reflection,
The day becomes clearer than the reality
On which it was based.

—David Puckett

If neither of these options appeals to you, ask yourself why. Perhaps an additional small step will make a difference to you. For example, some find that knowing the research base behind the practice is helpful; others find that hearing a colleague's story of the impact of the practice on a student is all the incentive they need. Again, the better you understand yourself as a learner, the easier it will be to find the mind-changing options that work for you.

Learn More About Changing Your Mind

Howard Gardner has been trying to change our minds about intelligence for years, so he understands the difficulty first-hand. His book *Changing Minds: The Art and Science of Changing Our Own and Other People's Minds* (2006, Harvard Business School Press) provides a fascinating theoretical and practical account of his seven factors that will help to change our own and others' thinking.

The problem with these two options is that they make the process of changing your mind sound so simple. It isn't—not for anyone, and especially not as you get older and have some long-held and strongly held perceptions.

Educators know change. We spend a lot of time talking about how much change there is in our profession (lots), how often (constant), and how we feel about it (the gamut from resistant to enthusiastic, depending on personality and circumstances). Change can take a long time—three to five years seems typical—and educators know all about how difficult or even impossible it is to sustain a change in education. There is also the dreaded implementation dip—where what you are trying to change actually gets worse before it gets better.

> "In the process of the ongoing education of teachers, the essential moment is that of critical reflection on one's practice."
> —*Paolo Freire*

AUTHOR TALK

Gardner's 7 Ways to Change Minds

> "All changes, even the most longed for, have their melancholy, for what we leave behind is part of ourselves; we must die to one life before we can enter into another."
> —*Anatole France*

HARK, IS THAT THE WIND OF CHANGE BLOWING AT MY DOOR?

ROAR

I THINK THAT WAS A "YES."

Copyright Grantland Enterprises; www.grantland.net.

I agree with all of these claims about change—for organizations. On an individual level, however, I would suggest that all this chatter about change simply offers an excuse not to change. It may help if you think of change as simply a step in your lifelong learning process. Learning gives you an understanding you didn't have before, a new way of doing something, a new way of looking at some aspect of the world. Quite simply, the changes we are talking about are learning; they are growth. Why would we, of all professions, be resistant to that?

Simply changing your mental models doesn't necessarily mean you are ready to change your actions; the process of change isn't that easy. There are many, many things you know you should do, but don't. But if the change is rooted in your own actions and is owned by you, it doesn't need to be ominous. Let's have some fun with it!

Copyright Grantland Enterprises; www.grantland.net.

Even after embracing a change, many of us live the experience that is one of Barbara Coloroso's often-told jokes: You return from an inservice, full of enthusiasm for the great new ideas you've heard, try one of them out the very next day, and your students groan, "What did you go to *this time*?" The following day or week or month, you are back to doing what you've always done. What happened?

New practices are difficult to sustain because they may clash with your mental models. For example, teachers may have trouble successfully implementing new practices if they don't believe that they can influence how well unmotivated or difficult students learn (Berman & McLaughlin, 1978, cited in Guskey, 2000). Problems can also develop if your experience of the new learning doesn't resonate with who you are as a learner, if you are not supported after the learning or, worse, if your colleagues are scornful about the changes you're trying to make. And, of course, there's the matter of implementing a new practice when in front of 30 students and every spare minute is already used up just getting ready for the next day.

> There is one fault that I must find
> With the twentieth century,
> And I'll put it in a couple of words:
> Too adventury.
> What I'd like would be some nice dull monotony,
> If anyone's gotony.
>
> —*Ogden Nash*

It is helpful to have a theory of change—a sort of road map to guide you through the steps along the way. The road map that makes the most sense for me, because it was researched and developed especially for teachers, is the Concerns Based Adoption Model (CBAM). According to its developers (Hord, Rutherford, Huling-Austin, & Hall, 1987), the change process for an individual involves seven stages divided into four categories of concern.

Stages of Concern

Category	Stage	Label	Key Concern
Awareness	0	Awareness	What innovation? What is it?
			You either don't know about the change (innovation, new practice) or don't want to know about it.
Self	1	Informational	I need to know more about this.
			This is the research stage. You want details.
	2	Personal	How will it affect me?
			At this stage you are worried about how you will fit the new practice into your life and whether you are able to meet its demands (i.e., are you going to feel foolish and incompetent as you attempt to make this change?)
Task	3	Management	How will I find time to do this?
			Your attention is devoted to organizational and management issues, as well as to time demands.
Impact	4	Consequence	How is my use of it affecting students?
			You may start looking at the data, deciding which student outcomes are being influenced, and what further changes you might need to make to improve results.
	5	Collaboration	I would like to discuss my ideas and feelings with others.
			This stage is about collaboration and cooperation with colleagues.
	6	Refocusing	I have an idea for improving it.
			You "own" the innovation now, and understand it so thoroughly that you may decide to make major alterations and improvements to it.

Source: Adapted from Hall and Hord (1987).

The Concerns Based Adoption Model confirms that change is highly personal. While we are dedicated professionals and might therefore imagine that our first response to a proposed change will be "How will it affect my students?," the reality is that without personal meaning attached, no change will ever be effective. The next time you put your own concerns before those of your students and wonder "How will it affect me?," remember CBAM and know that a little self-interest is perfectly normal!

You will be at different stages of concern for different components of the Success for Every Student model. You may find that you don't proceed through the concerns in a lockstep fashion; you may even have several concerns at once. The goal is to work through personal and task concerns as quickly as possible so that you can begin to see the positive impact of effective differentiated instruction on your students' achievement. You do this by identifying your concerns, reflecting on them, discussing them with colleagues, and working on them in your classroom. Since management of time and classroom demands is often an overwhelming concern for teachers under any circumstances, and especially when beginning to differentiate instruction, this book will explicitly address these issues. Look for helpful suggestions in the "In Your Role" and "Book Study" segments.

REFLECT

Defining Characteristics of Teachers Who Differentiate

Starting Where You Are

Appropriate challenge for students means knowing what they understand and are able to do without help, and then pushing them a little beyond that. Appropriate challenge for adults is exactly the same. If you have ever worked with a personal trainer, taken ski lessons, or learned to throw pots or paint landscapes, you know that your success is dependent on your instructor understanding what you can do and helping you progress from that point of competence. Your instructor doesn't expect you to participate in an Ironman competition, ski the black diamond runs, or exhibit at a gallery immediately after your first lesson, but does have every expectation that you will keep improving. By *starting where you are*, your instructor can make that happen.

So far in this book, you have made a preliminary diagnosis of where you are with respect to your knowledge and skill in implementing effective differentiated instruction in your grade 6, 7, 8, or 9 classroom. Just as knowledge of your students is enriched by an accumulation of various forms of evidence, you will add depth and detail to your diagnosis by completing the self-assessment quizzes at the beginning of each chapter. The quizzes will save you time by helping you decide which segments of the book you would like to focus on.

Refer back to the chart you completed on page 11. Use your responses to the quiz on page 18 to confirm or modify how you prioritized your reading. Did you prioritize your reading by selecting chapters from the first column (area of greatest need) to read before the chapters from the second column? If so, you may want to reconsider. Research shows that change is easiest to implement when you start from a position of strength because you experience positive results faster and with less effort. Since differentiated instruction is a framework for effective and responsive teaching, not a new initiative to be added to your existing workload, you are likely already differentiating to some extent in some components of the framework. It makes sense to identify those areas of strength and grow from there.

To establish a reading and learning plan (Blackline Master 2.2):

→ Align your priority chapters to your current stages of CBAM for each chapter. Decide where you are going to begin by determining where the best fit is in terms of time, resources, and energy needed for the next stage.

→ Compare your priority chapter to your prioritized list of benefits of differentiated instruction from page 12. Your priority benefits should align with your chosen area of focus.

→ Finally, compare your priority chapter to the barriers to differentiation that you listed (see page 17). If you keep the relevant barriers in mind as you work on a component, you should find that you are able to think of a number of creative ways to diminish or disregard these barriers.

Note: If you prefer to give yourself a more comprehensive pre- and post-assessment, refer to the 50-item quiz in Chapter 12.

3

Start Where They Are: Characteristics of Young Adolescents

QUIZ

Characteristics of Young Adolescents

Students between the ages of 10 and 14–15 are referred to as *young adolescents*. Their stage of development is called *early adolescence*. Read each pair of statements. Choose the one you believe to be most true. The correct answers are provided.

1A Young adolescents are more alike than they are different.

1B Young adolescents are more different than they are alike.

2A Early adolescence is one of the most dramatic periods of change in the human life cycle.

2B Early adolescence is a time of getting ready for the dramatic changes of adolescence.

1B, 2A Early Adolescence: A Defining Time of Life, pages 39–40

3A Physical maturation implies maturation in other developmental areas.

3B Physical maturation does not imply maturation in other developmental areas.

4A The appropriate response to the growth spurt of young adolescents is competitive sports.

4B The appropriate response to the growth spurt of young adolescents is movement and exercise.

3B, 4B Physical Development, pages 41–42

5A Learning is enhanced when students are allowed to work with friends.

5B Learning is diminished when students are allowed to work with friends.

6A Young adolescents have a heightened ability to read social cues.

6B Young adolescents have a reduced ability to read social cues.

5A, 6B Social Development, pages 43–46

7A A young adolescent's self-esteem is consistently very high or very low.

7B A young adolescent's self-esteem varies with the situation.

8A Young adolescents should be given lots of freedom and choice in school.

8B Young adolescents should be given consistency, predictability, and limited choice in school.

7B, 8A Emotional Development, pages 47–49

9A Early adolescence is a time of unique opportunity for adults to influence students' attitudes and beliefs.

9B Because peers are so important, early adolescence is an inappropriate time for adults to influence students' attitudes and beliefs.

10A Neuroscientists suggest that the courts should consider a young adolescent of 14 as capable of making a reasoned decision.

10B Neuroscientists suggest that the courts should consider an adolescent of 16 or 17 as capable of making a reasoned decision.

9A, 10B ▷ **Moral Development, pages 50–51**

11A The best way to promote learning in early adolescence is to stress its importance to subsequent years of schooling.

11B The best way to promote learning in early adolescence is through hands-on, active experiences.

12A Traditional schooling usually challenges the intellectual capacities of young adolescents.

12B Traditional schooling seldom challenges the intellectual capacities of young adolescents.

11B, 12B ▷ **Cognitive Development, pages 52–57**

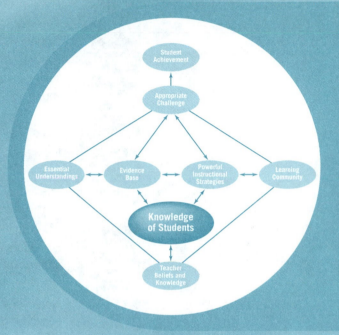

Recognizing Early Adolescence as an Important Developmental Stage	
1762	Jean-Jacques Rousseau calls adolescence a "second birth" in *Emile*.
1904	*Adolescence* is published, in two volumes, by G. Stanley Hall. He thought adolescents were primitive savages.
1977	Joan Lipsitz publishes *Growing Up Forgotten*, bringing attention to young adolescents as a neglected group.
1981	Hershel Thornburg founds the *Journal of Early Adolescence*. It's the first scholarly research devoted to 10- to 14-year-olds.
1980s	The terms *young adolescent* and *early adolescence* come into favour because of their frequent use in Thornburg's work.
Late 80's to present	Educators pay attention to the developmental needs of young adolescents and their impact on classroom practices.
1999	Neuroscientist Jay Giedd helps us to see early adolescence as the second most dramatic period of growth and change in the human life cycle. The first is ages 0–2.
2000	Young adolescents are half a billion strong worldwide and 6.6 percent of the Canadian population. Marketers pay a lot of attention, as do groups such as the World Health Organization.

Source: Adapted from "Timeline: selected milestones in early adolescence thought" from M. Lee Manning, *Developmentally Appropriate Middle Level Schools*, © 1993, Association for Childhood Education International, page 4.

Early Adolescence:
A Defining Time of Life

I f asked to choose a single word to define the young adolescent, many of us might suggest some variation of "hormonal." Young adolescents are, by definition, students going through puberty. The hormonal changes a body goes through as it gets ready for the biological process of reproductive maturation are anything but quiet and unobtrusive; it makes sense that they come to mind when we think of this age group.

However, to describe the defining characteristic of young adolescents as "hormonal" discounts the complexity of this developmental stage and furthers the myth that all 13- or 14-year-olds are alike. That isn't true. *Diversity* is the hallmark characteristic of young adolescents (Thornburg, 1983).

This diversity has not always been acknowledged. Early adolescence wasn't seen as a distinct developmental stage until the 1970s, and even then it wasn't considered particularly important. Researchers used to think that brain development was essentially finished by the time a child was three years of age, so talk of young adolescent development was about growth spurts and hormonal changes. It has only been in the last decade that neuroscientists realized they were wrong and that "the adolescent brain undergoes a massive remodelling of its basic structure, in areas that affect everything from logic and language to impulses and intuition" (Strauch, 2003, p. 13). We now know that early adolescence is a dynamic time, second only to the first two years of life for growth spurts in all areas of development. With every aspect of each student's development on an individual timetable, diversity is inevitable.

"Diversity is the one true thing we all have in common."
—*Anonymous*

Implications for the Classroom

REFLECT

The Young Adolescent Learner

Young adolescents are not a little bit "more" than a grade 4 student and a little bit "less" than a grade 10 student. Because of their unique developmental needs, they can't be taught as if they were simply slightly more mature than junior students or slightly less mature than secondary students. Young adolescents need an education that has been *designed for them*.

IN YOUR ROLE

Mentally walk through a typical day, jotting down each routine and activity in one of the three columns of a chart similar to the one shown here. Alternatively, just make note of those activities that are developmentally responsive. This is a perfect example of easy-to-collect data that have the ability to inform classroom practice, especially if you are surprised by the results.

Discuss your memories of your own early adolescence or your experiences with children going through this developmental stage. Focus on diversity: do you agree that it is the defining characteristic, or would you argue for something else?

Repeat of Earlier Grade	Developmentally Responsive	Prep for High School
Using flashcards to drill multiplication facts. If they haven't got the skills in place, I have to go back.	Had students build the insulated containers to keep their ice cubes frozen; I think hands-on active learning is perfect for this age group.	Told Jeff that no one would be looking over his shoulder in high school, making sure he got his work done. Gave him a zero for last night's homework.

Learn More About Young Adolescents

For often humorous and always heartwarming and insightful perspectives on this age group:

- Linda Perlstein (2003), *Not Much, Just Chillin': The Hidden Lives of Middle Schoolers*. Toronto: Random House.

- Faith Conlon and Gail Hudson, eds. (2005), *I Wanna Be Sedated: 30 Writers on Parenting Teenagers*. California: Seal Press.

Physical Development

You are daily confronted with evidence of the massive physical diversity that marks the period of early adolescence: the grade 7 girl who towers above her male peers; the boy whose voice deepens six months before his best friend's. Physical growth spurts, made evident by rapid changes in weight and height, happen first to girls around age 12 and then to boys around age 14. Over the full span of adolescence, students may gain more than 20 kilograms and grow 25 to 30 centimetres. Although 9 out of 10 girls and 4 out of 5 boys achieve puberty by grade 8, the rate of development is so variable that it is entirely possible for a grade 7 class to contain, biologically speaking, women, men, and children. There is no other time period in the entire human life cycle that rivals this age group for physical diversity.

I remember, with regret, telling my then 10-year-old niece that she was too big to sit in my lap after taking one too many knees in the chin. Because she was already taller than her 155 cm aunt, I mistakenly assumed that her emotional maturity matched her physical maturity. I wish I had known then that a physically developed body does not mean that a young person is emotionally or cognitively developed.

Inevitably, though, the process of physical development does mean that young adolescents are restless and fatigued. This is due to hormonal changes; it cannot be controlled by your students. The solution is movement and exercise, but not competitive activities unless you can ensure that competitors are evenly matched. Competitive activities that require size and stamina for success are unfair when physically immature students are pitted against their physically mature classmates. The experience can be particularly unsettling for friends who used to be physically matched and can no longer compete against each other fairly.

Implications for the Classroom

As you set up your classroom, take into account the lack of coordination and the discomfort that are byproducts of growth spurts. Make sure there is ample room between desks for students to extend their arms and legs. Students need lots of opportunity to move around the classroom. If you don't provide it, they will take it in repeated trips to the washroom or water fountain. Keep them in the room and learning by incorporating physical activity into academic lessons.

De-emphasize competitive activities for a while and encourage activities that allow equal participation.

For Example

Kathy uses a text-mapping activity to help her grade 6 and 7 students understand how to read textbooks from different subject areas. Students gather at the board as Kathy models the activity, then disperse in small groups to various corners and surfaces of the classroom where they map chapters of their history, geography, science, and math textbooks.

Keep them in the room and learning by incorporating physical activity into academic lessons.

IN YOUR ROLE

Take some time to observe a student who is physically out of step with his or her friends. What do you notice about the interactions within the group? Specifically, how is the student you are observing handling the physical differences? Is he or she drawing attention to them or ignoring them? What are the friends doing and saying? Is there anything from the Implications for the Classroom suggestions that might help the individual or group you are observing?

 If you find it helpful to focus on one student, continue observing that student throughout this chapter, observing his or her physical, social, emotional, moral, and cognitive development. This activity will show you the interconnectedness of various developmental characteristics. You can use Blackline Master 3.1 to note selected characteristics and chart the implications for classroom practice.

Social Development

Social networks enlarge during early adolescence; most students begin to expand their circle of friends and spend more time with them. Friendships start the shift from same sex to opposite sex and allegiances shift from parents to peers. Peer influences, positive and negative, are apparent in students' speech patterns, clothing choices, and behaviour.

It seems ironic that, just at the time when students want to distance themselves from their parents to assert their individuality, they tend to behave most like their peers. Of course, the significant variations in physical development contribute to this behaviour. A slowly maturing girl who notices that the early maturing girls have more friends, or a slowly maturing boy who doesn't yet have the coordination to skateboard like his early maturing peers, will find a way to fit in, by whatever means necessary.

Conforming to a peer's standards doesn't seem the ideal environment for learning, especially if those standards are low. It may not make sense to allow friends to work together if, for example, you have the sense that one student is going to imitate another student's poor work ethic through a desire to belong. That said, friendships are crucial to the young adolescent's social development. When possible, use cooperative learning structures to allow students to work with friends and to put students in situations that encourage new friendships.

Adolescents

I
do
see
them:
lively,
young,
growing
by leaps
and bounds;
bursting out
of poorly sewn,
mass-produced jeans,
to become individuals;
secure in their uniqueness;
No longer dependent on parents
Or the uniformity of their own conformity:
Castings dissatisfied with the constraints of the mold.

—David Puckett

Note the title. Our students are working toward the adolescent's recognition of uniqueness.

> "You don't have to suffer to be a poet. Adolescence is enough suffering for anyone."
> —John Ciardi

We also need to realize that, no matter how much we prepare them for successful group activities, young adolescents can have difficulty in these situations because they may literally see the social world differently than adults do. The cerebellum is the part of the brain that recognizes social cues and handles social interactions. Jay Giedd, neuroscientist at the National Institutes of Health, has discovered that the cerebellum is the last part of the brain to develop. Neuroscientist Robert McGivern and his colleagues found that "as children hit puberty, around eleven or twelve, the speed at which they can identify emotions drops by as much as twenty percent" (Strauch, 2003, p. 68). Young students need adults to be positive role models for many things, not the least of which is helping them to interpret social cues they may misinterpret. As Strauch suggests (2003, p. 68), "Lacking sufficient experience that would help them correctly sort out social cues and lacking a fully developed and functioning prefrontal cortex that can provide context (perhaps she frowned at me because she is having a bad-hair day or because her boss yelled at her and not because she hates me), they may not always get it right."

Implications for the Classroom

Provide students with experiences that build trust and teach social skills. *Discovering Gifts in Middle School* (2001) by TRIBES originator Jeanne Gibbs is one example of a cooperative learning book filled with inclusion activities for young adolescents.

Role plays help your students explore various ways of dealing with challenging situations, including times when they may need to rethink their loyalty to peers.

For Example

Bryan uses simple improvisations in his classroom. Here is one example:

> The Scene: Two students are talking after having stolen a bicycle.
>
> Goal A: You want to return the bicycle before anyone realizes it is missing. You feel guilty about having taken it.
>
> Goal B: You believe that since no one has noticed the theft yet, luck is with you. You want to go steal a second bicycle.

Our students need a safe environment where they can practise making good decisions.

He reads the scene to the whole class, but assigns goals privately. He encourages the role-playing to build a line of argument, but if it isn't working, to try another. Bryan instructs his students to play to each other, not the audience, so that they are clearly involved in the situation rather than trying to act a part. In his debriefing afterward, Bryan discusses the verbal strategies students used to achieve their goals.

If your students are in an assigned seating plan that does not take account of friendships:

Have each student write and circle their own name on an index card, then list the names of four students they would like the opportunity to sit beside and sometimes work with. Since friendships can change quickly, this may seem a questionable strategy, but if your students are not currently allowed to interact with friends during class time, you will find that they will make the effort to ensure success.

Start with partners before you move to larger groups. During whole class lessons, when you want to be sure your students understand a concept, have them think about the concept for a minute, then turn to their friend and do a partner-share or Think-Pair-Share of the most important information for a minute or two.

If your students already have the opportunity to learn with their friends, but you notice that work distribution is uneven, noise is an issue, or they talk about everything except the assignment:

Take a bit of time to observe. You may notice that there are certain conditions under which the problem occurs. For example, noise level may be especially high as students begin a task, or off-task conversation may indicate you have allowed too much time for the activity. If you notice conditions that cause the problem, you can vary the conditions. If not, you can at least be specific, although perhaps without using names, when you talk with your class. In a responsive classroom, students share in problem solving and decision making with you. (See Chapter 5, page 110.)

If you already give your students lots of opportunity to work with friends and it's going quite well:

In an effective learning community, all members need to feel accepted by and respectful of all others. Since you've already got a strong foundation in your classroom of partnerships or work groups based on friendship, this is a good time to teach students about their learning profiles. You can then create opportunities where they benefit from working with others whose profile varies significantly from their own. (See Chapter 4.)

Emotional Development

The hypothalamus, located under the thalamus in the reptilian part of the brain, controls hormones and is responsible for primitive emotions such as fear, anger, and aggression. Not surprisingly, many researchers believe that the hypothalamus is at its most active level during adolescence. Even if hormones aren't causing your students personally to feel sensitive, vulnerable, and highly emotional, many of their peers are experiencing these feelings, and young adolescents, as we know, are strongly influenced by their peers.

Learning tends to be memorable when connected to an emotion, but not to the emotions of the hypothalamus. Hypothalamus emotions shut down learning, so that part of the brain needs to be kept as quiet and calm as possible. You can do that by providing students with choice in their learning.

"THE CHALLENGE IN TEACHING JUNIOR HIGH IS THAT THE MATURITY LEVEL CAN FLUTUATE FROM 12TH GRADE TO 3RD GRADE IN A MATTER OF SECONDS."

Source: www.CartoonStock.com.

Personal choices address the young adolescent's developmental need for freedom from adult authority without you actually relinquishing that authority. Choice significantly reduces hypothalamus-driven behaviours and, by allowing students to choose activities according to their learning preferences, removes the need for you to be the sole decision maker in your classroom.

Young adolescents are convinced that their feelings and problems are unique to themselves; this isn't surprising, since it is the one period in their lives when, because of the diversity in this age group, they will find the greatest differences between themselves and others of the same age. It is a time of preoccupation with self, and often a period of self-consciousness.

The young adolescent's sense of self is situational—adolescents may feel great about themselves in physical education class, but lousy in English class. Your kind suggestions for how to improve their work in English may be met with loudly voiced claims that they will *never* be good at English. Emotional responses tend to be inconsistent, unpredictable, and impossible for the young adolescent to explain. Remember, however, that while emotions can reduce learning in both early adolescence and adolescence, positive emotions can also enhance it. Allowing your students to make choices, within the parameters of the curriculum, assists with positive emotional engagement and can improve learning, particularly if you are willing to advocate for your students and help them learn to make good choices.

Implications for the Classroom

If differentiated instruction were a wheel, choice would be the hub. Differentiated instruction is important at all grade levels, but its role in allowing students choice makes it particularly important for young adolescents. At the same time, concern for peer approval, shifting self-concept, and self-consciousness can make it challenging for students to freely access the choices you give them.

Take the time to teach your students about their own learning needs, preferences, and strengths so that they can assess themselves accurately and appreciate that variation in learning is not only normal but also a distinguishing positive characteristic of being human. (See Chapter 4.)

Young adolescents crave encouragement and approval. They are sensitive to criticism and are easily offended. Do not use sarcasm even if it seems to be appreciated.

About Choice

Providing Choice

IN YOUR ROLE

If you are new to providing students with choice:

Start small. Both you and your students need to see that choice will work in your classroom. Here are some options:

→ If you are providing students with a writing prompt, provide two or three instead and let them choose one.

→ If students have multiple tasks, allow them to choose the order of completion.

→ If you are assigning a series of math problems of a similar type, allow students to choose the ones that best demonstrate their understanding of the concept.

If you already provide students with choice:

You may already have your students demonstrating their understanding through a choice of products, for example, writing an essay, teaching the class, or taping a radio show to discuss symbolism in the novel they have just read. A comfortable next step for you might be to partner with a visual arts teacher and structure a product assignment that allows students to represent their understanding visually.

Review choices you are currently providing against what you know about your students' learning profiles and interests. You don't need to address everyone's preferences in every assignment, but you should address them over a series of assignments.

Moral Devlopment

While it is true that young adolescents are preoccupied with themselves and sometimes keen to emulate the "less than savory" behaviour of some of their peers, they are also in transition from "what's in it for me" to a concern for the rights and feelings of others. This is a time when students are caring and idealistic, especially about animals and environmental issues. They want to make the world a better place, but don't understand why that task should be so difficult to achieve. Teachers of young adolescents can have a tremendously positive influence on their students' attitudes and behaviours by approving of and supporting their growing moral consciousness. For example, although minimum age requirements of various organizations may prevent your students from participating in ongoing initiatives like soup kitchens, they can still raise money and awareness for an endangered animal or write letters to Santa Claus for kindergarten students.

Concern for others does not mean that young adolescents make good decisions—on the contrary. Giedd, a neuroscientist at the National Institutes of Health, has discovered that the brain's frontal lobes, nicknamed "the police officer" because they help you to do the right thing, may not be fully developed until well past the age of 20. Statistics bear this out. Measures of childhood delinquency begin their curve at age 12 and peak at age 17 before falling off (Willms, 2003). Of course, bad behaviour is influenced by many factors; no one simply shrugs it off as due to slowly growing frontal lobes. We step in to teach decision-making skills to help young people who may not always make good decisions, and, where necessary, use our own fully developed frontal lobes to compensate for their underdeveloped ones.

Implications for the Classroom

Emotions attached to thinking enhance learning; so, to the extent that it is acceptable in your community, this is an ideal time to highlight moral and ethical concepts embedded in various curricular units. Here are some examples:

- Explore sexism in English or media studies, cloning in a science unit about cells, or global poverty issues in human geography.

- Look for the issues and points of contention in an upcoming unit, and turn them into questions that form the basis for inquiry, reflection, and lots of discussion and debate. For help in framing good, essential questions, refer to *Understanding by Design* (2005) by Grant Wiggins and Jay McTighe, or to the tips provided in this book in Chapter 6.

- Provide students with structured activities that require them to analyze issues from various points of view. *Creative Controversy* (1992) by David and Roger Johnson uses cooperative learning structures to help students advocate for a position, then reverse perspectives and advocate for the opposing position before finally synthesizing and integrating the best reasoning from both sides into a collaboratively created joint position.

- Use class meetings or community circles (see page 111) to provide students with regular opportunities to resolve personal and social issues.

> Good questions "pose dilemmas, subvert obvious or canonical truths' or force incongruities upon our attention."
>
> —*Jerome Bruner*

IN YOUR ROLE

Discussion webs (Alvermann, 1991) will help your students learn to make decisions through a format that also furthers their social and intellectual development. Students are asked to respond to a higher-level thinking question by:

1. Thinking individually, referring to the text and personal experience for information that might support their opinion

2. Discussing their ideas with a partner, sharing text and personal references

3. Pairing up with another set of partners, and working as a group of four to come to consensus on the idea that a spokesperson then shares with the class

Discussion webs support differentiated instruction by providing all students with the opportunity for active participation in various formats (individual, partner, small group, and whole class) and in all four literacy modalities (reading, writing, speaking, and listening). Blackline Master 3.2 is a graphic organizer you can use for discussion webs.

Cognitive Development

We have as many neurons (nerve cells) in our brains as there are stars in the Milky Way—a hundred billion, give or take (Sousa, 2006, p. 22).

However, the brain cleans house every so often, leaving only those neurons that have made lots of connections—the ones we use, in other words. Early adolescence and adolescence are a time of tremendous production of new neural connections; this is also the time when more than 50 percent of neural connections are eliminated in certain areas (Strauch, 2003, p. 138). In other words, the brains of your students are in the process of becoming what they will be for the rest of the students' lives. As their teacher, you have an awesome responsibility and an equally awe-inspiring opportunity. You must act on your professional knowledge, fostering and furthering your students' intellectual capacities far beyond what is generally provided in schools.

off the mark.com   by Mark Parisi

The following suggestions highlight a dozen aspects of brain research that speak to the needs of young adolescents and help you understand individual variability so that you can more effectively differentiate your work with your students.

Try This	Because
Provide lessons and activities that require problem solving and critical thinking. (See page 203.) Example: History lessons should be about cause-and-effect relationships, not chronologies of facts and events.	There is ongoing growth during early adolescence and adolescence in the areas of the brain that support logic, spatial reasoning, and language (Giedd as cited in Strauch, 2003).

Try This	Because
Explicitly teach students about how they learn. (See Chapter 4.) Provide both concrete and abstract experiences wherever possible. Example: Manipulatives are as necessary and appropriate to the 14-year-old math student as they are to the six-year-old.	Some young adolescents start to exhibit abstract, critical, and metacognitive thinking skills in some subjects at some times. According to Piaget, students may be thinking concretely in one area and abstractly in another (Strauch, 2003).

Try This	Because
Have students process the same information in a variety of ways—such as talking, writing, drawing, role-playing, and so on. (See Chapter 4 and page 45.) Teach through cross-curricular and interdisciplinary studies as often as possible. (See Chapter 8.)	Connections in the brain are strengthened if they are reinforced with a variety of stimuli (Sousa, 2006).

Try This	Because
The best solution to sleep deprivation in adolescents is to start school later in the morning. Since that's rarely possible . . . • Make sure students and their parents are aware of the importance of sleep for both learning and the processing of emotions. • Re-examine, with parents, the number of hours devoted to homework and after-school commitments. Teens need to find balance in their lives.  **Actually, my species is not nocturnal: I'm just a teenager...** Source: www.CartoonStock.com.	Sleep is important to brain maintenance. Teens need an average of nine hours of sleep a night, but tend to get far less than that. Researchers think that, in addition to their increasingly busy lives, teens are secreting melatonin (a sleep chemical) up to two hours later than when they were younger. Some young adolescents may already be experiencing the sleep deprivation common to older teens (Strauch, 2003).

Try This	Because
Limit the amount of new information you provide at any one time to five chunks or fewer. Teach students a repertoire of memory strategies, including categorization of information. (See page 183.) Example: Each of the eight chemical groups of the periodic table represents a chunk, making it possible to eventually learn the table in its entirety if you decide that is important.	There are age-related limits to the capacity of working memory. For students between the ages of five and fourteen, the average capacity is five chunks (Sousa, 2006).

Try This	Because
Make sure students are retrieving information in the environment where they learned it. Do tests in the same room where the learning for the test happened. Explicitly connect new information to previous learning. More Experiences ➜ More Categories ➜ More Cross-Referencing Options = More Learning	Learning is different from memorization. When you learn, you cross-reference new information to multiple other categories so that you can detect new patterns and relationships (Nunley, 2003). When you memorize, you have simply categorized new information so that your brain can retrieve it later.

Try This	Because
Support risk-taking. Make sure students feel comfortable and safe in your classroom. Do not use sarcasm, even if your students seem to enjoy it. (See Chapter 5.)	Stress releases chemicals that kill neurons in the area of the brain responsible for memory retrieval (Nunley, 2003).

Try This	Because
Where possible, connect content to emotions. Performance tasks such as simulations and role plays provide for this, as do activities such as journal writing. (See page 111.)	You are more likely to remember learning that has an emotional connection for you (Sousa, 2006).

Try This	Because
Increase novelty of presentation and the use of visual cues. Address physical needs such as hunger and thirst. Incorporate opportunities for choice. (See pages 106–109.)	Your brain has to notice new information before it can remember it. The reticular activating system in your brain screens all incoming information and prioritizes it in a hierarchy of physical need, novelty, and choice (Nunley, 2003).

Try This	Because
Give students a minute or two of break time between episodes of learning. Let them go off-task by allowing them to move around or chat with friends, or keep them on task by having them move into a new grouping arrangement for the next part of the class. (See Chapter 8.)	Retention improves when you teach in 20-minute episodes with a couple of minutes of downtime or transition between the episodes (Sousa, 2006).

Try This	Because
Establish meaning by making connections between topics and across subjects. Wherever possible, have students analyze data that is important to their lives.	New information can make sense (be logical) and can have meaning (be relevant). Ideally, you want both, but if it comes down to one or the other for a learner, relevant information has a greater likelihood of being stored as new learning. This seems to be especially important to adolescents who often question the relevance of what they learn (Sousa, 2006).

Try This	Because
Vary your instructional strategies, keeping students actively engaged as much as possible. Minimize lectures; they are the least effective teaching method. If something is really important, make sure students have an opportunity to teach it to others. (See Chapter 6.)	A study conducted by the National Training Laboratories in the 1960s (see page 162) still holds true: the more actively involved students are in the learning, the more rehearsal they do of the information, and the greater the retention and, therefore, the learning (Sousa, 2006).

For more information, refer to the work of the following brain-research experts:

- David Sousa (2006), *How the Brain Learns*, Third Edition. Corwin Press.

- Kathie Nunley (2003), *A Student's Brain: The Parent/Teacher Manual*. (Try to attend one of her enlightening and entertaining presentations. More information is available at **www.brains.org** or **www.help4teachers.com**.)

- Eric Jensen (1998), *Teaching with the Brain in Mind*. ASCD.

- Laura Erlauer (2003), *The Brain-Compatible Classroom*. ASCD.

- Patricia Wolfe (2001), *Brain Matters: Translating Research Into Classroom Practice*. ASCD.

To focus specifically on the adolescent brain, including the young adolescent, read *The Primal Teen* by Barbara Strauch (2003, Anchor Books) or watch the Association for Supervision and Curriculum Development's four-part DVD *Teaching the Adolescent Brain* (2006).

IN YOUR ROLE

Of the 12 aspects of brain research highlighted above, where are your strengths?

Identify the opportunities you already provide for your students, and refer to the appropriate pages for ideas to make them even better.

Start Where They Are: Knowledge of Your Students' Learning Preferences and Interests

QUIZ

Knowledge of Your Students' Learning Preferences and Interests

Refer to the pages listed in the scoring guide for more information, and sometimes answers, to any of the following statements or questions that pique your curiosity.

1 List 10 ways in which individuals differ.

2 Explain the difference between intelligences and learning styles.

> 1 Individual Differences, page 61

> 2 Intelligences, page 70

3 Most learning style theories describe learner differences in how many ways: three, four, five, or six?

4 What, if anything, do people have to know about themselves before learning style inventories can be useful to them?

> 3 Learning Styles, page 62

> 4 Usefulness of Inventories—Implications, page 63

5 How many pictures are hanging on your living room wall?

6 Describe your preferred learning style.

> 5 Observation Skills—Implications, page 63

> 6 Learning Styles, page 64

7 Identify two learning conditions that work for your style and two that do not.

8 List four ways you have recently accommodated kinesthetic learners in your classroom.

> 7 Learning Styles, page 64

> 8 Kinesthetic Learners—Implications, page 68

9 Robert Sternberg's three intelligences are practical, analytical, and ____?

10 Describe a "searchlight profile" of intelligences.

11 When is the ideal time to use multiple representations in your teaching?

12 Have you ever given a preferences or interests inventory and then wondered what to do with the results?

13 Is the "Strengths Revolution" an educational movement? Should it be?

14 What are the pedagogical advantages to knowing a student's interests?

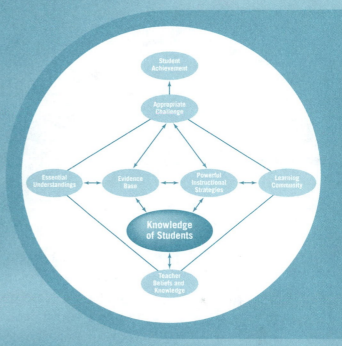

One day in 1666, 24-year-old Isaac Newton was at home in Cambridge, conducting yet another of his experiments that would change our understanding of the natural world. On this particular day, Newton made two discoveries: that white light is composed of all the colours in the visible spectrum and, concomitantly, that the only way to create white light is to combine all the colours into a single beam.

"There is an incredible amount of variability in talent, and the forms of mind are no less varied than the forms of bodies."

—*Quintilian*
Ancient Roman orator

Newton's experiment is a good metaphor for this chapter and the next. At the beginning of the school year your understanding of your students is limited, so, of necessity, you treat them as if they are all the same. The rainbow is trapped inside the prism. However, as you get to know your students as individuals—their learning preferences, interests, and needs—you will come to see them in all the richness of their diversity. You can then increase your effectiveness by differentiating your responses to them based on your developing understanding. At this stage, you can now see the rainbow—the visible spectrum.

However, as you read in Chapters 1 and 3, your classroom won't function—at least, not a classroom of young adolescents and not at optimum effectiveness—if you focus exclusively on the individual. Therefore, in this chapter and Chapter 7, you will refract the single light beam of your class into a rainbow of colours. Then, in Chapter 5, we create a strong and effective learning community by recombining all of those colours into a single beam.

Students differ from each other in so many ways that it might at first seem impossible to offer them an education that is responsive to these differences. However, a closer look at a list such as the one in the margin should reassure us that we already do an excellent job of taking many individual differences into account in our classrooms. Our classroom libraries include boy-friendly resources; we are respectful and inclusive of the diverse cultural backgrounds of our students; we make sure projects happen exclusively at school if we know that family support is limited; and all our students have opportunities to connect new information to their existing and varied background knowledge.

The difference between these common practices and differentiated instruction is that differentiated instruction delves deeper into understanding and then making use of each student's *learning preferences*. When you take a student's learning preferences into account in your teaching, you will see improvements in the rate and ease of their learning, self-esteem, interest in school, and relationships with you and with their peers.

How we differ
- Emotions
- Interests
- Family support
- Goals
- Cultural background
- Talents
- Strengths
- Fears
- Personality
- Self-concept
- Attitudes and values
- Gender
- Experiences
- Background knowledge
- Intelligences
- Socioeconomic status
- Learning styles
- Readiness to learn a new concept

Peanuts: © United Feature Syndicate, Inc.

Learning preferences include both an individual's learning style and intelligences.

When it comes to thinking about ways in which humans are different, we seem to have had a historical preference for the number four (Silver, Strong, & Perini, 2000):

▶ The Greek physician Hippocrates thought there were four liquids, or "humors," in our bodies—blood, black bile, phlegm, and yellow bile. Equal amounts of each would confirm that we were properly "balanced."

▶ The eighteenth-century English poet William Blake believed that there were four life energies, corresponding to our body, heart, head, and spirit.

▶ The North American Plains Indians linked four personality traits to the animal world. These traits are wisdom, clarity of perception, introspection, and understanding one's emotions.

▶ In 1923, Carl Jung identified four psychological types based on combinations of how we take in information—through sensing or intuition—and how we process or make decisions about that information—through thinking or feeling.

Jung's theory was made popular by Isabel Briggs Myers when she and Katharine Briggs developed the Myers-Briggs Type Indicator (MBTI) in 1962.

"Looks aren't everything. It's what's inside you
that really matters. A biology teacher told me that."

Implications for the Classroom

The MBTI is a well researched, validated psychological instrument, superior to many of the quizzes you find on the internet or in magazines, but you have to be qualified as a trainer before you can access the full inventory. That said, before using any inventories to determine personality type, learning style, or intelligence with your students, please remember that none of them (and that includes the heavily researched MBTI) should be used to label, define, or limit the learner. Rather, they are intended to emphasize a learner's natural strengths. In the case of multiple intelligences, inventories simply allow students to indicate an interest in a particular intelligence. To determine strength, you will need to observe students in multiple, varied demonstrations of that intelligence.

Also keep in mind that inventories are self-reporting; in other words, the usefulness of the results is directly related to the self-knowledge of the individual providing the information. If you decide to use inventories with young adolescents, remember that, by definition, they are both ultra-sensitive to peer opinion *and* are just beginning to learn about themselves. Inventories can be fun for students to complete and make great discussion starters, but use them to complement and enrich your observations and professional judgment.

Who Am I as a Learner?

You can learn about your students' preferences without inventories by providing activities of sufficiently rich variety through which students can demonstrate their strengths. Watch for instances where a student learns a concept rapidly, is engaged in the learning, and/or expresses confidence in the work to you or to a peer. Be careful of the last instance, however; students at this age may pretend a confidence they do not feel.

When a student demonstrates a strength, determine what aspect of the activity worked for that student. As already noted (see page 53), our students are at a perfect age to develop their metacognitive skills, so be sure to involve them in determining their strengths by asking questions about what they think works for them and why. The goal is to have students develop increasingly nuanced understandings of their own learning preferences so they know the conditions that will be most helpful to them in more challenging learning situations.

If you want to use inventories, four are provided with this chapter. Free inventories are also readily accessible online by typing "free learning styles inventories" or "free multiple intelligences inventories" into a search engine.

You can use Blackline Master 4.1 to track your observations and the results of any inventories you administer. Note that this master includes *all* the learning preferences discussed in this chapter, as well as gender and culture, so that you can create learner profiles. Make one copy of the master for each student you are observing. If you teach multiple classes of students, minimize the workload by sharing the profiles with other teachers.

 Blackline Master 4.2 is a class profile form that clusters students according to preferences.

Provide each student with a copy of a mandala. (See Blackline Master 4.3 for the template and guidelines for use.) Over the course of this chapter, students will have a number of opportunities to identify their learning preferences and interests. They can add to their personal mandalas with each new inventory they complete, and can display their finished products for review by peers and parents.

Learning Style by Type   Q 6 & 7

After the development of the Myers-Briggs Type Indicator, several theorists looked at how the concept of "type," or human difference, could be applied to education. Each theorist (Gregorc, Kolb, McCarthy, and Silver, Strong, and Perini) describes four types of learners. Although their descriptors and labels vary, the similarities among the models are greater than the differences. The four types of learners can be summarized as I have done in the chart. I use the highlighted words to refer to the learning style type, but you and your students should feel free to substitute whatever terms you find most descriptive.

Learn More About Learning Style Types

Anthony Gregorc (1982), *Inside Styles: Beyond the Basics*. Columbia, CT: Gregorc Associates.

David Kolb (1984), *Experiential Learning: Experience as the Source of Learning and Development*. Englewood Cliffs, New Jersey: Prentice Hall.

Bernice and Dennis McCarthy (2006), *Teaching Around the 4MAT Cycle: Designing Instruction for Diverse Learners With Diverse Learning Styles*. Thousand Oaks, CA: Corwin Press.

Harvey Silver, Richard Strong, and Matthew Perini (2000), *So Each May Learn: Integrating Learning Styles AND Multiple Intelligences*. Alexandria, Virginia: ASCD.

Prefers	Learns Best When	Learns Less When
• Choice • Experimentation • Doing things in own way	• Allowed to make choices in what activities to complete and how to complete them • Given a variety of challenging hands-on and open-ended activities • Competing against self and others	• Told what activities to complete and precisely how to complete them • Given written, repetitive tasks (i.e., responding to a daily journal prompt) • Activities don't permit exploration or discovery
• Practicality • Facts and details • Straightforwardness	• Given predictable activities with detailed directions provided in advance • Examples are practical, not theoretical • Activities emphasize problem solving	• No direction, support, or feedback is provided with activities • Required to take risks and try new approaches • Can't see an obvious or immediate benefit to the activity
• Research • Theories • Working with ideas	• Has access to a wide range of expert resources • Has time to think things through • Allowed to explore a topic as deeply and thoroughly as desired	• Situations are open-ended, especially if they are based on opinion and emotion rather than logic and analysis • Required to work with others • Activities require expressing emotions (i.e., role playing)
• Feelings • Imagination • A variety of perspectives	• Allowed to work with others • Activities include various perspectives or opportunities to discuss opinions and beliefs • Support and feedback are provided by teachers and peers in a collaborative, not competitive, environment	• Required to work alone • Feedback is negative or peers are negative, challenging, or competitive • Work doesn't have personal relevance

Even a cursory glance at this chart confirms that optimal conditions for one learner are less than ideal conditions for another. Kolb and McCarthy have each resolved that problem by creating cycles of learning that ensure that each learner's preferences will be addressed some of the time during a unit of study. This book is also full of ways to address each student's learning style.

IN YOUR ROLE

If you haven't already done so, identify your learning style. Next, think of two students in your class whom you find easy to teach and two who present a challenge. Try to identify their styles. Most likely, the students you find easy to teach share your learning style, while those you find challenging have styles diametrically opposed to your own.

Give students a copy of Blackline Master 4.4 and have them complete this simple inventory. A majority of A answers indicates a student who prefers choice, B answers a student who prefers practicality, and so on. Have students meet with others who have chosen the same type. Assign each group the task of elaborating on the answers they gave for their type and of determining a single word and an image or symbol that best captures the type's uniqueness.

(The coloured word in the chart on page 65 may end up being their keyword, but not necessarily.) When groups share their work, emphasize that a learning style is an individual mixture of styles; no one is all one type. Students should listen carefully for any descriptors from other groups that also describe them, and note these for use on their personal mandala.

Individually record what you think are the learning styles of each member of your group, including yourself, then compare notes. The group member being discussed should offer a self-assessment last, preferably accompanied by examples of typical actions that support the selected learning style so that the connection between the description of type and what might be observed in the classroom is reinforced.

Learning Style by Senses

Your knowledge of your students will be further enriched if you know whether a student is a predominantly visual, auditory, or tactile/kinesthetic learner. This learning styles model, also known as VAK (or VARK if you want to include Reading, or VACT if you separate kinesthetic from tactile), is based on the senses of sight, hearing, and touch, respectively. Of course, we all use all of these senses every day. Remember that "learning style" refers to the ways in which a particular student *most readily and most easily* learns new information.

Learning Styles by Senses			
	Visual Learners	Auditory Learners	Tactile/Kinesthetic Learners
When Accessing New Information	Prefer reading it/seeing it for themselves (watching videos, viewing overhead transparencies, reading)	Prefer listening to someone (listening to stories, direct instruction, recordings, oral directions, lectures)	Prefer experiencing it through an activity (dramatizing, demonstrating, playing games and doing puzzles, using manipulatives, going on field trips)
When Working with New Information	Prefer to write and/or draw it (mind mapping, drawing, painting; creating timelines, diagrams, charts, graphs, and maps; writing)	Prefer to discuss it (telling stories, interviewing, participating in class discussions, choral readings, readers' theatre, debates, using voice-to-text software, teaching others)	Prefer to manipulate, touch, or create with it (conducting experiments and simulations, constructing, drawing, painting, multi-tasking, i.e., labelling a diagram while reading)

Learn More About Sense-Based Learning Styles

Ken and Rita Dunn (1993), *Teaching Secondary Students Through Their Individual Learning Styles: Practical Approaches for Grades 7–12*. Needham, Maine: Allyn & Bacon.

While there is some overlap across categories, it is safe to say that kinesthetic learners don't tend to fare as well as visual or auditory learners in our classrooms. Since most teachers are visual learners, it can be a real challenge to think of meaningful yet simple ways to address the kinesthetic learner's need for touch and movement while still dealing with the content of the curriculum.

Here are seven ideas that will help you with your kinesthetic learners:

- Have students stand to answer a question, make a choice, or vote their preference for something.

- Use the flexible pairings and groupings indicative of differentiated instruction and frequently change them. Refer to page 109 for suggestions on how to quickly move students into short-term configurations.

- Use activities that involve physical movement, such as
  - the text-mapping activity described in Chapter 3 (see page 42)
  - a four-corners activity where students move to the corner of the room that best represents their opinion on an issue and remain there, discussing that issue with like-minded individuals (see the activity described on page 66 in this chapter)
  - the ball-toss activity explained in For Example below

- Many of the activity structures particularly appropriate to differentiated instruction are also, not coincidentally, highly appropriate to your kinesthetic learners. See Chapters 8 and 9 for several examples.

- Try to make sure the furnishings in your classroom allow for students to lounge on a pillow or in a comfortable chair while they read. Before dismissing this idea as impractical in a busy rotary classroom, think of your students sitting for six hours on a plastic chair.

- Whenever possible, have students physically interact with their textbooks. They can use sticky notes, bookmarks where they record questions and comments, and overhead transparencies laid on top of the textbook page and marked with coloured transparency pens to argue with the author, highlight important points, summarize their understanding, and make personal connections.

- I once taught a grade 7/8 class that would burst into song whenever someone was sad or upset. The song was "How Much Is That Doggie in the Window?" (don't ask—I have no idea) and it was accompanied by appropriately placed "arf, arfs," and gestures, some more kinesthetic than others, particularly at "the waggly tail." I'd love to pretend I had something to do with this very physical way my students strengthened our classroom community, but I was flabbergasted and hugely amused the first time they did it ... and the fifteenth. I borrowed the concept and, in subsequent years, my students and I would develop gestures to represent everything from "piece of cake" (an easy task) to "haven't got a clue."

For Example

At different points throughout a unit, Candace has her grade 9 science students stand in a large circle and toss a ball to each other. Whoever receives the ball has to state a concept or fact from the unit being studied. If the student fails to do so, he or she remains standing in the circle, but with folded arms to indicate that the ball shouldn't be tossed to him or her.

Candace uses this ball toss as a whole-class activity when there is a lot of material to cover, and as a small-group activity when there is less material or when she wants to ensure that students have more opportunities to participate.

Ball toss is an enjoyable way to review material. Of course it doesn't have to be a ball. Plastic snowman toss in January, anyone?

IN YOUR ROLE

Give students a simple VAK inventory to complete (Blackline Master 4.5). While they are doing the inventory, take a class list and, based on observations you have made, note whether each student is predominantly visual, auditory, kinesthetic, or a combination of styles. Compare your assessments with your students' self-assessments, reflecting on the accuracy of your observations or of their self-knowledge.

Intelligences

Learning styles deal with the how of learning—how we prefer to acquire, process, and remember new information. Intelligences theory, on the other hand, describes the *formats* (Gardner, 2006, p. 42) in which our mind thinks. In Robert Sternberg's work, there are three different intelligence formats; according to Howard Gardner, there are eight or nine.

Sternberg's Triarchic Intelligences   Q 9

Robert Sternberg argues that there are three different kinds of intelligence:

▶ practical (real-world applications)

▶ analytical (problem solving; making critical judgments)

▶ creative (imaginative; looking for new ways to do things)

We use these different intelligences in varying amounts. According to Sternberg, to be "successfully intelligent" we should be able to use all three intelligences together; however, we should teach through a student's preferred intelligence as often as possible, particularly when introducing new ideas.

In a study of 326 high school students, students were grouped according to whether they had tested high in practical, analytical, or creative intelligence or a combination of the three (Sternberg, 2006). Students were then randomly assigned to four instructional groups with each intelligence represented in each group. Students in all four groups participated in a summer course in introductory psychology, using the same textbook and listening to the same lectures, but attending discussion groups that emphasized one of memory-based, practical, analytical, or creative instruction. All students were evaluated for memory, practical, analytical, or creative quality of work on homework, two exams, and an independent project.

> "When we teach and assess in ways that respect different strengths, students learn and perform better."
> —*Robert Sternberg*

Students who happened to be in the groups that matched their pattern of intelligences outperformed students who were mismatched. "In other words," says Sternberg, "when we teach students in a way that fits how they think, they do better in school. Students with creative or practical abilities, who are almost never taught or assessed in a way that matches their pattern of abilities, may be at a disadvantage in course after course, year after year" (Sternberg, 2006, pp. 33–34).

Implications for the Classroom

Asking a variety of intelligence questions on assignments or tests need not be overly difficult or time-consuming. For example, here are some test items used to assess students' geometry learning:

Memory
A square has four sides of equal length. Circle the formula that shows how you would calculate the perimeter of the square.

a. $y - y + y - y$
b. $y + y + y + y$
c. $y \times y$
d. $y + y - y$

y ☐

Analytical
You have two pipe cleaners of equal length. Make a circle with one and an oval with the other. Which shape has the greater area? Why?

Practical
You can have the square piece of your favorite chocolate bar or you can have the rectangular piece. Circle the piece that will give you the most amount of chocolate.

Creative
Young children learn new words best when there is a picture or a symbol for them to remember. You want to help children remember the new word area. Come up with a symbol or simple picture that helps young children remember what area is.

Source: From "Recognizing Neglected Strengths," p. 32, by Robert J. Sternberg, in the September 2006 Issue of *Educational Leadership*, 64 (1). Used with permission.

Learn More About Triarchic Intelligences

Robert Sternberg (1996), *Successful Intelligence*. New York: Simon & Schuster.

Robert Sternberg (1997), *Thinking Styles*. New York: Cambridge University Press.

Gardner's Multiple Intelligences   Q 10 & 11

Howard Gardner has been introduced to audiences as the man who single-handedly changed the way teachers think by simply adding an "s" to the word "intelligence." He challenged the idea that intelligence is a single construct, positing instead that there are many different intelligences, or, more accurately, "potentials," that we all possess to varying degrees.

Gardner's multiple intelligences can be roughly divided into three categories (Gardner, 2006), as shown in this diagram.

Based on Material Objects	Based on Symbols	Based on Personal
• visual-spatial • bodily-kinesthetic • naturalist *Associated more with skills*	• verbal-linguistic • musical-rhythmic • logical-mathematical *Associated more with concepts, stories, theories*	• interpersonal • intrapersonal • existential *Associated more with knowing humans*

IN YOUR ROLE

 Use the Multiple Intelligences Observation Checklist (Blackline Master 4.6) to give you a better understanding of what each intelligence might look like in your classroom.

And/or

 Have students complete the Multiple Intelligences inventory (Blackline Master 4.7).

When Gardner first developed his theory, his intention was to engage other cognitive psychologists in a discussion of how the mind works. He did not set out to make teachers' lives more challenging, although that is what happened. Many of us have spent years making heroic efforts to develop learning centres for each intelligence, trying to teach a single concept in eight different ways. Despite our best efforts, the results were too frequently a trivialization of education: spelling by contorting bodies into the letters of the alphabet, singing the multiplication table, or building words with twigs so that our students could be naturalistic and linguistic at the same time.

In recent years Gardner has clarified that, when considering student preferences, it is most useful to think in terms of a *profile* of intelligences that interact, one with another, rather than a number of distinct intelligences by which students do all their learning through one or two intelligences of their greatest strength.

There are three basic profiles (Moran et al., 2006):

▶ laser—one or two intelligences are exceptionally strong, while others are quite weak

▶ jagged—some intelligences are stronger than others

▶ searchlight—differences among intelligences are not pronounced

Individuals with laser profiles can be enormously successful in life if they develop their peak intelligence; on the other hand, if that intelligence is neither linguistic nor logical-mathematical, they may be spectacularly unsuccessful in school. Most people have jagged profiles, meaning some types of information are easier to process than others. People with searchlight profiles can have a difficult time finding a career that appeals to them. The relationship between intelligence potentials and future success in life makes it even more important that we help our students be aware of their preferences, and of the careers that might be of interest to them.

"Adopting a multiple intelligences approach can bring about a quiet revolution in the way students see themselves and others. Instead of defining themselves as either smart' or dumb,' students can perceive themselves as potentially smart in a number of ways."
—*Howard Gardner*

"Minds seek and should find their best ways of functioning during their school years, a period during which brains give off little signals that reveal what they are and are not wired for."
—*Mel Levine*

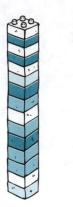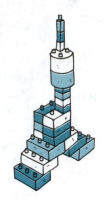

Although intelligences are independent, they do interact with one another. Moran et al. (2006, p. 23) compare the intelligences to interconnecting building blocks. If you have only one kind of block (or one dominant intelligence), you are limited in the range of structures you can build. But if you use various block shapes (or intelligences), you can create a variety of patterns and structures (or explore careers that suit your particular combination of intelligences). A dancer, for example, has musical, spatial, and bodily-kinesthetic intelligences, while a paramedic needs bodily-kinesthetic, verbal-linguistic, and interpersonal intelligences.

The implication for teachers is that, while there is no need to teach a concept in eight different ways, it is equally unreasonable to expect that all students should be learning all material through the two intelligences that dominate our educational system, namely, linguistic and logical-mathematical.

To apply Gardner's theory in your classroom:

- ▶ introduce new topics through *multiple* entry points *and*
- ▶ encourage students to demonstrate their understanding through *multiple* representations *and*
- ▶ vary teaching according to intelligence when the subject lends itself to it. For example, when teaching classification in science, use the natural world; when teaching it in English, use genre.

Entry Points

Entry points correspond to the various intelligences. They describe both what *you* might do when introducing new material to your class, and what *your students* might do when working with that material. The intention of using multiple entry points is to introduce and to encourage students to work with multiple representations of the same core ideas.

> "The biggest mistake of past centuries in teaching has been to treat all children as if they were variations of the same individual and thus to feel justified in teaching them all the same subjects in the same way."
>
> —*Howard Gardner*

New Information

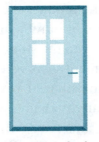

| **Narrative** (tell a story) | **Logical/Quantitative** (share a graph, organizer, or chart) | **Foundational** (consider the theory behind the idea) | **Aesthetic** (use an art form) | **Experiential** (involve students in a hands-on activity) |

Five entry points that are particularly useful, and possible, for classrooms

Implications for the Classroom

When you present new material through various entry points, you give all students initial access to the learning through their various strengths and, because expertise is demonstrated through the ability to represent an idea in multiple forms, you increase their understanding of the information. However, because multiple representations take time, it is important that you:

→ make sure the topic is worth the effort

→ identify essential understandings (see Chapter 6) so that you remain focused on what matters

→ teach in an interdisciplinary or cross-curricular manner when possible

→ use inquiry learning (see page 163) when possible; during inquiry, students automatically have and use a range of entry points and representations

IN YOUR ROLE

Review a recent unit of study, using Blackline Master 4.8 to note the entry points you used and to develop new ideas for the next time you teach that unit.

You are undoubtedly familiar with the product choice charts that suggest it is equally useful to sing, dance, or draw your understanding of anything, from the plot of a short story to the study of global warming. My experience has been that engagement soars when students are permitted to use a preferred intelligence to demonstrate their understanding; their work demonstrates greater creativity than is generally evident in daily assignments. Sometimes the results are downright spectacular.

But every silver lining has its cloud. Spectacular results can take tens, sometimes hundreds, of hours to achieve. There are particular skills necessary to designing websites, creating comic strips, writing research reports, and performing plays; students need to be taught these skills if they are going to produce quality work. And a student's enthusiasm for working in a particular mode can completely derail your intended focus on a demonstration of conceptual understanding.

The dilemma reminds me of a conversation I had with a friend who had just been divorced. When I asked him what his wedding day had been like, he responded, "I thought it was the greatest day of my life. It was only later I realized that under the tinsel, there was more tinsel." Cynical certainly, but perhaps, like me, you've had some of these tinsel moments in your classroom: moments where you are simultaneously overwhelmed by the attractiveness of the final product and underwhelmed by the learning being shared. Tinsel times become especially evident, and especially problematic, if the rubric or other form you use for assessment gives weight to production quality. This can result, for example, in a student with limited understanding of the periodic table scoring an A because his "Element Man" comic strip was well drawn. (See Chapter 11 for examples of summative assessments.) Refer to Chapter 6 for a discussion of essential understandings and of when it is and isn't worth the time and energy of either you or your student to be involved in time-consuming demonstrations of learning.

Learn More About Multiple Intelligences

- Howard Gardner (1999), *Intelligence Reframed: Multiple Intelligences for the 21st Century*. New York: Basic Books.

- Howard Gardner (2006), *Multiple Intelligences: New Horizons*. New York: Basic Books.

Using your knowledge of your students' intelligence preferences and your own comfort level, decide on the product skills you are going to teach throughout the year. Choose an appropriate product for each of the intelligences most strongly represented in your class and teach all students to create quality work in this product form. Then you can give students choice in the product they create for a unit's summative assessment, or you can require that all students demonstrate their understanding in one or more specific forms. The following chart shows examples of products that are worth teaching because of their use in a variety of subject areas.

Incorporate multiple representations of understanding into your next test. For example, in addition to answering questions, students could complete a graphic organizer, create an outline of key points, make a sketch, or suggest an analogy. (See pages 243–245 for test construction ideas.) Remember that, for a test to be a fair assessment of understanding, the test formats need to be familiar to students. In other words, teach the graphic organizer before asking students to complete one in response to a test question.

Verbal-Linguistic	• reports or essays • speeches • poems • storytelling	Musical-Rhythmic	• songs • choral reading • musical performances
Logical-Mathematical	• charts and graphs • flow charts • surveys or opinion polls • problem-solving steps	Interpersonal	• interviews • debates • organization of an activity or event
Visual-Spatial	• cartoons or comic strips • maps • slide presentations • posters	Intrapersonal	• journaling • statements of personal belief
Bodily-Kinesthetic	• role plays or improvisations • experimental designs • models	Naturalistic	• methods of classifying objects or ideas • methods of comparing characteristics • displays or exhibitions of artifacts

Student Interests

REFLECT

Learning About Your Students II

Determining a student's interests is fairly straightforward: you just ask. There are several good reasons for making the effort to know your students' interests:

▶ Learning is easiest when the information is personally relevant. In order to be relevant, the information has to link to something the student already knows. Therefore, if you know what your students are interested in, you have some established points of connection for new learning.

▶ Paying attention to your students' interests is paying attention to their experiences. You forge personal connections with your students to validate who they are as human beings. Encouraging them to explore an aspect of a unit through their particular area of interest validates them even further.

▶ Knowing your students' interests reminds you that they have lives outside of your classroom. Tapping into their interests can give you the privilege of witnessing strengths and talents you didn't know they possessed.

▶ Interests can give you clues as to a student's intelligence preferences. For example, if a student tells you she wants to be an architect, she may have a preference for logical-mathematical or visual-spatial tasks.

ALMEIDA

"EINSTEIN!!! Stop fooling around and pay attention!"

Source: www.CartonStock.com.

Scott uses the R.A.F.T. strategy, developed by Santa (1988), to provide his students with an extended writing opportunity based on their interests in a unit they have just completed about Canada's Native peoples.

Students choose their assignment from a chart organized according to Role (whose perspective they are taking as the writer), Audience (who they are writing to), Format (type of writing), and Topic.

Heather assumes the role of chair of a fact-finding commission looking into the issue of Aboriginal land claims. She is preparing a summary for her boss in the government.

IN YOUR ROLE

 Have students complete the interest inventory (Blackline Master 4.9).

Or

Instead of interest inventories, have students:

→ share three objects that represent their interests

→ share a favourite TV show, song, book, or game and explain why it is a favourite

→ identify one aspect of an upcoming unit for which they are prepared to become the class expert

→ play "Two Truths and a Lie." Students each write three facts about their interests. Only two of these facts are true, but they should be made to sound as if they could all be true. Students read their statements aloud and classmates guess which one is untrue.

→ choose a book from the classroom or school library and explain to the class why it is worth reading

→ design a week of classes, explaining what you would be doing in each class

For your own reference, keep a class list, recording for each student an interest you have learned about. At some point over the next few weeks, ask a question or make a comment to each student about their interest.

 Read the excerpt from Peter Applebome's short story *The Accidental Boy Scout,* provided on Blackline Master 4.10, and discuss the questions.

Many of us have asked our students to complete various learning inventories. We review the inventories and they confirm our suspicion that Sarah's incessant and annoying pencil tapping is indicative of her preference for the musical rhythmic intelligence, that more than half of our class are kinesthetic learners, that Sunjay, who creates havoc in every group, really means it when he says he is better at working alone, or that Mark is keenly interested in skateboarding.

The difficulty is not in administering the inventories, but in making effective use of the results. Gardner's theory of multiple intelligences, for example, has been around for more than 25 years and, while it certainly has had an impact, Gardner ruefully acknowledges that he has "assembled a massive amount of data about how difficult it is to change people's minds about intelligence . . . " (2006, p. 30).

What's going on when we return to our schools, enthusiastic after a workshop about learning preferences, and have our students complete learning inventories, then do nothing or very little with our new knowledge? Do we, as Gardner suggests, possess mental models that contradict and limit the usefulness of the inventories? Consider the following three arguments and the counterarguments that could be made by a teacher who differentiates instruction.

When Mental Models Are the Problem   Q.13

Argument 1

Young adolescents' interests and strengths are still forming. It is too early for them to have any real idea of who they are or even of how they learn best. As teachers, it is our responsibility to expose them to *all* learning preferences. Those with strong learning preferences in a particular area may well develop a corresponding talent over time, but if that's going to happen, it will do so with or without our help. John Lennon did just fine.

> "People like me are aware of their so-called genius at 10, 8, 9 . . . . Why didn't they put me in art school? Why didn't they train me? I was different, I was always different. Why didn't anybody notice me?"
>
> —*John Lennon*

Counterargument 1

Yes, students' interests and strengths are still forming, but young adolescents are not blank canvases. Two children raised in the same household, under the same conditions, are completely different individuals. Buckingham and Coffman (1999) argue that many preferences are inborn, and it is our filtering of the world through these preferences that creates "four-lane highway" pathways in our brains, in contrast to the "trail through the desert" pathways of our non-preferences. Paying attention to our preferences, they argue, is paying attention to our destiny. Although we can learn new knowledge and skills, our preferences are our recurring patterns of behaviour, our attitudes, and our habits. They define who we are and the contribution we will make to the world.

That said, Buckingham and Coffman acknowledge that our environment—including culture, family, and schooling—influences the development of our preferences. Behaviour is always dynamic; we need to know when we can use our natural preferences and when it is more appropriate to set them aside. These influencing factors are of even greater importance to the still-developing young adolescent than to the adults Buckingham and Coffman have studied.

Sometime between birth and adulthood, our preferences are formed. It is still possible to influence the preferences of young adolescents in some respects, but decidedly not in others. This reinforces the argument made in Chapter 3 that early adolescence is the ideal time to teach students about who they are as learners *and* to expose them to the widest possible variety of alternative ways to learn—including ways that we adults don't tend to use. Some students, particularly at-risk learners (Hanson & Dewing, 1990), struggle in school not because they aren't capable but because their learning preferences are routinely ignored.

> "We neither get better or worse as we get older, but more like ourselves."
> —**Robert Anthony**

> "My experience is what I agree to attend to. Only those items which I notice shape my mind."
> —**William James**

Learn More About The Strengths Revolution

Marcus Buckingham and Curt Coffman (1999), *First, Break All the Rules: What the World's Greatest Managers Do Differently*. New York: Simon & Schuster.

Rosanne Liesveld and Jo Ann Miller (2005), *Teach with Your Strengths*. New York: Gallup Press.

Argument 2

Students will not be able to choose how they do their work once they leave school. They will have to perform specific tasks under conditions set by their employers. Therefore, our job is to teach students to be well-rounded individuals who are capable of doing quality work under a variety of circumstances. We do that by focusing our attention on the remediation of our students' weaknesses.

Counterargument 2

When our students leave school and join the workforce, we hope they base their choice of work on a deep understanding of their preferences and passions. We also hope they find work with an enlightened employer who understands that quality performance happens when the steps to achieving specific outcomes can vary and be based on individual strengths.

This isn't as farfetched as it might sound. Consider research that took place over a 25-year period and consisted of 90-minute interviews with 80 000 managers, resulting in 120 000 hours of tape and 5 million pages of transcripts (Buckingham & Coffman, 1999). This staggering effort was on behalf of the Gallup organization, Buckingham's and Coffman's employer, and was completed in order to determine the distinguishing characteristics of particularly effective managers running highly successful divisions within otherwise ordinary companies.

Expecting their research to result in a shopping list of great management characteristics, Buckingham and Coffman were astonished to learn that the managers had only one thing in common, namely: their belief that employees are individuals with individual strengths, and that you get the best performance when you encourage people to use their strengths to get the job done, rather than assuming that every employee should be equally competent at every task.

Argument 3

Despite the conclusions of Buckingham and Coffman's research, this thinking is considered radical—so radical it goes by the name of the "Strengths-Based Revolution." Since assigning tasks according to individual strengths and preferences is still far from accepted practice in the workplace, why should we focus on our students' strengths when they are at an age where they still have so much to learn and so many weaknesses that need attention?

Counterargument 3

I am not arguing that we should ignore a student's weaknesses or needs, but that equal time should be given to the identification and development of strengths and preferences. In school, that means allowing students to work often in their areas of strongest intelligence and preferred learning style. Doing so builds self-knowledge and self-confidence. It also supports academic achievement by allowing students to make sense of new information through the intelligence or learning style they use best. This process is referred to as "translation" and it is something we adults do on a regular basis. For example, as a predominantly linguistic learner, I prefer that directions be given to me as a list of instructions rather than shown to me on a map. If both are provided, I ignore the map. If I'm given only a map, I translate it to my own list of directions because I know that studying the map while en route is going to be problematic for me. It doesn't mean I can't read a map if I have to, but when the stakes are high—I have to get there!—I am going to opt to use my preferred area of strength.

> "Glance at weaknesses, gaze at strengths."
> —*Unknown*

REFLECT

Inviting the Learner

Implications for the Classroom

Students should be allowed to work from their strengths when the stakes are personally high. That might be when students feel incapable and you need to boost their confidence, or when an assignment or test represents a significant portion of a student's grade. Provide for choice to honour preferred response modes on some assignments.

Think about the most challenging student in your class—the one you have the most difficulty teaching. Try to identify at least one strength the student possesses and think about ways that strength might be accessed in your classroom. (See Blackline Master 10.3 for a list of strengths.)

Consider the student's preferred learning style and reflect on the relationship between style and strength.

Talk together about teachers from your lives who noticed a strength in you that you didn't know you had, and what difference that recognition made to you.

"Appreciating learning differences is the first step. Celebrating the differences is the goal."

—*Mel Levine*

When Students Are the Problem

Sometimes the obstacle to using your knowledge of learning preferences to support your students is your students themselves. Young adolescents are very aware of the differences between themselves and others. In their desire to belong, they may be unwilling to acknowledge that they aren't great at everything, and they may be hard on students whose strengths don't match those of the "in" group. Fairness is important to this age group, so if you match learning preferences to assignments and there's a perception among your students that one task was more challenging than another, you will hear about it from them, and perhaps their parents.

All these potential problems call upon you to educate, not capitulate.

". . . and give me good abstract-reasoning ability, interpersonal skills, cultural perspective, linguistic comprehension, and a high sociodynamic potential."

If students don't believe they have different preferences:

Have students sign their name with their non-preferred hand. Record on the board adjectives they offer to describe the process. Next, have them sign their name with their preferred hand and record the adjectives. Discuss how preferences are simply part of who we are, and how preferences (like handedness) that are now considered perfectly normal were once questioned and rejected (Kise, 2006).

If students are resistant to acknowledging differences:

Repeatedly stress that people have different strengths, and provide opportunities that demonstrate and reinforce this. Opportunities can include everything from doing a people search (see Blackline Master 4.11, which is designed for multiple intelligences; you can modify it to use it for learning styles or interests), to having students identify a strength of each group member and the contribution that strength made to the group's achievement, to noticing when a student is doing something well and, with the student's consent, publicly acknowledging it and explaining why it is important.

Discuss and model alternative strategies. If there are different ways an activity can be completed, talk about these. Encourage students to prepare for an upcoming test using study techniques specific to their learning style preference—visual, auditory, or kinesthetic (Blackline Master 4.12). Talk also about how you handled similar work when you were in school or about the various ways your own children approach different tasks.

Have students determine the dominant intelligences or learning style of a character in a novel they are reading, a famous person from history, or a scientist, mathematician, or geographer whose work they are studying. Modify Blackline Master 4.13 to include the terminology of the intelligence and learning style theories you have discussed with your students.

If students perceive differing tasks as unfair:

Make sure all tasks are focused on a common essential understanding. (See pages 121–122.) Make the equity of the assignment obvious by using a common assessment tool. (See pages 253–254.) Be explicit about the fact that paying attention to differences doesn't mean that "anything goes"; your students are always going to be appropriately challenged and ultimately held accountable for their learning.

Keep exemplars of student work so that students can see what quality work through different intelligences or learning styles looks like. Discuss the qualities of exemplary work and work with your students to create criteria for assessing projects.

Creating an Effective Classroom Learning Community

QUIZ

Creating an Effective Classroom Learning Community

Please refer to the appropriate sections for any statements you are not able to check as currently true for you.

1 I believe that the development of a classroom community is up to me, and not dependent on the personalities of my students.

2 I know exactly what I want my class as a whole to achieve.

3 I can imagine, or I have experienced, a wonderful classroom community.

1–3 ▶ **The Goal of a Classroom Community, page 89**

4 I can identify the characteristics of a learning community.

5 I am aware of the relationship between resiliency and classroom community.

6 I work to ensure that all members of our community understand and appreciate the diversity of learners in the room.

4–6 ▶ **The Characteristics of a Learning Community, page 91**

7 I can explain why belonging is essential to a young adolescent and what can happen if a student doesn't experience a sense of belonging.

8 I am a "withit" teacher.

9 I am able to be emotionally objective in high-intensity moments.

7–9 ▶ **Participants Are Caring, page 92**

10 I believe that I need to teach students to be responsible.

11 I establish beginning-of-year agreements with my students based on my beliefs.

12 I can list a dozen procedures essential to successful differentiation.

13 I work at creating an attractive and inviting physical environment for my students.

10–13 ▶ **Participants Are Responsible, page 98**

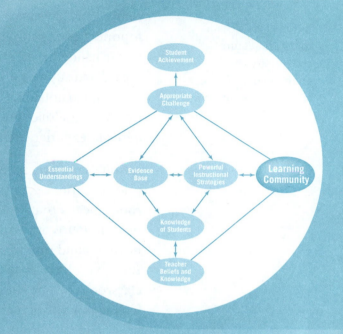

14 I provide choice for my students according to a variety of criteria.

15 I regularly debrief issues with my students in a manner that is interpreted as dialogue, not lecture.

16 I make extensive use of flexible, short-term learning groups based on student readiness, interest, or learning preferences.

17 I recognize the value of shared experiences in building community, and provide these experiences on a regular basis.

18 I believe that choice allows students to work on tasks that are at an appropriate level of challenge so that neither boredom nor frustration will derail success.

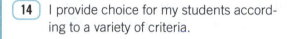

14–18 ▶ The Individual in the Community, page 106

When I want to describe the feeling of community in a classroom, I think of those moments that happen on some rainy days, when the fluorescent lights cast a warm glow in contrast to the dark skies outside, students' voices are soft and calm against the steadily falling rain, and everyone is productively and happily engaged, content to be together and cocooned from the outside world.

Many of us have experienced such moments. We remember them with fondness from our childhood and enjoy them when they happen in our teaching. In an effort to recreate that rainy-day feeling of mutual regard and support more often, we invest a great deal of energy in creating and maintaining a strong classroom community. In many ways our classroom is a microcosm of Canadian community, and we want our students to experience the feeling of belonging to a caring community.

It isn't easy. Sometimes, no matter how hard you work, your students' prior experiences or the particular combination of individuals in your room means that your community falls a little or a lot short of greatness. If you work with a different group of students every hour, you have to build multiple classroom communities, which can be difficult. But if you have ever experienced a really great community—in your classroom or elsewhere—or even if you just imagine that rainy-day feeling multiplied many times, you will keep striving because the people in a great community "become better than themselves . . . able to see more, achieve more, and have a far better time doing it than they can working alone" (Bennis & Biederman, 1997, p. 196).

Learn More About Incredible Communities

Warren Bennis and Patricia Ward Biederman (1997), *Organizing Genius: The Secrets of Creative Collaboration*. New York: Addison-Wesley.

It may be unrealistic to expect consistently amazing classroom communities, but you owe it to your students and to yourself to plan for and create effective communities each and every year. Although it takes something beyond your control to nudge effective into amazing, effective requires only intention, commitment, and hard work. It is solely within your Circle of Influence. (See page 136.)

> "School gets a chance to be a miniature community, an embryonic society."
> —*John Dewey*

The Goal of a Classroom Community

The first step in building community is to be clear about the exact nature of the community you are trying to create. The mutual regard and support I mentioned earlier are wonderful. They are visible signs of the values of respect and responsibility in action. But after years of studying community development in my own classrooms and those of my colleagues, I am confident that effective classroom communities cannot be built or sustained on warm feelings alone. They also need a goal—a clear collective purpose.

Just as individual goals give meaning and relevance to our work, a shared goal gives meaning and relevance to a community. During the Second World War, engineers from all over the United States were recruited and brought to Los Alamos, New Mexico. They were expected to sit all day, every day, at primitive computers and perform energy calculations and other tedious tasks. The United States Army was so obsessed with security it didn't tell the engineers that their work was part of a project to develop the atomic bomb—a weapon that, it was hoped, would end the war. The engineers were simply told that the relevance of their work would become clear in time, and that they should be pleased to be contributing to the war effort.

The engineers' supervisor, physicist Richard Feynman, found the men slow and their work shoddy and badly done. These were men specifically recruited for their skills; it wasn't that they didn't know how to do the tasks assigned to them. Feynman persuaded his boss, Robert Oppenheimer, to meet with the men, explain the project, and detail their contribution. Feynman describes what happened afterward as a complete transformation:

> *They began to invent ways of doing it better. They improved the scheme. They worked at night. They didn't need supervising in the night; they didn't need anything. They understood everything; they invented several of the programs that we used. (Bennis and Biederman, 1997, p. 205)*

Feynman calculated that progress on the project was 10 times faster once the work had meaning for the engineers.

Implications for the Classroom

Young adolescents are at a time in their lives when meaning, relevance, and making a contribution in the company of their peers is crucial to who they are and who they hope to become. Capitalize on your students' energy, interests, strengths, and desire to have a positive impact on their world by building a strong classroom community focused on the goal of learning together.

"Lack of something to feel important about is almost the greatest tragedy a man may have."

—*Charles C. Noble*

IN YOUR ROLE

One dictionary definition of *community* is simply "a body of people with something in common." What is the "something in common" in your classroom? What is the collective goal? After considering the question for yourself, ask your students. If either you or they identify "learning" as the goal, probe a bit further. What is it about learning that makes it a *collective* goal in your classroom? Is there something about the learning that requires people to work in community, or is the learning in your classroom a solitary, perhaps even competitive, process?

A strong learning community is equally important to teachers. As noted educator Parker Palmer writes, "The growth of any craft depends on shared practice and honest dialogue among the people who do it" (Palmer, 1998, p. 144). As a group, identify three simple actions you could take in the course of studying this book together that would increase your "shared practice and honest dialogue."

D on't be dismayed if you tried the above activity and found it difficult to define or describe a community focused on learning. (See Chapter 6 for more on the goals of learning.) Most of us struggle, partly because the term *learning community* has become a meaningless shorthand reference to any group of people in a school.

If you were to imagine an effective learning community, what would it look like? Roland Barth (1990, p. 9) says it is "a place where students and adults alike are engaged as active learners in matters of special importance to them and where everyone is thereby encouraging everyone else's learning." Myers and Simpson (1998, p. 2) provide a similar definition: a "cultural setting in which everyone learns, in which every individual is an integral part, and in which every participant is responsible for both the learning and the overall well-being of everyone else."

So, not only does each individual learn in a learning community, but each individual carries some responsibility for encouraging and supporting the learning of others. In this way, students in a strong classroom learning community assist the teacher in providing some of the protective factors that help all members of the community bounce back from life's adversities and stresses.

> "Resiliency is what happens when one regains functioning after adversity."
> —*Norman Garmezy*

To be resilient, individuals need (Benard, 2004)

- caring relationships

- opportunities for participation and contribution

- to use their strengths and interests as starting points for learning

In a learning community, individuals demonstrate (Sergiovanni, 1994)

- care and concern for each other

- responsibility for their own and each other's learning, and for the classroom environment

- understanding and appreciation for the diversity of learners

Participants in a Learning Community Are Caring

It is easy to recognize when a sense of caring is at the heart of a classroom: members are kind to each other, respect each other, and help each other grow as learners and as people. No one is isolated or ostracized; everyone feels connected and valued. Students feel they belong, that every student is a class favourite, and that their absence would be noticed.

"No greater burden can be borne by an individual than to know none who cares or understands."

—*Arthur Stainback*

It has been more than 50 years since Abraham Maslow created his hierarchy to show that belonging, or group affiliation, is a basic human need. The absence of a sense of belonging—of a connection with others who accept, value, and care about them—is considered at least partially responsible for the aggression, poor self-image, inability to defer gratification, resentment toward authority, and juvenile delinquency that we see in some of our students (Bluestein, 2001). While we may expect some rifts between adolescents and the adults who have authority over them and consider this as something of a developmental rite of passage, Thomas Sergiovanni (1994) is one of the many who fear that "the rift is becoming a chasm."

Belonging to a community changes that. A sense of community can make "peer-group dynamics . . . work in support of, rather than contrary to, the school's goals and values" (Schaps, 1999). Community has also been linked to "increased engagement in school activities, lower rates of student burnout, class cutting, and thoughts of dropping out, and a higher likelihood of feeling bad when unprepared for class" (Bluestein, 2001, p. 100). In a longitudinal study examining protective factors for adolescent health (Schaps, 1999), two factors emerged as the most significant in preventing negative outcomes for students. One was a feeling of connectedness at

Maslow's Needs Hierarchy

home; the other, connectedness at school. *Connectedness* at school is defined as feeling close to and cared for by others, and getting along with teachers and peers. If students don't feel cared for, they won't feel they belong in the community. Belonging is central to our sense of emotional safety. Learning simply doesn't happen unless and until students feel emotionally safe.

The development of an ethos of care and respect begins with the teacher. Author and therapist Chris Crutcher writes:

> *When I work with a student who is having trouble in school and ask in which class they are having the greatest success, it's never what they're best at; it's which teacher they like, which teacher shows them the respect of being a witness to their lives.* (Kittle, 2005, p. 116)

Learn More About Making Connections

This book is a short, quick read filled with practical suggestions. It makes the point that making a connection with some students, especially those with dysfunctional home lives, can spell the difference between success and failure—in life, not just in class.

Allen N. Mendler (2001), *Connecting with Students*. Virginia: ASCD.

Implications for the Classroom

A differentiating teacher is responsive to individual students based on a deep knowledge of and concern for each student's personal interests, learning preferences, and needs. In other words, you already demonstrate care and respect and your students know it.

However, if it's early in the year, your ethos of care won't yet have taken hold as "the way we treat each other in this class." Students may be making jokes at each other's expense, complaining if they have to work with someone who isn't their friend, and generally demonstrating their feelings about their peers in ways both subtle and overt. It is a mistake to allow *any* of that behaviour, regardless of whether you don't see it, or don't have the time or skill to deal with it, or simply consider it part of the developmental stage of early adolescence. If the comment is a putdown of another student and you don't stop it, you are on the slippery slope of having to decide which of the increasingly frequent comments are funny and which are hurtful.

"Take care of each other. Share your energies with the group. No one must feel alone, cut off—for that is when you do not make it."
—*Willi Unsoeld*
Mountain climber

"Relation, except in very rare cases, precedes any engagement with subject matter."
—*Nel Noddings*

Make the contrast in your responses to acceptable and unacceptable behaviour very clear. For example, I am warm and friendly in my interactions with students until someone makes an inappropriate comment, at which point my warmth vanishes. I utter the single word "Unacceptable," and I give my best "This comment is beneath our community of mature young people" look. I also become completely still, instantly creating a much greater formality and distance from my students than is usually the case for me.

Examine your own method of handling inappropriate comments, and make sure the message you are sending is consistent and clear.

 Discuss Maslow's entire hierarchy in terms of the young adolescents in your school. All levels are important. Is there a need for you to address basic needs such as nutrition, sleep, or safety? If these needs and the need for belonging have been met, what can you do to address esteem needs or self-actualization?

> "Nothing you do for children is ever wasted. They seem not to notice us, hovering, avoiding our eyes, and they seldom offer thanks, but what we do for them is never wasted."
>
> —*Garrison Keillor*

Expressing positive regard for students is easier on some days than others, and easier with some students than others. It is difficult to be a paragon of virtue when events in your personal life are creating some tough days. And it is tempting to respond in kind to a student who doesn't seem to respect or care about anyone or anything. These are the times when you remind yourself that successful teaching of young adolescents means letting them know they matter to you and that you care about them regardless of their behaviour. You do this by making generous use of the two most effective forms of classroom management: "withitness" and emotional objectivity (Marzano et al., 2003).

Caring Teachers Are "Withit"

Jacob Kounin (1970) coined "withitness" to describe the characteristic of teachers who seem, according to their students, to "have eyes in the back of their heads." While withitness is usually described as a proactive and preventive discipline strategy, I suggest that it can also describe the variety of meaningful ways that teachers can demonstrate care in daily interactions.

Withit teachers are fully present in the classroom. They greet students at the door. They remember who had a game the night before and ask about it; they listen to and empathize with students. And, whether teaching the whole class or working with a small group, they constantly scan the room, making eye contact with students, smiling, encouraging, and remaining vigilant for signs of trouble, such as students who don't treat their peers with respect.

IN YOUR ROLE

If you are working at your own desk when students are working:

Take five minutes to observe your students and the classroom atmosphere. Don't say anything and don't move from your desk—unless, of course, there's a safety issue and you must intervene. If students make eye contact with you, smile, nod encouragingly, or give a pointed look, as the situation warrants. Scan the entire class, not just the troublemakers. Once the five minutes are up, can you identify who is having a good day and who is not, or who seems comfortable in the class and who does not? What clues gave you this information?

The next day, observe your students for five minutes again. This time, however, make your observations from various points in the room. Reflect on the differences you notice when you are moving about the room. For example, misbehaving or off-task students may become industrious when you are standing near them. Acknowledge the improvement in behaviour with a smile and nod or with a positive (not sarcastic) comment and move on. During this observation, try to make each student aware that you have noticed them and that you are there for support and encouragement.

Proximity does this as long as it's more than a fast patrol up and down aisles looking for problems. Students will know you are recognizing them if you make eye contact, smile, or slow down to offer a positive comment.

If you aren't happy with the work output or behaviour of other students while you are busy working with individual students or a small group:

Students need to know that you care about how they're feeling and how their day is progressing before they can settle to work. If you are going to be busy with others, the start of the period may be the only time that all students will feel acknowledged. Make it count by greeting students at the door as they arrive, making a small personal connection with each individual. Then, while working with the group or individual, position yourself so that you can still observe the class and check in frequently by scanning the room and making eye contact with individuals. If a few days of individual acknowledgment doesn't improve work effort or behaviour, another issue is at work. You'll need to backtrack and build stronger independent work habits in your students. (See pages 99–103 in this chapter.)

If you teach several different classes and find that there is significant variation between them in the feeling of a caring community:

Check to see if you are fully present or "withit" for each class. Perhaps post-lunch drowsiness makes it especially difficult for you to teach your grade 9 French class, so you tend to give the students in that class more individual seatwork than your other classes. Maybe the advance warning you received of that "challenging" class you now have for grade 7 geography put you on the offensive and you have been a brusque taskmaster since your first day with them to make sure they didn't dare challenge you. Maybe you're learning grade 8 algebra while you're teaching it, so you've set up a predictable, and tedious, pattern of "take your seats, open your books, show me that your homework is done," after which you take up the homework, teach the new concept, assign the work, and so on.

Although it is true that your students need to work with you to build a caring community, your actions are the decisive factor. If there are minimal points of connection, there's minimal opportunity to demonstrate care and concern for individuals. Self-assess your classroom presence by charting a week of classes. (See Blackline Master 5.1.) If you find there are times when you aren't as withit as usual, choose one of the suggested actions from the blackline master and experiment with adding it to that time period.

Discuss the concept of "withitness." Do you think it's appropriate to link teacher awareness or presence to students' perceptions about whether their teacher cares about them? If a teacher has difficulty multi-tasking—scanning the environment and being aware of individual students while teaching the lesson—does that mean the teacher won't be perceived as caring? Are there other ways for a teacher to demonstrate care?

"I don't need to go to a gym. One of my classroom management strategies is to circulate frequently around the room. I figure I walk three miles a day."

Source: www.CartoonStock.com.

Caring Teachers Demonstrate Emotional Objectivity

The heading may appear oxymoronic—caring requires attachment, whereas you have to be detached to be objective. But as those who successfully teach or parent young adolescents will attest, success comes when you are able to care *without* the expectation of a positive response from the teen. An emotionally objective teacher neither romanticizes nor demonizes students. They are neither your best friends nor your sworn enemies. Emotional objectivity means that you can't be crushed when students are angered by your calm application of consequences for disciplinary infractions, or personally wounded when a student walks past you without responding to your greeting at the door. Demonstrate caring by recognizing and responding to students as individuals, but also by consistently reinforcing rules of behaviour, regardless of the student's home life or your personal regard for them. Adolescents value fairness and want equitable treatment for all in the classroom.

IN YOUR ROLE

Our efforts are sometimes superhuman, but when it comes to responding to difficult students, teachers are human beings. If you are having trouble appearing emotionally objective with some of your more challenging young adolescents, try any of these strategies suggested by Marzano et al. (2005):

→ Reframe. Explain a student's behaviour so that it has nothing to do with you. For example, "John didn't respond when I said hello. I wonder what has him upset. I'll check in with him later."

→ Don't let anger be obvious in your demeanour. Look at the student directly, but don't glare or stare. Stand close enough that you can speak quietly and calmly, but not so close that you loom over the student. Keep your facial expressions neutral as you state what angers you.

→ Give yourself a break. After a negative encounter with a student, actively seek healthy ways to alleviate the tension you are feeling. Watch a show that makes you laugh, do a workout, have coffee with a friend—whatever works for you and helps you make a fresh start with that student and others the next day.

Responsibility is a contentious issue among teachers of young adolescents. Teachers all want the same result: that their students become self-directed, independent learners, able to make good decisions and solve their own problems, committed to taking care of others and of the world. But teachers do tend to have widely varying beliefs about how best to achieve this goal.

IN YOUR ROLE

Start from the actions you take with students and work backwards to determine the corresponding mental model or belief that you have about students taking responsibility for their learning. Here are two examples:

If	Then
Your action is to record a zero in your mark book for the six assignments that Hannah didn't complete, even though you talked to her about the implications and gave her opportunities to submit the work later	Your mental model is that students of Hannah's age will hopefully become responsible by experiencing the consequences of their irresponsibility. If they don't, they have made a poor choice and it is their problem.
Your actions are to call Hannah's parents after the first or second missed assignment, talk with Hannah and help her make a plan to complete the missed assignments and, if she fails to honour the plan, work with her parents in setting up a new plan that would be impossible for Hannah to avoid	Your mental model is that students of Hannah's age don't necessarily possess the maturity to make decisions that have long-term consequences. It is your job to assume that responsibility and gradually release it to the students as you teach them to make good decisions.

Most students will be kinder and more caring toward one another when they are in a nurturing environment where care is consistently demonstrated toward them. Responsibility, however, is different. Most students have to be taught how to be responsible. If you don't teach responsibility, directly and through modelling, and if you don't create an environment that supports students in becoming responsible, you will find it very difficult to differentiate instruction effectively.

The good news is that young adolescents crave the opportunities we offer. They *want* to be independent, to make a contribution, to be treated more like an adult and less like a child. But they also want it recognized that, as my niece once suggested, they've "only been on the planet for 12 years."

Students need support, modelling, and guided practice. If you are prepared to teach them to be responsible, then sharing ownership, providing choice, and debriefing are three actions you can take to help build a strong community and support effective differentiated instruction. Inspiring students with your trust and confidence in them will encourage them to take new risks with your guidance.

Share Ownership

Classrooms are run, whether smoothly or with difficulty, on a combination of beliefs, rules, procedures, and routines. As you read in Chapter 2, your beliefs are the first and most important determinants of the classroom you are going to create. By constantly living your beliefs and by sharing them in conversations with your students, you reassure them that the classroom will be a safe and supportive place where it is possible to take risks because they can count on being treated as thoughtful and mature people.

Implications for the Classroom

Many teachers like to establish with their students a set of agreements as to how they will function together in the classroom. These agreements are based on the teacher's non-negotiable beliefs, but emerge from discussion by the whole class and are personalized to the language and needs of the class. If you want students to assume some responsibility for a smoothly functioning classroom and the well-being of its participants, it's important that beginning-of-year efforts result in agreements, not in lists of rules.

> "Many of the teachers and parents who grumble that kids just don't take responsibility' spend their days ordering kids around—as though children could learn how to make good decisions by following directions."
> —*Alfie Kohn*

> "Few things help an individual more than to place responsibility upon him, and to let him know that you trust him."
> —*Booker T. Washington*

Assess any agreements created in your class against the following criteria.

Class agreements that support student ownership of the classroom community

→ *are about fostering relationships*

→ *consist of positive, affirming language rather than a list of prohibitions ("We believe in respecting each other" rather than "No putdowns")*

→ *use student language as much as possible so they don't sound like school policy documents*

→ *are short, to reflect that they're a thoughtful summary of what matters*

→ *are written in a student's handwriting, signed by all students, or artistically represented by a student*

Procedures are ways of doing things, routines are a sequence of procedures, and rules are expectations of behaviour. Procedures and routines are critical when students are moving about the room and engaging in a variety of tasks. If students are involved in the development of workable procedures, disruptions are minimized and there is little need for rules. If needed, post rules for easy reference.

Implications for the Classroom

The following procedures are especially important to the smooth operation of a differentiated classroom. A suggestion is provided for each procedure, but the best suggestions will probably come from your students. Let them own the procedure whenever possible. Post procedures for student reference.

Managing Movement

Moving furniture	Decide what furniture groupings you need for various activities, then have students practise putting the furniture in those groupings until they can do it quickly and quietly.
Leaving the room for washroom, library, computer lab . . .	Establish a quota for each destination, a time limit, and a method for logging in and out. Students who abuse the privilege should be privately placed on restricted access and have to earn back your trust in their ability to be responsible for their actions.

Managing Resources

Distributing supplies	Assign and rotate responsibility to "materials managers." Multiple managers will get supplies distributed faster and with less fuss than a single manager.
Cleaning up at the end of a class	Make good use of bins and other organizational tools. If there are places for everything and people have assigned responsibilites, clean-up doesn't need to be an issue. Refer also to ownership of the physical environment (see page 105), which significantly reduces clean-up problems.
Storing materials	Have a bin per table stocked with scissors, sticky notes, rulers, pencils, pens, glue sticks, and other supplies. Tape a list of supplies and quantities to the inside of the lid; make sure the bin is an appropriate size and has compartments so that everything can be easily viewed and counted; and colour-code the items so that it's clear what bin they came from. Give students the responsibility of ensuring that all items are returned to the appropriate bin at the end of the period.

Managing Interactions

Assigning partnerships or small groups	Use a variety of ways to assign students to flexible partnerships or groups. (See page 109.)
Adjusting noise level	Determine acceptable noise levels for different kinds of activity and then practise, practise, practise until students are able to produce the appropriate level on command.
	Make a game of sustaining the right noise level. For example, a class may enjoy trying to beat their previous scores as they record the length of time they were able to maintain the appropriate level of noise.

Note: The routine of moving from whole class to small-group activity would involve a particular sequence of a number of procedures.

Managing Work

Distributing assignments	Have one file folder per student, colour-coded according to the student's group. One student acts as group leader and is responsible for inserting assignments into each student's folder, distributing the folders, and returning them to the cabinet at the end of the period. (Note: This is also a quick way to take attendance if you ask the group leaders to return the folders of absent students at the start of the class.)
Knowing what to do if help is needed	Use an adaptation of the primary teacher's "three before me" rule: Have students ask their question of the other members of their group. If no one knows the answer, they all raise their hands and you know that help has been sought appropriately. Provide group leaders with the information they need to handle most requests for help.
Knowing what to do in a small-group or paired activity	Give groups assignment sheets, task cards, or an audio recording of the assignment. Alternatively, provide instructions to the group leaders who in turn share them with the rest of the group. Avoid having all students sit and wait while you explain each group's assignment.
Completing work on time	Teach students to "chunk" their work, especially larger assignments, into a number of smaller tasks. They can use a calendar to work backward from the deadline, assigning various tasks to specific dates. Check in, especially with struggling students, at points along the way.
Knowing what to do when work is finished	Have a list of interesting and meaningful activities that students can turn to when they have completed an assignment.
Handing in completed work	Require students to check their work against a list of criteria for the assignment before they hand it in as completed. Have a tray (if it's an individual assignment) or a folder (if it's a group assignment) where students put their completed work. In either case, provide a class list where students initial that they've submitted the work.

CLASS ROOM

When Work Is Finished

Finding out about missed work during an absence	Staple file folders to a bulletin board where you immediately put extra copies of handouts, newsletters, and so on.
	Have students exchange phone numbers with a homework buddy, and hold buddies responsible for keeping each other informed.
	Have a rotating roster of class secretaries who are responsible for keeping a detailed log of the day's activities.

IN YOUR ROLE

List all the responsibilities you have tomorrow. Delegate to students any responsibilities that do not absolutely have to be carried out by you.

 Individually, order the above list of procedures from most to least difficult to implement. Compare your lists, and share ideas for some of the most challenging procedures. Invite your students to contribute their suggestions and tell them you'll share their ideas with the rest of your colleagues.

The Physical Environment

Teachers spend more days in their classrooms in a year than they do in their own homes. Yet, whereas most homes are attractive, comfortable, and inviting spaces, many classrooms can be impersonal, messy, sometimes grubby, and often depressing. Consider each of the following sights common to many grade 6–9 classrooms. What beliefs are being communicated to students through each example?

▶ 25 percent of the classroom space is taken up by the teacher's desk, bookcase, filing cabinets, and worktable.

▶ Stacks of papers and books lie on all of the above surfaces.

▶ Bulletin boards are empty or are never updated.

▶ The tops of bookcases and cabinets are used for long-term storage.

▶ Bookcases contain class sets of texts no longer in use, stacks of *National Geographic* magazines that no one ever references, and donated sets of outdated encyclopedias.

If you believe that your students should be enthusiastic about learning, positive about themselves and others, willing to take risks, and constantly striving to do their best work, consider capitalizing on the power of the physical environment in fostering progress toward those goals.

The two key considerations for the set-up of a differentiated classroom to enhance student responsibility are:

The Classroom Environment on Rotary

Posters Help Me

The Classroom Environment

▶ Flexibility—There are spaces in the room for whole class, small group, partner, and individual work, or students are adept at quickly and quietly moving their desks into these configurations (see page 100). Regardless of grouping, you and your students should be able to circulate easily from one area of the room to another.

▶ Organization—Students have access to a wide variety of resources, from art supplies to assistive devices. They know where to find the material they need and how to access it. You have taught them to be responsible for returning resources to their proper places, and have organized the classroom so that these places are clearly identified (see page 101). If organization is not your strong suit, there are always students in your class who will be delighted to assume this responsibility. Approach your principal for a small budget for plastic bins, coloured file folders, et cetera, and give your students ownership of planning, purchasing, and putting an organized system in place for you.

There are easy ways to personalize classrooms so that they're comfortable, inviting, and reflective of the interests, strengths, and intelligences of the people who inhabit them. Here are a few suggestions:

→ Hang a bulletin board devoted to student interests and celebrating individual or class achievements, with various groups or individuals responsible for updating it on a regular schedule.

→ Have science and math puzzles and toys readily available for student use.

→ Set up a class library. Display the books attractively with the covers visible to pique interest.

→ Display interesting three-dimensional objects such as mobiles, kites, or a rope ladder with toy monkeys.

→ Write on the board a daily quote that is inspirational, or humorous, or just a great conversation starter. (See Blackline Master 5.2 for some examples to get you started.) Have students take turns adding their daily quotes.

→ Have available a CD player with a wide selection of music for a variety of purposes. Allen (2001, p. 119) suggests that you buy a few compilation CDs—best of a time period, artist, or genre, for example—and that you:

→ Play an up-tempo selection to energize and slow-tempo to calm.

→ Play music during transitional activities, such as when students move their desks into new groupings.

→ Play a Baroque selection to focus participants.

For Example

One year my students decided to write a class dictionary of the interesting objects in our classroom. It was a great way to encourage student ownership of the classroom, a feeling they shared with their parents when they presented the dictionaries at the end of the September open house. As an added bonus, they learned about dictionary structure in a relevant and interesting way.

The dictionary included the many unusual features of our classroom, features we had worked together to put in place during a room set-up and meet and greet party at the end of the summer.

Provide Choice

Choice makes the young adolescent's desire for control and freedom possible—without the power struggle. Choice builds confidence and fosters independence. Choice tells students their interests are important and allows them to demonstrate responsibility. Choice helps students learn to make good decisions, which is a far more difficult and useful skill than following directions.

In a differentiated classroom where students have learned about their strengths, preferences, and needs (see Chapter 4), and where they have developed the values of care, respect, and responsibility that allow them to function as interdependent and supportive members of a learning community, choice allows them to personalize and take more ownership of their education.

Choice in the classroom can be thought of as a continuum.

| completely the teacher's choice | student choice from a range of teacher options | completely the student's choice |

Jane Bluestein cites a study that claims "98 percent or more of assignments are teacher-selected, with no student input involved at all" (2001, pp. 216–217). That is clearly not a position from which to teach responsibility or build community. But neither is the other end of the continuum. Unlimited choice is overwhelming for students, way too much work for you to tie their choices to essential understandings and assessment structures, and of limited value in the development of community because students are scattered in 30 different directions doing 30 different things.

> "Man ultimately decides for himself! And in the end, education must be education toward the ability to decide."
> —*Victor Frankl*

Choices are in *how* students do their learning, not in *what* they are learning.

Choices are always focused on the same essential understandings. (See Chapter 6.)

The rule of thumb when providing students with choice is to allow a maximum of four to six options *after* students have learned how to make choices. To teach them how to make choices, begin by providing no more than two options; for example, "You can answer Question 7 either by drawing a food chain or by writing about it." For each choice you provide, make sure students have already had the opportunity to practise or apply the skill to a high level of quality. For example, if you tell students they can compare and contrast the creation of Frankenstein's monster to the development of the atomic bomb by either creating a computer animation or writing a free-verse poem, your days will be challenging and your assessments unfair if you haven't taught them how to animate on the computer and how to write free verse. Remember also to discuss criteria for exemplary work and, where possible, provide some exemplars so that students know what excellence looks like. (See Chapter 11.)

Young adolescents need to develop their skills not just in making but in creating wise choices. In addition to the choices that you provide, encourage students to share their ideas. Requiring them to connect their choice suggestion to the essential understandings of the unit reinforces your learning goals.

Students can be offered choices in just about anything: homework, daily assignments, major assignments, and tests. However, they don't need to be offered choice all the time. It's up to you to select those times when choice would be beneficial. For example, offering a choice is helpful when you want students to have the opportunity to

→ work in an area of strength in order to further develop that strength, or to build their confidence, or to give them the chance to do well on a test or performance-based assessment

→ work with friends or with students of similar strengths, needs, or interests

→ work on a particular skill or concept to develop mastery

Choice isn't necessarily wide open. You can provide your choices using a grid called a Choice Board. (See Blackline Master 5.3 for a blank grid. Add additional columns and rows to increase from a 4 x 4 grid to 5 x 5, 6 x 6, or whatever you need.) Here are some examples of how you can use a Choice Board:

→ Develop one Choice Board for all multiple intelligences.

→ Develop a Choice Board for each multiple intelligence to give to certain students, so that the students have choices, but within parameters set by you.

→ Create a Choice Board for Bloom's Taxonomy questions and direct specific students to specific columns on the Choice Board.

→ Use the Choice Board as a bingo or tic-tac-toe game, and require students to either complete all the activities in a row of their choice or to complete certain activities and then choose which of the rest to complete.

If you use Choice Boards frequently you can set up a permanent grid on a bulletin board, writing the activities on large cards that can be rearranged or rewritten. This option works only if you have all students use the same Choice Board. Use paper copies of Choice Boards if you want to provide different choices to different students. (See Blackline Masters 9.6 and 9.14 for samples of completed Choice Boards.)

When you offer choice to your students, keep in mind that young adolescents, when given the option, will want to work with their friends. While friendships are critically important at this age and students should be given some opportunity to select partners or groups on the basis of friendship, be aware that someone is always left out, work production frequently suffers, and your cohesive classroom community where everyone cares for, respects, and encourages each other may not come to pass. To help students make choices based on interest in a topic rather than what their best friend is doing, make frequent use of randomly assigned partnerships or groupings so that all students experience working with all of their classmates. This fosters the development of teamwork, which is essential in schools and later in the workforce.

Try any or all of these suggestions for placing students randomly with partners or in small groups. You may hear fewer complaints because the process is truly random and, at least the first few times, a bit novel. Arrange several variations of random groupings or partnerships to allow you as much flexibility as possible in your classroom.

Partners

→ Hand out cards, of which students need to find the other half. The cards can be related to the curriculum; for example, math problems and their solutions, names of short stories and their authors, or terms and their definitions from any subject area.

→ Use two suits from a deck of playing cards and have students find the matching number or face card of the other suit. For variation, use cards from Monopoly or another game.

→ Provide each student with a copy of the Learning Partners Clock on Blackline Master 5.4. Have each student go to 12 other students, asking them to write their names on the different hours of the clock. The student also writes his or her name on the same hour of the other person's clock. For example, if Rishi is Travis's 11 o'clock partner, Rishi writes his name at 11 o'clock on Travis's clock and Travis writes his name in the same place on Rishi's clock. When you want students to work with a partner, tell them to meet with their partner of a particular hour. This allows students to move around the classroom, which is good for your kinesthetic learners, and gives you and the students lots of variation in partnering. If you want to set up specific partnerships, such as pairing a strong math student with a struggling one, you can always pre-assign certain partners for a particular hour before students complete their clocks, and call out that hour when you want those individuals to work together.

Small Groups of Four

→ Buy a package of coloured popsicle sticks and have students sit in colour groups.

→ Write each student's name on a popsicle stick and draw names for each group or partnership. Note that you can also draw name sticks for roles on teams such as materials manager, or for the order in which people will be asked to share their ideas.

→ Use all four suits of a deck of playing cards and have students sit with others of their number.

→ Hand out cards that can easily be clustered into groups of four, such as four quotations that deal with the same theme or four facts about the same concept.

Debrief

In recent years literacy teachers have been encouraged to do think-alouds when teaching students a new strategy. Think-alouds, as the name suggests, involve the teacher or a student verbalizing their thinking process as they work through a piece of text. Teachers share connections, clarify confusions, and show students how to mentally question a text.

Debriefing with Students

Grouping Students

One of the best actions you can take in building an effective classroom learning community is to do a great many think-alouds about classroom issues. Talk about everything: from how you went about making a particular decision to what interpretations someone might make of a sarcastic comment and ways to rephrase it. The difference between literacy and community building is that in community building you want to move very quickly into dialogue. Students should do as many think-alouds as you do, otherwise your best intended advice will become the meaningless sound of Charlie Brown's teacher—"Wah wah wah, wah wah . . . ."

When you debrief with students in a respectful and supportive manner, you accomplish a number of important objectives:

▶ You give students a language for their feelings and a different perspective on situations, both of which are needed by the young adolescent. (See page 44.)

▶ You model respectful, reflective, and thoughtful discourse.

▶ You teach decision-making and other higher level critical and creative thinking skills.

▶ You demonstrate concern for your students and your belief that they are mature young people who are learning to be responsible and self-directed and therefore do not need to be treated as children.

▶ You foster the appreciation of multiple perspectives.

IN YOUR ROLE

Watch your language! If you want students to assume responsibility, always say "our" classroom, never "my" classroom. If you want students to feel mature, consider addressing them as "ladies and gentlemen."

Provide students with private opportunities to share their thoughts and feelings with you. This will help them practise how to share their ideas, make them feel safer in the classroom, and give you useful insights into each individual. Once a week you could have students respond to the prompt "How's it going?" in a journal of the same name.

Students should also be encouraged to share their suggestions for future instruction. This will foster shared ownership for success in the classroom.

Class meetings or community circles are well worth the time and effort. They build a commitment to community and help students develop democratic citizenship skills. Establish some ground rules, such as offering a positive comment about the week before saying anything negative, refraining from using names, and focusing on solutions rather than the problems. Have students take turns as circle leaders (and with you participating as a member of the circle). When a community circle goes well, both you and your students will recognize it as the achievement of an excellent classroom community.

Remember that shared experiences are invaluable for building community. Something as simple as your daily read-aloud of the latest novel chapter, poem, or nonfiction text gives students a pleasurable experience that they have in common and enjoy referencing.

Essential Understandings

Essential Understandings

Imagine that the following information is in a unit you are going to teach, then answer the questions that follow. Refer to the appropriate pages for more information about each question.

- In early hypotheses about the universe, Earth was at the centre.
- This view of the universe corresponded to Christian beliefs of the time.
- Claudius Ptolemeus thought the Earth remained stationary, and the moon, sun, planets, and stars revolved in circular orbits around it.
- Nicolas Copernicus thought the stars were fixed, and that Earth and the other planets revolved in circular orbits around the sun.
- This solved some problems in explaining the movement of stars and planetary orbits, but it created other problems.
- The theory meant that Earth was no longer the centre of the universe.
- Copernicus was afraid he'd be found guilty of heresy and burned at the stake. His theories weren't published until he was on his deathbed, and even then he stressed that they were just a hypothesis to resolve certain mathematical difficulties.
- It took Galileo, looking through a telescope and taking a public stand, to bring about an intellectual revolution in the way we understand the structure of the universe.

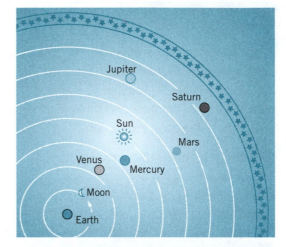

1. What essential understandings could this unit be about other than the structure of the universe? (page 121)

2. What are the four aspects of quality curriculum that are especially important to young adolescents? (page 117)

3. Which of these questions are essential? (page 123)

   (a) What is the main difference between Ptolemeus's and Copernicus's hypotheses about the universe?

   (b) Why would it matter if Earth is not the centre of the universe?

   (c) Are ideas worth dying for?

4. Would your students be interested in exploring the answers to challenging questions or would they just want the facts? (page 119)

5. After you have framed an essential question and shared it with your students, what would you do next? (page 126)

6. What do essential understandings have to do with differentiated instruction? (page 128)

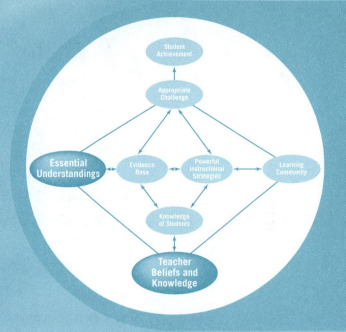

"I don't pretend to understand the universe; it is a great deal bigger than I am."
—*Thomas Carlyle*

After English Class

I used to like "Stopping by Woods on a Snowy Evening."
I liked the coming darkness,
The jingle of harness bells, breaking—and adding to
—the stillness,
The gentle drift of snow . . . .

But today, the teacher told us what everything stood for.
The woods, the horse, the miles to go, the sleep—
They all have "hidden meanings."

It's grown so complicated now that,
Next time I drive by,
I don't think I'll bother to stop.

—Kate Bloomfield in *Hey World, Here I Am!* by Jean Little

Whether it is a poem they're studying in English, a historical event they're reading about in social studies, or a hypothesis they are experimenting with in science, we want students to "bother to stop." We want them to discover the pleasures of learning, to feel the exhilaration that comes from understanding, from connecting the pieces, from seeing the patterns and gaining insights. We have experienced these pleasures ourselves; it may be one of the reasons we became teachers. For some, this is *the* reason we teach young adolescents: the desire to ignite a passion we feel for a particular discipline in others at an age when they may decide to make that passion their life's work.

It is scary to see how quickly passion for learning can be buried under the pressure to address curriculum guidelines, standardized, high-stakes tests, and the ever-growing demands of accountability for achievement. Feeling pressured and overwhelmed, it is a small step for teachers everywhere to start saying, and ultimately believing, that their job is to cover the curriculum, to explain the hidden meanings

Hopefully you have had many positive experiences of times when you were acutely aware of your learning. One of mine happened during a summer course on the teaching of primary mathematics that I took early in my teaching career. One day we were doing an activity with base 10 blocks. That day, the borrowing and carrying I'd learned 20 years earlier made sense to me for the very first time. I'll never forget the "eureka" moment when I understood the concept of bases, when I could see the pattern and apply my understanding to adding and subtracting in other bases.

Share your story of an exhilarating learning moment with the group. Then look for commonalities among the stories.

rather than allow students to discover them, and to "get as many students through" as possible, knowing the others will simply have to catch up on their own time.

These kinds of statements are, of course, completely contradictory to the two central themes of this book:

▶ Teaching must be *effective* by making a significant and enduring positive impact.

▶ Teaching must be *responsive* by differentiating to meet the varying needs of individuals.

If you believe teaching to be more than the one-way transmission of information, if you think it has to do with helping students make sense of information and developing an understanding of important concepts and skills, then, when students don't learn, can you really say you have fulfilled your responsibility? Have you really *taught*?

Copyright 1997 by Randy Glasbergen.

"Class, I've got a lot of material to cover, so to save time I won't be using vowels today. Nw lts bgn, pls pn t pg 122."

This chapter is about how you can be both effective and responsive and how you can uncover understanding, not just cover curriculum. If you believe this to be impossible in your work environment, however, you will find yourself putting up mental barriers in response to every suggestion that follows. Refer to the mind-changing options discussed in Chapter 2 (see pages 27–28) or look at the problem of too much curriculum and too little time from these creative perspectives:

Make It Worse

Make the problem worse. Imagine you have no choice in planning your day whatsoever. You are given a list of facts to teach (forget about concepts) for every minute of every day and are constantly racing against the clock. Elaborate on what your day would look like if the situation were as bad as it could get. Then, imagine that you do not have the option of quitting your job. Make a list of ways you would retain your integrity as a teacher under these conditions. Is there anything in the list that gives you ideas for improving your current conditions (Schenck, 2007)?

Host a Dinner Party

Imagine hosting a dinner party to which you invite six people whose opinions and experiences you value. Your guests can be living or dead, famous or infamous, or your next-door neighbours. (Note: You will get better ideas from people who aren't educators. For example, Kris Kristofferson is my personal favourite.) Put your dilemma to the group and imagine their responses.

Challenge Your Assumptions

Turn your assumption (e.g., the only way to address all curriculum outcomes or expectations in this unit is by lecturing) into a provocation (e.g., all curriculum outcomes or expectations in this unit can be addressed through one really great question). Use the provocation to start thinking in a new way. Schenck reports that Federal Express was formed by crop-dusting pilot Fred Smith when he turned an assumption ("It takes an average of three to five days to deliver a package") into a provocation ("A package can be delivered overnight") (Schenck, 2007, p. 188).

Practise the Principles of *Koinonia*

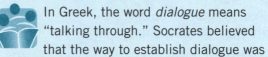 In Greek, the word *dialogue* means "talking through." Socrates believed that the way to establish dialogue was to honestly exchange ideas, suspending all untested assumptions and making no attempt to change each other's mind. The rules of dialogue for the ancient Greek philosophers were "Don't argue," "Don't interrupt," and "Listen carefully."

These principles were known as *koinonia,* meaning "spirit of fellowship." *Koinonia* allows the members of a group to focus on developing ideas rather than winning arguments (Michalko, 2001).

Quality Curriculum for Young Adolescents

igh-quality curriculum is a non-negotiable and non-differentiated component of an effective classroom. If you are not focusing on what your students absolutely need to know, understand, and be able to do by the end of their time with you, you aren't preparing them for life, never mind the next grade. If you differentiate *what* you are teaching to the extent that some students get the essentials and some do not, you are also differentiating their likelihood of success—in life and in the next grade.

This does not mean, however, that curriculum is not part of the discussion of how to create effective differentiated instruction for young adolescents. On the contrary, as the National Middle School Association argues in the position paper *This We Believe* (2003, p. 24), nothing is "as important as creating developmentally responsive curriculum."

A high-quality curriculum for young adolescents has the following characteristics (NMSA, 2003):

▶ It is *relevant*, allowing students to connect to areas of personal interest, answer questions they have about themselves and the world, see the connections across subject boundaries, and create new areas of interest and opportunity. (See page 56.)

▶ It is *challenging*, examining important concepts from a variety of perspectives, helping students to "start where they are" and moving them forward from that position, and furthering each student's ability to take increasing responsibility for their own learning. (See page 99.)

▶ It is *integrative*, focusing on the big ideas that cross subject boundaries and that connect with students' lives, teaching literacy and mathematical literacy skills not as isolated subjects, but wherever and whenever they are useful, and helping students reflect on their experiences and progress so they become aware

> "To be able to be caught up in the world of thought—that is to be educated."
> —*Edith Hamilton*

of their learning, not just in school but throughout their lives. (See page 56.)

▶ It is *exploratory*, recognizing that young adolescents need the opportunity to "engage in activities that will broaden their views of the world and of themselves" (NMSA, 2003, p. 24). (See page 50.)

Today Miss McIntyre, our guidance counselor, said, "You have to decide who you are and where you're going." . . .

Right now I could be anybody, Miss McIntyre. Can't you understand that? I could be anybody at all.

I'm not ready to choose and besides, I'm choosing more than one road. I'm putting myself together, Miss McIntyre. But it is like a jigsaw puzzle. I keep on finding new pieces.

If you were once a puzzle, you soon found the edge pieces and fitted yourself inside. There is no edge to me yet. I hope the picture turns out to be worth the work. I hope I never discover an edge.

—**Kate Bloomfield in *Hey World, Here I Am!* by Jean Little**

It sounds so easy, doesn't it? Make the curriculum relevant, challenging, integrative, and exploratory and you will be successfully teaching young adolescents *and* capably preparing them for an unknown and unknowable future. But we all know it isn't that easy, and that lack of time, standardized tests, curriculum documents, and parental expectations aren't the only problems. Sometimes the students themselves get in the way of your best efforts to be developmentally responsive.

When Students Are Part of the Problem

Dysfunctional mental models aren't the exclusive property of adults. Some students, for example, have what is referred to as a shallow understanding or conception of learning. These students favour classroom activities that allow them to look smart, such as spelling tests or computation drills, over those that help them to become smart, such as inquiry and problem solving (Dweck and Bempechat, 1983). The difficulty, of course, is that learning tasks aren't good for helping us look smart. They are often "difficult, involve errors, confusion, or revelations of ignorance, and they require a lengthy presolution period" (Dweck and Bempechat, 1983). Additionally, they require a high tolerance for ambiguity and uncertainty.

A shallow conception of learning is often accompanied by what Dweck and Bempechat (1983) refer to as an "entity model" of intelligence. In the entity model, which seems to be independent of both subject difficulty (Stodolsky, 1988) and academic ability (Dweck and Bempechat, 1983), students believe both that an objective truth exists and resides in the teacher and that every issue is simply a matter of personal opinion, which is immune to criticism or change.

I'm not a fan of laying blame for students' difficulties at the feet of their previous year's teacher. That simply moves the problem out of your Circle of Influence and into the Circle of Concern (see page 136), which isn't particularly helpful. But it can be helpful to know that some of your students' beliefs come from multiple years of "doing school" in a certain way and that the cumulative impact of these years shapes not only student understanding but also your own pedagogy (Gabella, 1993). It is helpful to know that, when faced with a class where the majority have a shallow conception of learning, you may unconsciously use strategies that avoid disturbing the balance of order and control in the classroom. These strategies might include avoiding controversial topics, simplifying complex issues, and fragmenting tasks and information into smaller, more easily managed pieces (McNeil, 1986).

> "Education is about learning to deal with uncertainty and ambiguity. It is about learning to savor the quality of the journey. It is about inquiry and deliberation. It is about becoming critically minded and intellectually curious, and it is about learning how to frame and pursue your own educational aims."
> —*Elliot Eisner*

You may be among the last of your young adolescents' teachers who have enough time with them at a point in their lives when they are still open to influence. This is the time to help students become smart, rather than look smart. You can do that through inquiry-based learning, where students are actively engaged in exploring interesting questions, making observations, and building knowledge about important concepts.

If your students have trouble tolerating ambiguity and uncertainty:

Some students are not developmentally ready to tolerate ambiguity and uncertainty, so you will need to choose your battles. One place where the battle is worthwhile is at the end of an inquiry. If students believe there is a definitive answer that you will eventually hand to them, they will not bother to search. "On the other hand, if the outcome is truly a puzzle, and we have the chance to develop a solution that is both unique and powerful, we are far more likely to plunge in. Not only do ambiguity and uncertainty serve as the starting point of any inquiry, they are the necessary conditions for anyone to take inquiry seriously" (Gabella, 1993, pp. 9–10).

If your students are focused on looking smart:

Make sure your teaching practices reinforce students' efforts to become smart. Relentlessly acknowledge and applaud growth and risk-taking. Talk about all the different ways to be smart (see Chapter 4) and provide activities using a variety of entry points (see page 74) so that students are bombarded with evidence that they don't need to look smart because their strengths and preferences give them many different ways to become smart.

If your students think you are the source of objective truth:

When you don't have an answer to a question, say so. Let your students see you searching for the answer. Congratulate yourself and them if they ask you a question you can't answer; it shows they are digging below the surface of a subject.

If your students constantly fall back on "I'm entitled to my opinion":

Require that their opinion be supported by evidence. Use Anticipation Guides (see page 132) and structures such as debates (see page 123) to create controversy. Model the importance of supporting opinion with evidence in community meetings (see page 111) and whole-class discussions.

Essential Understandings

No matter how many ways you do the math, there is a distinct and troublesome imbalance between the amount of instruction time available and the number of learning outcomes students are expected to be introduced to, work with, or master in that time. When the diversity of students' backgrounds and knowledge—and the particular social, emotional, and cognitive needs of young adolescents, including their need for the development of a strong and supportive learning community—are factored in, some tough choices have to be made about what life in your classroom will look like on a daily basis. Fortunately, a focus on essential understandings allows you to find the middle ground between the extremes of a forced march through a master list of outcomes or expectations and a classroom where students' learning is secondary to whether they are getting along and feeling good about themselves. Neither position provides effective education; a focus on essential understandings does.

Essential understandings—what Wiggins and McTighe call *enduring understandings*—are big ideas at the core of a subject, ideas that are of keen interest to experts in that subject and that are often the source of misconceptions for novices (Wiggins and McTighe, 2005). Because they are ideas at the heart of a discipline and with value beyond the classroom, essential understandings are a natural fit for inquiry-based units that encourage students to wonder, ask questions, and collaborate in building knowledge to answer those questions.

Determining the essential understandings of a discipline requires either that you understand the subject matter "deeply and flexibly" (Darling-Hammond, 1998, p. 6) or that you work in a team with colleagues who have that expertise. Essential understandings "have great transfer value; applying to many other inquiries and issues over time—horizontally' (across subjects) and vertically' (through the years in later courses) in the curriculum and out of school" (Wiggins and McTighe, 2005, p. 69).

An interdisciplinary team is an excellent means for teachers to share their subject expertise for the benefit of students by addressing how various concepts connect across the disciplines.

To determine big ideas or essential understandings (Wiggins and McTighe, 2005, pp. 73–74), try:

- Reading the descriptive text preceding the outcome or expectation statements

- Looking for recurring nouns and verbs in the curriculum documents; nouns highlight the big ideas, verbs the core tasks

- Thinking about your subject in terms of large transferable concepts such as conflict or discovery

- Asking yourself a question such as "What is a real-world insight about . . . ?" or "Why study . . . ? So what?"

- Asking yourself, "Is this idea worth knowing as an adult? Will learning it now make my students better adults?"

Understanding by Design

Essential understandings may be thought of as umbrella concepts that subsume specific facts. For example, you would talk to your students about intelligence (the concept) before you asked them to decide whether specific actions (facts) are examples of Sternberg's creative, practical, or analytical categories of intelligence. (See Chapter 4.)

Practise determining concepts by identifying, in one or two words, the big idea of a book you have read or a movie you have seen.

Examine the curriculum guidelines for the subjects you teach. If they do not already make the concepts clear, work from the expectations or outcomes to determine the important concepts, and cluster the expectations or outcomes under each concept.

t is helpful to phrase essential understandings or big ideas as questions or problems to signify that students will be actively involved in inquiry. As Jacqueline Brooks reminds us in *Schooling for Life,*

There's really no reason to be in school if there are no problems and no questions. Students are supposed to go to school to think about good questions and to solve important problems, or at least to attempt these activities . . . . The students I spoke with thought that all they needed to do was show up and follow directions. And for the most part, they were correct. When we help students "succeed" in school when they invest no effort, we're setting a terrible precedent for our youth. (2002, pp. 68–69)

Essential questions are the sorts of questions that we discuss, sometimes heatedly, at dinner parties, and that our students find engaging, relevant, and genuine.

> "Some say it is no coincidence that the question mark is an inverted plow, breaking up the hard soil of old beliefs and preparing for new growth."
>
> **—Saul Alinsky**

For Example

The boys in Raistlin's grade 9 remedial English class thought Arthur Miller's play *Death of a Salesman* was dumb until he invited them to debate the statement "Willie Loman is a wimp." The energy level in the class changed dramatically with a debate proposition worded in language students could relate to and when students were required to look at Willie's life from multiple perspectives so that they could take on different positions in the debate.

Essential questions not only provoke inquiry, but also keep us inquiring.

You meet all the conditions of a high-quality curriculum for young adolescents when you do much of your teaching through essential questions. Essential questions have the following characteristics:

	Relevant	Challenging	Integrative	Exploratory
They have no single or obvious right answer.		✔		✔
They connect to students' lives.	✔		✔	✔
They are worded to engage students' interest.	✔	✔	✔	✔
They foster higher-order and creative thinking skills.		✔	✔	
They are central to a discipline's big ideas.	✔	✔	✔	✔
They ignite students' curiosity and sense of wonder.	✔	✔	✔	✔
They lend themselves to multidisciplinary study.	✔	✔	✔	✔

Essential Questions

Essential questions have tremendous power, but they aren't always easy to write. If, for example, the question simply requires students to look information up in books and transfer that information to a report or display, it is not an essential question. If the question is so large and complex that no one, including you, has any idea how to break it down to a number of smaller questions, the question may be essential, but it is not very helpful to your students' learning.

Implications for the Classroom

To develop good essential questions, follow these steps:

1. Know the most important concepts of the unit or of the subject as a whole. (This depends on whether your questions are for a unit or for a year. Note that a single lesson is too small for an essential question.)

2. Think about the controversies and misconceptions inherent in the topic. What questions will encourage students to discuss and to inquire?

3. Pre-assess your students to determine their interests related to the topic, their knowledge, and their misconceptions. (See Chapter 7.)

4. Write questions in student-friendly language or, better yet, involve your students in crafting the questions.

5. Remove any value-laden terms. (For example, "How does the media negatively influence teenagers?" assumes that it does.)

6. Think about what students will need to do to address the question. Find Bruner's medium questions that will take them somewhere.

7. List the smaller questions that will help your students answer the essential question. Be sure that each question deals with a different aspect of the essential question. Avoid repetition.

8. Review your list of learning outcomes or curriculum expectations for the unit to ensure that your essential questions deal with as many as possible.

9. Decide what skills your students are going to need in order to address the questions. In the For Example box above, Debbie's students needed to know how to debate.

> " . . . it is easy to ask trivial questions . . . . It is also easy to ask impossibly difficult questions. The trick is to find the medium questions that can be answered and that take you somewhere."
>
> —*Jerome Bruner*

IN YOUR ROLE

 You can use Blackline Master 6.1 to assess a number of sample essential questions.

 Use Blackline Master 6.2 to write essential questions for an upcoming unit in the subject area of your choice.

Learn More About Big Ideas and Essential Questions

Grant Wiggins and Jay McTighe (2005), *Understanding by Design*, 2nd ed. Virginia: ASCD.

Jay McTighe and Grant Wiggins (2004), *Understanding by Design Professional Development Workbook*. Virginia: ASCD.

After the Questions

Ideally, your students will be involved in writing the essential questions that will drive their inquiry, but this isn't always possible, especially if they or you don't have prior experience in inquiry-based learning. In either case, to make sure the experience is successful, you will probably take responsibility for generating the first round of questions.

Then, by all means, try the questions out on your students. Build ownership early on by modifying the wording of the questions in response to your students' suggestions. Talk about the questions and post them in the classroom. Get students to make conjectures, pose smaller questions that will address the larger ones, and give personal examples; in other words, create commitment to the inquiry.

Demonstrate your own commitment by joining the inquiry as participant rather than observer. It's a great way to demonstrate that learning is a lifelong adventure and to build a strong classroom learning community. (See Chapter 5.) Quoting Jacqueline Brooks once again:

> *Teaching for big ideas keeps classrooms honest, real, fresh, and intellectual. Honest because teachers and students ask questions they truly want to answer. Real because the process of investigating answers takes the class down some unpredictable pathways. Fresh because teacher and students need new resources based on the new pathways. And intellectual because all members of the class, regardless of background, can find a conceptual leading edge—that place and that time that challenges them to consider what they think they know. (2002, p. 32)*

"I prefer the errors of enthusiasm to the indifference of wisdom."
—*Anatole France*

"Curiosity fuels every Great Group. The members don't simply solve problems. They are engaged in a process of discovery that is its own reward."
—*Warren Bennis and Patricia Biederman*

Implications for the Classroom

Resource-based learning is essential in an inquiry classroom. A single text-book is never adequate. An assortment of textbooks is better, but by their very nature textbooks chunk big ideas into small, digestible bits, often to the point where it is difficult to recognize the big idea and difficult to see connections among the bits of information. Students need access to a wide range of oral, print, and other media resources, including artifacts, DVDs or videos, the internet, photographs, works of art, and print materials of all forms. Public libraries, school board media libraries, school libraries, and the lending programs of art galleries and museums all help, but there is no denying that a resource-rich classroom does require extra time, ingenuity, and sometimes expense.

Another issue in inquiry-based learning is assessment. Many teachers struggle with the logistics of assessing students who are constructing knowledge rather than remembering or even applying information. It seems messy, difficult to do, and inequitable. However, if you create your assessments as you plan the unit, assessment in an inquiry-based classroom doesn't have to be difficult. (You will read about assessment in greater detail in Chapters 10 and 11. See also the *Understanding by Design* resources listed in Learn More About Big Ideas and Essential Questions on page 125.)

> "Where is the knowledge we have lost in information?"
> —*T.S. Eliot*

IN YOUR ROLE

Send a newsletter home advising parents and family members of the essential questions of an upcoming unit and your need for resources. Encourage parents to take their young adolescents to the public library to pursue inquiry questions and to build the habit of accessing library resources. Ask parents to think about how they would address these questions, and the connections they would make to other disciplines and prior experiences. You will find that parents may not only provide some interesting resources in the form of print material and artifacts, but often offer themselves or colleagues and friends as human resources.

 Think of the essential understandings or big ideas of a unit you would like to teach through an inquiry approach. Brainstorm with others a list of resources that would support the inquiry. Assist each other in gathering the resources for various units, sharing where possible.

Differentiation and Essential Understandings

As mentioned at the beginning of the chapter, all students need to work with the big ideas or important concepts of a discipline; clarity about those essential understandings is what makes it possible for you to differentiate instruction to support learners "where they are." This does not mean that you think of essential understandings as the pinnacle of achievement, reachable only by your most advanced learners while struggling learners labour at the base of the pyramid, endlessly hauling the sand and constructing the bricks of basic skills and knowledge. It is not true that struggling students cannot handle concepts until they have learned facts. Struggling students certainly need "the basics," but the basics will only make sense and be useful to them if work on those basics is liberally interspersed with opportunities for application in relevant contexts. (See Chapter 10 for more information about appropriate challenge for different learners.)

When you are clear about the essential understandings, you differentiate to provide a wide variety of ways for your students to work with the important concepts, and a range of resources to support students' varied learning preferences and interests. Inquiry-based learning is a valuable teaching approach for differentiation because it is a natural for multiple entry points (see page 74), which allow students to learn and to demonstrate their understanding through a variety of intelligences. Inquiry-based learning is also supportive of student choice (see page 106) and of varied assessment formats (see Chapter 11) because it is expected that there will be many different paths to the same destination.

IN YOUR ROLE

 Discuss whether you believe it is possible to teach essential understandings other than through student inquiry.

The 17 boys and 7 girls in a grade 6/7 combined class I once taught were all identified as gifted. I used the following inquiry-based process with this particular class (Hume, 2001). I also used the same process with another non-gifted class of grade 7/8 students and the results were similar, although less sophisticated.

Day 1: It is early in the year and I'm choosing our first inquiry. I will do a science unit about light because my students will like using hands-on materials and because they will be able to resolve problems through experimentation. I notice they like to retreat to books as the final authority. I would like to change that.

Day 2: I pre-assess student knowledge through a whole-class Know Wonder Learn chart. Students have a lot of information about light from a unit they did in grade 4. They can rhyme off the order of colours in the visible spectrum, quote the figure for the speed of light, and talk about which colours are primary, which secondary, and how to mix them.

What they wonder about is a lot more interesting. They want to know, for example, why light travels faster than sound, and why light creates heat. I am panicking. I have absolutely no idea what to do with these questions—other than to retreat to books as the final authority.

Day 3: After a night of reflection I still have no idea what to do next, so I stall. I put out a table of supplies—flashlights, prisms, a holograph kaleidoscope, Fresnel lens, mirrors, and magnifying glasses. My students are so interested

The development of the knowledge-building wall is the central activity in most of our inquiries.

that they don't even remove their coats before starting to explore.

Day 6: We have spent a few days in small-group and whole-class work with diffraction gratings to look at the visible spectrum, and with mirrors to examine the path of light in reflections. I am feeling very teacherly and knowledgeable, but my students are not seeing any point to my efforts to teach them how to use diagrams as well as text to record their thinking, or my insistence that they keep detailed written records in order to note subtle differences in their experimental observations.

Day 7: I have read through my students' "How's it going?" journals and had my conviction that they are bored resoundingly confirmed. I address the issue head on in a class discussion. I begin by saying, "I think you need to take ownership and responsibility for the way you are feeling. Dylan Thomas said, 'Somebody's boring me. I think it's me.' In our classroom, the only reason you are bored is because you expect to be entertained. So here is my request: If somebody's boring you, look to yourself.

Decide for yourself what it is you need to understand about light that you are not currently understanding, and make use of the resources we have available—hands-on activities, print materials, other people, and your personal knowledge—to try to deepen your understanding."

We then summarize what we have learned so far in our work on light. I reiterate that our work can take any direction, especially now that we have a common base. I emphasize that questions are most useful when you can actually do something with them in the attempt to build understanding. Finally, I ask my class to tell me the questions they would really like to address and I record them on a whiteboard.

Essential Questions in the Light Inquiry

My students ask 28 questions, the majority of which are more open to experimentation, more focused, and yet broader in scope with more possible connections and applications than the questions they asked on Day 2. For example, "If you bounce light off a mirror and put a prism up to it, would the colour spectrum reverse?" and "Can light be trapped or slowed down enough to become an object you can touch?"

There is such a marked difference in the quality of the questions that I ask for an explanation. David says, "We can get a lot more interesting puzzles because now that we know more and are learning more, we've started to see like shades of grey and more questions that we wouldn't have thought about before

because we didn't know enough to think about them." I guess there are advantages to our days of whole-class work.

Day 8: The process we use for inquiry is a low-tech invention of mine. The seven metres of chalkboard running across the front and down the side of my classroom are soon covered with yellow, fluorescent pink, and neon-green sticky notes, written by my students and arranged by them beneath their questions that were recorded on manila tagboard and fastened with magnets to the top of the board. Students take responsibility for different questions, which means that they begin their work with those questions and post their ideas to the wall. They encourage other students to add their ideas or to disagree with what has been said, all by having a written conversation in postings on the wall so that everyone can track the development of work on the question.

Day 9+: When students aren't posting their notes, they are engaged in a wide variety of related activities: reading the notes already posted; standing at the board and discussing the notes with others; or writing notes at their desks, based on reading, conversation, and experimentation, and then returning to post them. Eventually the board is so full of sticky notes that I ask my students to summarize the responses to each question. I meet with vehement resistance until I reassure them that we are not ending the inquiry, but rather are writing a progress update for each question and then carrying on. The inquiry that started so tentatively is now a source of pleasure for everyone involved.

At the time of the light inquiry, I was satisfied with what I had done, and couldn't imagine doing anything differently. However, having learned more about the relationship between essential understandings and differentiated instruction, if I had the chance to do it over, I would make some changes. What would you do? Are there any aspects of the For Example that you think might work in your class? What would you improve upon?

I invite you to compare my work with the information provided in this chapter and discuss the strengths and the challenges you discover. You might want to do that before looking at my reflections provided below.

Seven Years Later

Committing your actions and your thinking to paper not only clarifies thought but allows you to return weeks, months, or years later and relive the experience from a new—and hopefully more nuanced—perspective. Here is what I would do differently in the first eight days of the light unit discussed in For Example.

▶ Pre-assess a couple of weeks before beginning a unit, not the day before. Pre-assessing at the last minute caused me unnecessary anxiety.

▶ Used observation of my students' hands-on exploration of the Fresnel lens, et cetera, as a form of individual pre-assessment. Then I could group students for the Days 4–6 activities based on my knowledge of their readiness to engage with the essential understandings of the unit.

▶ Speaking of essential understandings, I would discuss the intended learning outcomes with my students at the very beginning. The skill work of Days 4–6 likely would have received more attention if my students had known where we were headed.

▶ I might reduce the number of questions we would explore, but I'm not sure about that. The questions were all student-initiated, some were smaller questions that could be clustered under the essential questions, and some just naturally "fell off the radar" as students worked.

> "Sometimes when learning comes before experience it doesn't make sense right away."
>
> —Richard Bach

Knowledge of Your Students' Understanding

Decide your position for each of the statements in the Anticipation Guide before you read this chapter, and then again after reading. As you respond, reflect on the difference in your level of engagement if, instead of indicating your agreement or disagreement, you were simply asked to indicate if a statement was true or false. Refer to the appropriate section any time your response is the <u>same</u> as the answer noted in the scoring.

1 It is my responsibility to cover the curriculum with all students, so there's little point in pre-assessing knowledge.

Before Reading	Agree	Disagree
After Reading	Agree	Disagree

1 ▶ **Agree: Why Pre-Assess?, pages 134–136**

2 All assessments should be marked and count toward a student's grade.

Before Reading	Agree	Disagree
After Reading	Agree	Disagree

2 ▶ **Agree: Why Pre-Assess?, pages 134–136**

3 Pre-assessments should be used to determine a student's strengths as well as needs.

Before Reading	Agree	Disagree
After Reading	Agree	Disagree

3 ▶ **Disagree: The Purpose of Pre-Assessments, pages 137–138**

4 A good pre-assessment of an upcoming unit would tell me which students already know the important concepts.

Before Reading	Agree	Disagree
After Reading	Agree	Disagree

4 ▶ **Disagree: Designing and Administering Pre-Assessments, pages 139–141**

5 Standardized diagnostic assessments are often not as useful as the assessments I write myself.

Before Reading	Agree	Disagree
After Reading	Agree	Disagree

5 ⟩ Disagree: Designing and Administering Pre-Assessments, pages 139–141

6 I am aware of at least six different ways to pre-assess my students.

Before Reading	Agree	Disagree
After Reading	Agree	Disagree

6 ⟩ Disagree: Ways to Pre-Assess, pages 142–150

7 I know how to use pre-assessments to determine student growth over the course of a unit.

Before Reading	Agree	Disagree
After Reading	Agree	Disagree

7 ⟩ Disagree: Using Pre-Assessment Information, page 151

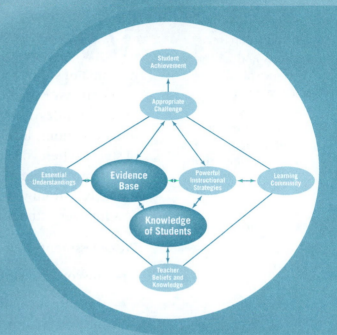

Why Pre-Assess?

Whether you call it pre-assessment, diagnostic assessment, or assessment for learning, determining what your students already know, understand, and can do before they start a new unit of study is a cornerstone activity of a differentiating teacher. Good pre-assessments give you valuable information about an individual student's background experience, knowledge base, misconceptions, level of skill, and attitude relative to a particular unit of study. When you combine this information with your knowledge of their learning preferences and entry points (see Chapter 4), you have a solid base from which to differentiate your instruction and build success for every student.

Pre-assessments help you determine:

- ▶ the content, skills, and strategies you need to teach

- ▶ the misconceptions students may bring to the unit (whether misconceptions of content or of themselves as learners)

- ▶ how to group students for instruction

- ▶ the kinds of activities that will best support various students

Good pre-assessments allow you to be both more effective and more efficient in your instruction because you don't waste time and energy working on material students have already mastered or are not yet ready to master. You can also compare pre-assessments to post-assessments to measure student growth over a unit of study, which will help you evaluate the effectiveness of your instruction.

If you decide to measure growth by comparing pre- and post-assessments and you provide this information to your students, they receive specific, meaningful feedback and many become more aware of the relationship between effort and success. Both are pivotal to appropriate challenge. (See Chapter 10.) Even if you don't compare assessment results, administering pre-assessments informs your students of the learning priorities of the work they will be doing. Robert Marzano identifies instructional goals and feedback as one of the nine categories of powerful instructional strategies. In fact, the setting of instructional goals is so powerful that you have to be careful not to make a goal too specific. If you do, research shows that students will ignore useful information that is only incidentally related to the goal (Marzano et al., 2001).

IN YOUR ROLE

Pre-assessments should *never* count toward a student's grade. It is unfair to evaluate students on material you have not taught. If anyone in your study group disagrees with this statement, use the rationale for pre-assessments provided above, along with your understanding of your colleague's learning preferences, to craft an argument that will be compelling for them.

Walk into any classroom during the first month of school and you will see your colleagues engaged in finding out as much as possible about their students. At the very least, all teachers want to know if students are working at grade level, if they are struggling, or if they require enrichment. However, after administering a reading interest inventory, a general interest inventory, a spelling test, and either informal or commercially prepared and sometimes standardized math and language assessments, you may be overwhelmed by the range of your students' needs.

In any class, there are students who are:

▶ anywhere from one to five years below grade level (sometimes identified as special needs, sometimes not)

▶ facing significant gaps in their learning (for a variety of reasons, from frequent moves to poor attendance)

▶ new immigrants and new to the language of instruction in your classroom

▶ soaring well beyond their peer group

▶ able to do grade-appropriate work (although perhaps not always motivated to do so)

The range of student ability can cause some teachers to believe that they can only instruct to the middle of the pack: they will teach the curriculum content and skills appropriate to the grade level, support students on either end as much as they can, and advocate for students to receive specialized assistance. In complex classrooms such as these, beginning-of-the-year diagnostic assessments may be the only pre-assessing that is done. The reality of student variance and the feelings of hopelessness and helplessness that can result are simply too painful to repeat with each new unit of study.

Stephen Covey (1989) talks about this dilemma in his book *The Seven Habits of Highly Effective People*. He provides an image of a large circle, which he calls the Circle of Concern. Inside that circle is the Circle of Influence. Reactive individuals, explains Covey, put most of their time and energy into the Circle of Concern. They focus on circumstances they cannot control (in our context, the variability of student need) and neglect the issues they can do something about. The result is that their Circle of Influence shrinks and the individual becomes lost in blaming, judging, and being negative.

In contrast, proactive people devote most of their time and energy to the Circle of Influence. They work on what they can change, their positive attitude inspires and engages others, and their Circle of Influence actually grows.

Pre-assessments of your students can help you stay strongly within your Circle of Influence.

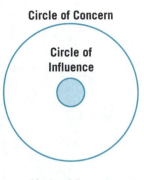

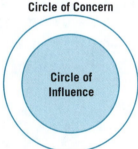

The Purpose of Pre-Assessments

You may have noticed that I referred earlier to beginning-of-the-year assessments as *diagnostics*, but to all other situations as *pre-assessments*. The distinction was deliberate. Doctors diagnose health problems; auto mechanics diagnose problems with cars. I believe there is a negative connotation to the word *diagnostic*; it focuses on looking for problems, gaps, weaknesses, needs, or deficiencies.

Our training and our very natures as caring professionals may embed in us a drive to identify and focus on our students' weaknesses, particularly at the start of the school year.

I am not suggesting that you should ignore your students' weaknesses. They are within your Circle of Influence and need your attention. I am, however, reiterating the argument I made in Chapter 4 that you need to devote at least *equal time* to identifying and building on your students' strengths. (See pages 80–83.) Imagine the difference in your students' self-efficacy and their willingness to take risks in their learning if, through the diagnostics you employ at the start of the year and the pre-assessments you use for every new unit of study, you make the effort to highlight their strengths as well as their weaknesses.

Unfortunately, we do not usually have to imagine the reverse scenario. While students are often told that a new school year is a new beginning and a fresh start, some young adolescents have already experienced many years of failure by the time they get to your classroom. Their expectations and their behaviours are going to be different from those of students who have been successful for many years. Assessment expert Rick Stiggins summarized the differences between the two groups of students:

> "The artistry of teaching finds its source in the ability to start with where the learner is, in using that starting point to build bridges to new knowledge and outlooks . . . ."
> —*Seymour Sarason*

Successful Students	Falling Students
▶ Are driven by growing confidence	▶ Are driven by intense vulnerability
▶ Expect positive results	▶ Expect to fail and are pessimistic
▶ Have a strong desire to succeed	▶ Feel a sense of futility, hopelessness, and/or fatalism
▶ Put in a high level of effort	▶ Make a waning effort and are self-critical
▶ Are open to risk-taking	▶ Are defensive: trying is just too risky

Source: Adapted from Rick Stiggins, "Rethinking Assessment Dynamics," Assessment for Learning Conference, Toronto, April 3, 2006.

Implications for the Classroom

What may seem like innocuous assessments to you may make the first month of school rather stressful for the students in your classroom who are convinced they are failures. The timing and context of beginning-of-year assessments matters. Take the time to help students understand themselves as learners (see Chapter 4), and to build a learning community focused on the recognition and appreciation of individuals with different strengths (see Chapter 5) before assessing.

When sharing the results of assessments with students, begin by enumerating strengths as specifically as you can, then provide a short, numbered list of weaknesses. Mel Levine (2003, p. 218) refers to this as putting "limits around the deficits." It gives students the language for what they need to work on, and makes their difficulties manageable.

IN YOUR ROLE

The next time you assess a student, record a strength rather than a weakness, and a "next step" that builds on the strength.

Was it easy or difficult to think in terms of strength? What difference did this approach make to the ease with which you determined a next step? to the student's learning?

Designing and Administering Pre-Assessments

If you pre-assess students' knowledge, skills, strategies, interests, and attitudes several weeks in advance of a new unit of study, you will have time to use the data in your planning. Of course, this is possible only if the pre-assessment provides useful information about your students' strengths and learning needs. You will find it easy to construct pre-assessments and make use of the results only if you have a clear understanding of exactly what concepts your students need to understand (the essential understandings) and what skills they need to demonstrate at the end of the unit. (See Chapter 6.) In the case of concepts, this means you need to think beyond the factual information students may be expected to recall so that you can get at the essential understanding at the heart of the unit. In the case of skills, you must determine the sub-skills or entry skills students need to achieve the target skills.

The clearer you can be in determining the goals of the unit, the easier it will be to write a good pre-assessment and the more useful will be the results. This is why your own informally developed pre-assessments can be far superior to assessments you purchase, even if the commercially developed assessments are standardized.

Standardized tests consist of a common set of items administered to all students under uniform conditions. As long as those conditions are met, you can make valid comparisons between groups of students and among individual students. Standardized tests can be reassuring because of their high degree of reliability (scoring stays consistent across all students) and validity (the test measures what it purports to measure). The problem with standardized tests is that they are often standardized on large populations of students from a number of provinces or states, meaning that the questions usually cannot be specific to your curriculum. Since the purpose of pre-assessments is to identify your students' current level of understanding and skill relative to the specifics of your curriculum, standardized assessments become of questionable value for use as pre-assessments.

Examine any standardized assessments your school uses or is considering for diagnostic purposes. What is the degree of alignment between the questions asked on the assessment and the essentials of your specific curriculum? Discuss how useful the results would be in helping you identify students' strengths and the steps to take with a particular student.

Once you know what essential understandings and skills your pre-assessment should focus on, there are just a few tips to keep in mind as you develop it:

▶ Keep your pre-assessments short. One question that gets at an essential understanding is worth four that skirt around it. Since pre-assessments do not count for grades, you want to be able to scan the results and get the information you need quickly and efficiently.

▶ Group together all questions or activities about a particular understanding or skill. This will allow you to easily identify what students understand as well as the gaps in their understanding.

▶ Include questions at various levels so that you can determine which students have a concrete understanding of a topic and which have an abstract understanding.

▶ Identify any misconceptions that might hamper students' understanding of the topic and ask about them in your questions or activities. Misconceptions persist if they are not identified and addressed.

▶ Where possible, have the assessment method match the learning goal. For example, if students are going to have to demonstrate their ability to draw contour maps at the end of the unit, have them draw maps in the pre-assessment. It can be a good idea to write your summative assessment (whether a test or performance-based assignment) first, and then use elements of the summative assessment to construct the pre-assessment.

▶ Be clear about whether you are assessing content, skill, or attitude. They each require different assessment tools and each will produce a different result. For example, it's usually possible to determine that a student can or cannot perform a skill, but if you're pre-assessing understanding of the unit's big ideas, the results will be have to be interpreted in terms of levels of understanding, not as a binary "understands" or "doesn't understand."

▶ Know what you are going to do with the results of the pre-assessment before you collect the information. For example, if you pre-assess for student interest, you will be planning to give your students a choice of learning tasks or products, and/or you will be giving them access to varied materials. If neither is intended, there is no value in collecting information about student interests. Students will be watching to see how you make use of their pre-assessment information, and the effort they put into future pre-assessments will be influenced by your decisions.

IN YOUR ROLE

Review a pre-assessment you have used in the past. Begin by completing the pre-assessment yourself; this will show you whether your questions are clear and focus on essential understandings and skills. Then compare your pre-assessment with the seven tips above, and revise as necessary.

 Reviewing pre-assessments is more fun if you trade pre-assessments with a trusted colleague who will critique your work and offer suggestions.

Before reading the next section of the chapter, brainstorm a list of all the forms of pre-assessment the members of your group have used. Discuss which forms have been helpful and under which conditions.

Pre-assessments are not restricted to paper-and-pencil tests. Many pre-assessments simply look like engaging and interesting activities to your students, especially if you sometimes design them to match your students' learning preferences. An assortment of pre-assessments follows.

Anticipation Guides

An Anticipation Guide (Head and Readence, 1986, cited in Tompkins, 2004) is a before-reading strategy that can be used in any subject area and at any grade level. Its purpose is to activate prior knowledge so that the reader can begin to engage with the text, building connections between known and new information. When used as a before-reading strategy, an Anticipation Guide consists of five to ten controversial statements related to the reading. Controversy piques student interest, promotes their active reading of the text so as to converse or argue with the author, and encourages discussion. When used as a pre-assessment, Anticipation Guides are helpful for exposing student misconceptions. As

IN YOUR ROLE

Invite students to join with like-minded classmates to prepare the case for their position about a particular statement from an Anticipation Guide that they can put to the class. Alternatively, they can individually record their thinking. Either approach will give you more information about what students already know, as well as the source and nature of any misconceptions.

At the end of the unit, have students revisit their Anticipation Guides. They can individually circle their new responses and write or discuss reflections on any changes of opinion, or they might choose a single statement and, using the knowledge gained throughout the unit, share their understanding through the intelligence of their choice.

 An Anticipation Guide template is provided in Blackline Master 7.1.

you noticed in the Anticipation Guide provided at the beginning of this chapter, misconceptions can easily be worded to provoke controversy and therefore engage interest!

Cloze Procedure

The cloze procedure (Taylor, 1953, cited in Tompkins, 2004) is used specifically to determine a student's ability to handle the content of a text they are reading. To create a cloze activity, you select a passage from the book and retype it so that the first sentence stays exactly as in the original text. Then you choose a word in the second sentence to delete and replace with a blank. Every fifth word from that point on is also deleted and replaced. Students read the passage through once and then, on the second reading, fill in the blanks with the words they believe are missing.

Cloze passages are scored (Tompkins, 2004, p. 19) by awarding one point for each correctly identified missing word. To determine the percentage of correct answers, divide the number of points by the number of blanks. If the student has:

▶ 61 percent or more correct replacements, the text is at an independent reading level

▶ 41–60 percent of correct replacements, the text is at the instructional level

▶ Less than 40 percent correct replacements, the text is at frustration level

Learn More About Literacy Strategies

Kylene Beers (2003), *When Kids Can't Read, What Teachers Can Do: A Guide for Teachers 6–12*. Portsmouth, New Hampshire: Heinemann.

Gail Tompkins (2004), *50 Literacy Strategies Step by Step*, 2nd ed. New Jersey: Pearson Education.

Interview Students

Listening is taken to the level of art when you conduct informal interviews with your students. You may want to use interviews as a follow-up to another pre-assessment and just with those students who you suspect know more than they were able to share the first time around. To accomplish these interviews in a busy classroom, the emphasis is on the word *informal*. Stop beside the student when the rest of the class is engaged and invite the student to tell you more about the topic or to demonstrate a particular skill.

Graphic Organizers

Graphic organizers such as Venn diagrams and comparison matrices are particularly helpful in encouraging students to focus on the key characteristics of a topic. Have students list the differences between an upcoming topic and something related they have already studied. Alternatively, ask students to identify what they have already studied that would compare to the new topic, and explain the similarities. Or provide your students with terms from the new unit, and ask them to group them and give the rule for each grouping. (See Blackline Master 9.3.) Their choice of categories and rules will tell you what each student understands of the critical attributes of core concepts. All three activities encourage students to make connections to prior information and therefore think more deeply about what they already know about a new unit of study.

Self-Report Inventories

It is important to know your students' attitudes toward learning in general, but also toward different subject areas, and even toward particular units so that you can intervene if those attitudes are negative. Negativity is a significant barrier to learning.

You can't determine individual attitudes through self-report inventories—that can only be done through observation—but you can get valid group summaries of attitude as long as the self-report inventories are anonymous, and are perceived by the students as anonymous (Popham, 2003). This means no names and no handwriting (use checkmarks or Xs only) and have the inventories collected anonymously. Include a clear statement to indicate that you are asking students to complete the inventory in order to improve your teaching, not to evaluate them, and remind them that there are no right or wrong answers.

Two different self-report structures meet the needs of most teachers:

▶ Write a series of paired statements (one positive, one negative) about each variable you want to explore and have students rate their agreement on a four-point scale, such as Strongly Agree, Agree, Disagree, Strongly Disagree. Note that although the statements are paired, you should separate them in the assessment.

▶ Write statements describing activities students might be expected to do and skills they would be expected to demonstrate, and have students identify their degree of confidence if asked to carry out that activity. Again, you can use a four-point scale such as Very Confident, Fairly Confident, A Little Confident, Not Confident (Popham, 2003). Although some students will lack confidence but be competent, and others will be confident but lack competence, James Popham suggests that there is usually a positive relationship between confidence and competence.

If your students are comfortable indicating what they personally understand or don't understand, there are many other forms of self-asessment you can use. They include:

▶ Four-Corners Activity, where students go to the corner of the room with the sign indicating the aspect of a topic they know most about, or the one for which they are able to make the most connections

▶ Five Finger Assessment, where five raised fingers means the student could teach the topic, down to one raised finger meaning "I know nothing about this topic"

▶ Graphing, where students indicate their knowledge of or interest in subtopics of a unit through the bars of a bar graph or the slices of a pie graph

▶ Prioritizing a list of unit topics from most to least interesting. Students may be asked to choose one topic for which they are prepared to become a class expert (see Chapter 4, page 78)

Know—Want to Know—Learned

A KWL strategy (Ogle, 1986) is another prereading strategy that doubles as a useful pre-assessment. Students work alone, in partners or small groups, or as a class to record what they already know about a topic, and what they wonder about or would like to learn. As they progress through the unit, students also record what they are learning. As a pre-assessment, therefore, it might be better to call this a KW strategy.

The "know" part of the KW will help you determine if there's any content you can eliminate from the unit because your students already know it. The "wonder" part allows you to tailor some aspects of the unit to match students' interests.

To pre-assess individual students, you may want each student to record what they know about an upcoming unit before asking the whole class to share their knowledge and what they'd like to learn. Have students record their ideas in list form (perhaps challenging them to generate a minimum number of responses) or on a concept map, which can be blank or can include headings relevant to major subtopics within the unit to help students focus their thinking. (See Blackline Master 7.2 for a blank concept map.) Students with special needs could record what they know into a tape recorder or computer, or share with a partner who will do the recording for them.

Listen and Observe

Often, the easiest way to find out what students know, what they can do, and whether they care about a topic is to give them an activity related to an essential aspect of an upcoming unit and then stand back to listen and watch.

Observation is especially appropriate for assessing a student's attitude toward a topic, their motivation to engage in the learning, and their learning preferences. Because all these factors are behavioural, they have to be observed in order to be assessed.

Observation can be particularly powerful when you know what you're listening and looking for and when you know what steps you can take as a result of your findings, as in the case of the For Example below.

For Example

After the retirement of the school's math teacher a few years ago, Joanne took on teaching math to her grade 8 students. She worked hard, got help from colleagues, consultants, and conferences, and generally felt good about her teaching ... with the exception of geometry. This year, she decided she would research the essential principles of geometry so that her pre-assessments would give her useful starting points for each student in her class.

In her research, Joanne read about the five van Hiele Levels of Geometric Thought. She was amazed to find that it is experience with geometry, not a person's age, that influences advancement through the levels. Older students or even adults may be at level 0. However, Joanne learned that to successfully handle deductive geometry in secondary school, her students really needed to be at level 2 by the end of grade 8.

Before Joanne could plan for her students' growth, she needed to determine each individual's current level of thought. She

Determine levels of understanding by observing students working at an open-ended task.

had her students work in small groups to compare a rich variety of two- and three-dimensional geometric shapes according to their properties while she stood back and listened to the language her students used. Joanne used a simple chart to match her students' language to levels 0–2 of van Hiele's model. (See Blackline Master 7.3.) Although Joanne's knowledge of her students left her fairly confident that additional pre-assessments would be unnecessary, she decided in advance that if any students were at level 2, she would go back to the research to determine how she might support those individuals.

Learn More About Teaching and Assessing Mathematics

John Van de Walle and LouAnn Lovin (2006), *Teaching Student-Centered Mathematics Grades 5–8, Volume 3*. Toronto: Pearson Education.

Use Blackline Master 7.3 to practise listening and observing to determine your students' current level of geometric understanding. Then use the results of your pre-assessment to create

CLASS ROOM

Sorting Geometric Shapes

an activity for each level of students with the goal of having all students compare geometric shapes according to their properties. When you create activities for various levels, differentiated by complexity and depth according to student need, these activities are called **tiered**.

A quick litmus test of a well-designed tiered task is that, when the challenge is appropriate to the individual, the tasks at the different levels take approximately the same amount of time.

For help in developing activities appropriate to the various van Hiele Levels of Geometric Thought, refer to the following chart or go directly to the *Teaching Student-Centered Mathematics* e-book and review the 20 pages of activity suggestions, blackline masters, and video footage available in Chapter 7.

Level	Name	Appropriate Instruction
0	Visualization	Sort and classify physical shapes. Introduce specific characteristics or properties and challenge students to use these characteristics in their sorting. You want them to begin to see that observations made about one shape apply to other shapes of similar kind.
1	Analysis	Focus on properties of figures and apply these ideas to entire classes of shapes. Use geometry software such as *The Geometer's Sketchpad* (Key Curriculum Press) to explore many examples of a class of shapes. Challenge students with questions that involve reasoning, such as, "If the sides of a four-sided shape are all congruent, will you always have a square?"
2	Informal Deduction	Encourage students to make and test hypotheses based on properties of shapes. For example, "What properties of diagonals will guarantee that you have a square?"

Source: Adapted from John Van de Walle and LouAnn Lovin (2006), *Teaching Student-Centered Mathematics Grades 5–8, Volume 3*. Toronto: Pearson Education.

Quickwrites and Quickdraws

Quickwriting used to be called *freewriting* (Elbow, 1973). Its purpose is to give students limited periods of time, usually five minutes or less, to write everything they know about a topic. If you are assessing content knowledge only, make sure students understand that quantity and detail of response are more important than spelling and sentence structure. You may want to provide a list of key vocabulary terms without any definitions or explanation, and ask students to use them in their writing where appropriate. If you find that students aren't being very energetic in their quickwrites, and the urgency of a short time period isn't working, try having them circle a key concept from their quickwrite and then write another quickwrite based on that concept. Or encourage students to incorporate quickdraws into their writing or in place of it. They can sketch and label or they can create graphic organizers to explain their understanding.

> "Knowledge of specific terms is, for all intents and purposes, synonymous with background knowledge."
> —*Robert Marzano*

IN YOUR ROLE

Pre-assess student knowledge or attitude about an upcoming unit by giving them the unit's essential question and then having them write or discuss responses to any of the following pairs of prompts:

- I can explain/I can't explain
- I know/I don't know

- I remember/I don't remember
- I like/I don't like
- I am looking forward to/I am not looking forward to
- I am interested in/I am not interested in
- I am good at/I am not good at

Questioning

You can determine students' conceptual levels by asking questions at a variety of levels from Bloom's Taxonomy (see page 208). When you are questioning as a pre-assessment, don't be afraid to probe for further information. Students may have the knowledge but need your help in retrieving it from the dark recesses of their minds! In addition to your questions, pay attention to any questions students ask. In open, supportive classrooms, students ask real questions; these questions give you excellent indicators of their conceptual levels.

Pre-Tests

You can use simple pre-tests the day before teaching a particular skill, as Bob did in For Example.

CLASS ROOM

A Tiered Lesson on Similes

If you know exactly what you want to find out about your students, you can ask very specific questions. Bob gave his grade 7 students a simple three-question pre-assessment.

What is a simile?

Please provide an example of a simile.

Please identify what is being described and what is being compared in the following sentence: "Cole's binder has been dropped so many times, it looks like a beat-up old truck!"

Bob's pre-assessment is similar to a 3-2-1 card, where you give students an index card and ask them to tell you three things they know, two questions they have, and one application they can think of for the concept.

Simple pre-tests can be used to provide information prior to planning a unit or, as in Bob's case, to sort students into three learning groups prior to a lesson.

There was the group that didn't understand (several thought a *simile* was a misspelled *smile*), the group with limited understanding, and the group with emerging understanding.

Bob taught the lesson to the whole class, but the graphic organizers students used to complete the task were differentiated according to each student's level of readiness. Bob simply sorted the graphic organizers according to his seating plan and handed them out.

Organize Your Grade Book

If you label the column heads in your grade book by learning outcome rather than assignment, you'll be able to return to some of these headings to determine your students' skill levels prior to beginning a new unit. (See page 238.)

Use pre-assessment results to:

► group students temporarily for differentiated activities

► design student tasks

► determine and locate the necessary range of appropriate learning resources

► decide timelines and priorities for an upcoming unit

► build new work from a starting point of student strengths and interests

If you would like to be able to compare pre- and post-assessments in order to determine student growth over the course of a unit, there are two ways to do this:

► Write the pre- and post-assessments at the same time. The idea is that both assessments should be of equal difficulty. If you delay writing the post-assessment until after students have started the unit, it's likely that you'll make it more difficult than the pre-assessment, students will score lower, and you'll believe, incorrectly, that your instruction wasn't effective.

► Use the Split-and-Switch Model (Popham, 2003). Create two assessments, but give half your class one assessment and half your class the other as pre-assessments. At the end of the unit, switch so that students complete as a post-assessment the assessment they didn't complete before the unit. If you really want to enhance the credibility of your results, James Popham suggests that you code the back of each form as pre- or post-assessment, and then have someone else mark them using a scoring rubric.

Unit and Lesson Design in a Differentiated Classroom

QUIZ Choose your response to each question from the options below. Refer to the appropriate sections for any answers that do not match the answers provided.

1A Student differences are taken into account in unit planning before identifying essential understandings

1B Student differences are taken into account in unit planning before creating assessments

1C Student differences are taken into account in unit planning before planning lessons

2A To adequately integrate content into their knowledge base, students need two exposures to the material

2B To adequately integrate content into their knowledge base, students need four exposures to the material

2C To adequately integrate content into their knowledge base, students need eight or more exposures to the material

3A There are two types of knowledge: declarative and procedural

3B There are two types of knowledge: expository and informational

3C There are two types of knowledge: narrative and expository

4A It is better to have a consistent instructional approach because students need structure

4B It is better to have a variety of instructional approaches

4C It is fine to have either consistency or variety as long as you're effective with the instructional approaches

5A All instructional approaches are equally valuable in terms of student retention

5B All instructional approaches are useful in some situations with some students

5C All instructional approaches are not created equal; some are superior to others

6A Homogeneous or ability groups are beneficial for short-term gap-filling

6B Homogeneous or ability groups are beneficial to advanced students

6C Homogeneous or ability groups are beneficial to struggling students

1B, 2B, 3A ▸ **Unit Design, page 156**

4B, 5B, 6A ▸ **Instructional Approaches, page 161**

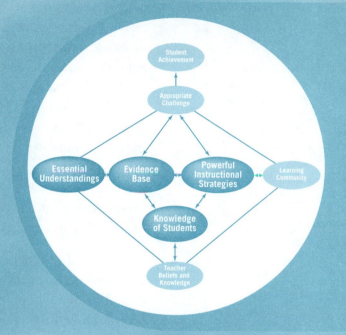

7A The purpose of a lesson "hook" is to capture student attention

7B The purpose of a lesson "hook" is to connect to students' prior experiences

7C The purpose of a lesson "hook" is both of the above, plus more

8A Advance organizers need to focus on what's novel or unusual

8B Advance organizers need to focus on what's important

8C Advance organizers need to focus on possible misconceptions

9A According to brain research, the appropriate length of time for a lesson segment is 10 minutes

9B According to brain research, the appropriate length of time for a lesson segment is 20 minutes

9C According to brain research, the appropriate length of time for a lesson segment is 40 minutes

7C, 8A, 9B ▶ Lesson Design, pages 166–177

As teachers, when we focus on essential understandings (see Chapter 6), we are doing so because it is smart learning theory and smart unit design, certainly, but also because it is a way to make teaching the mandated curriculum possible. The mandated curriculum—as provided through documents with lists of expectations, objectives, standards, and benchmarks—could be thought of as the part of teaching that falls within our Circle of Concern, and our winnowing it to essential understandings and questions could be thought of as our effort to move it to our Circle of Influence, where we can act on it rather than be acted upon. What we sometimes forget is that beyond the mandated curriculum there is a huge territory of curriculum that is solely within our control. Jerome Harste speaks of the envisioned curriculum, the enacted curriculum, and the curriculum that is co-constructed with our students. Others talk of the implemented curriculum, the achieved curriculum, and the curriculum that is tested. One author (Portelli, 1987, cited in Marsh, 2004) claims that there are at least 120 different definitions of curriculum, and that most of them have nothing to do with what is mandated.

Regardless of your definition of curriculum, beyond the mandated curriculum is where the artistry and the professionalism of teaching combine; it is the place where learning happens because our decisions and our actions make it so. Although we can, and often do, complain about the challenges facing us with a large and overwhelming curriculum, we have to acknowledge that what we do in the classroom on a day-by-day basis with each individual student will determine the success of that individual's learning and, by extension, of our teaching. *We* make the instructional decisions in our classrooms; regardless of the size of the mandated curriculum, we have the responsibility, and the pleasure, of combining our professional knowledge, our knowledge of our students and their developmental needs, and our own personal creativity in order to ensure student achievement in all its domains.

You might think about instruction as being like one of those plastic bands you wear when you've paid for an all-day pass at an amusement park. The only way to get the band off is to cut it, but once you do that, you can't put it back on. Now imagine that the band lists eight elements of instruction. No matter where you cut, you will be cutting one of those elements; your band won't have its original strength.

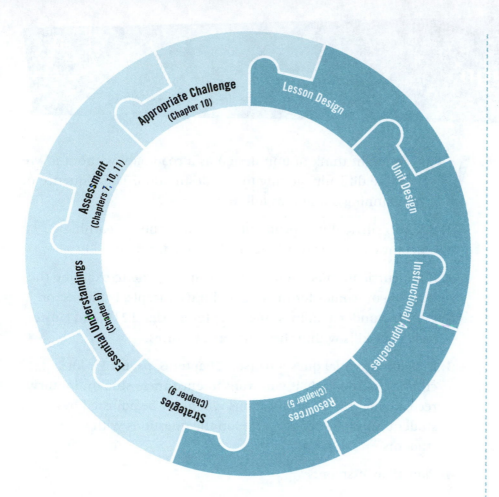

This chapter examines the four elements of instruction shown in colour in the above diagram. Staying true to the intention of being effective before differentiating, we will look at each element in light of what is known about effective teaching and connect that to what we know of the developmental needs of young adolescents. Then we consider how we can differentiate each element to support what we know about our individual students.

Learn More About Instructional Design

Barrie Bennett and Carol Rolheiser (2001), *Beyond Monet: The Artful Science of Instructional Integration*. Ajax, Ontario: Bookation.

This is a wonderful resource that provides a thorough and engaging explanation of the creativity involved in working with instructional skills, strategies, concepts, tactics, and organizers.

Unit Design

We might think of unit design as a roadmap; without it, we have difficulty getting to our destination. The sequence of planning a unit is as follows:

1. Refer to curriculum documents for expectations, learning outcomes, or objectives that need to be addressed.

2. If the curriculum documents do not specify them, examine the learning outcomes for the overarching concepts, big ideas, or essential understandings (see Chapter 6, page 121), and cluster facts and skills within these larger categories.

3. Develop essential questions (see Chapter 6, page 125, for criteria), particularly if you want to encourage student inquiry, recognizing that these questions will likely be adjusted by student input. Better yet, develop the questions with your students.

4. Plan all assessments:

   ▶ pre-assessments (assessments *for* learning) to determine students' knowledge, skills, strategies, and attitudes related to the upcoming unit (Chapter 7)

   ▶ formative assessments (assessments *for* and *as* learning) to administer during the unit to determine how you can alter instruction so that it is more responsive to student needs (Chapter 10)

   ▶ summative assessments (assessments *of* learning) so that students, parents, and you know the degree to which each student has mastered the expectations, objectives, or learning outcomes of the curriculum (Chapter 11)

5. Plan the learning experiences (individual lessons).

> "Only in education, never in the life of farmer, sailor, merchant, physician or scientist, does knowledge mean primarily a store of information."
>
> **—John Dewey**

Melissa Talks About Assessment in Mathematics

There is likely nothing about this sequence that is new to you; it is a sequence variously referred to as "design down," "backward design," or "planning with the end in mind," and discussed extensively in the work of Wiggins and McTighe (2005). (See Chapter 6 for more information.) It is an excellent and highly effective model for unit design; if more of us used it, there is little doubt that student learning would take a quantum leap forward.

However, I hope you are already thinking, "Where are my students in all of this? How do their needs, interests, and learning preferences factor into unit design?"

In Steps 1 and 2 you give priority to the dictates of the discipline and the requirements of your grade's mandated curriculum. Although it's helpful if you use your knowledge of student background and interests when framing essential questions (Step 3), it is likely that most of this recognition will come when you modify the questions in response to student input.

Structuring assessments and planning learning experiences (Steps 4 and 5) are the two places in unit design where it is both easy and critically important to review your class profile (Blackline Master 4.2) and create opportunities that are responsive to the needs, preferences, and interests of your individual students. Chapters 10 and 11 deal with structuring assessments in detail. For now, one small example of how you can use pre-assessments to refine your planning is by interjecting a gap of time between Steps 4 and 5 to allow you to use the results.

Implications for the Classroom

At the level of unit design, the planning of learning experiences can simply be a chronological list of headings to provide a focus for each day's learning. If you use a calendar page (see Blackline Master 8.1), recording the date when you want the unit to end, crossing out any dates when you aren't teaching that class, and filling in the remaining blanks, you will find your attention remarkably focused on essentials. Blackline Master 8.1 is equally helpful to students as you support them in learning how to organize themselves when working on large projects by assigning specific dates for specific tasks.

"What may be done at any time will be done at no time."
—*Scottish proverb*

"One of these days is none of these days."
—*English proverb*

As you list learning experiences, note that the research indicates that students need repeated, frequent exposures to content in order to "own" that content (Nuthall, 1999). Some suggest that four exposures with no more than two days between exposures is required. Content refers to *declarative knowledge* (facts, information, and concepts) as opposed to *procedural knowledge* (processes, strategies, and skills). Procedural knowledge needs more than four exposures, as it needs to be practised to a level where it is automatic or doesn't require much attention. Attention can instead be devoted to the content for which the process, strategy, or skill was learned.

Fortunately, repeated exposure to content does not mean repetitive drilling of basic facts. In fact, drills are useless for new learning because our level of understanding alters only when we have complex, meaningful interactions with content. Harmin (1994) reminds us that there are four kinds of content in any given subject:

▶ facts and details

▶ concepts and generalizations

▶ applications

▶ personal values

"Hey, it's helped me get this video game generation interested in math..."

As young adolescents demand relevance and want to be morally engaged in issues of personal importance (see Chapter 3), practical applications and personal values need to be included in any unit of study.

Regardless of the instructional approach used, complex interactions with content require multiple opportunities for students to make connections to previous experiences and understandings. There is, Marzano claims (2003), a preferred order to these experiences:

1. Begin with a dramatic representation of content that sparks student engagement through involvement or observation. Stories are the simplest example.

2. Accompany or follow the dramatic representation with pictures, graphic organizers, artifacts, models, and other visual representations of information.

3. In follow-up exposures, provide students with opportunities to discuss what they have learned and allow them to make choices and defend their decisions.

This order has been shown to result in effective learning both immediately after instruction and when measured again a full year later. Good unit design supports the developmental needs of young adolescents, including their diverse learning preferences and interests. Marzano's list provides entry points for bodily-kinesthetic, verbal-linguistic, visual-spatial, logical-mathematical, and both interpersonal and intrapersonal learners.

Learn More About Teaching Through Story

Kieran Egan (1992), *Imagination in Teaching and Learning: The Middle School Years*. Chicago: University of Chicago Press.

> "It is the business of drama to open up for scrutiny what we think we know and examine how it is we know it."
> —*Kathleen Gallagher*

> "Talk enhances the development of literacy. It is not a subject, but rather a condition of learning in all subjects."
> —*David Booth*

Blackline Masters 8.2 and 8.3 provide a plan for a unit on elements, compounds, and the periodic table developed by Janice and Bill, who teach grade 9 applied science. Both teachers planned their first unit for a new group of students using two ideas that were new to them: essential understandings and differentiated instruction. (See page 198.)

Note that the essential questions in Blackline Master 8.2 focus on application (Question 2) and personal values (Question 3), that the performance task combines both, and that both declarative knowledge (students will know . . .) and procedural knowledge (students will be able to . . .) are clearly defined and connected to the overall expectations.

Blackline Master 8.3 is a sequential list of what students would do over the 22 70-minute periods devoted to this unit. Note in particular the activities of the first day. The essential questions are discussed with students rather than presented to them in order to invite their engagement and ownership. Students are introduced to the culminating task so that they know what they're working toward in the unit. A multiple intelligences survey informs each teacher's development of the lessons, particularly the differentiated activity on Bohr-Rutherford models for lesson 9.

Choose a unit you've taught in the past, and review it to ensure that you've addressed all the components covered in Janice and Bill's unit plan. If you haven't, modify the unit, paying particular attention to the establishment of essential questions (Chapter 6) and the correspondence of assessments to established goals (Chapters 10 and 11).

The In Your Role activities will be easier and faster to do, and more useful, if you work on them as a team. Better still, if your study group includes several teachers who work with a group of students in different subject areas, you can form an interdisciplinary team to review and then teach the material from a variety of perspectives. Either choose a unit you would like to modify as a team (see above) or create a unit from scratch, focusing on the development of essential understandings, questions, and tasks as discussed in Chapter 6.

Instructional Approaches

When you design a unit of study, you have the choice of a number of different instructional approaches or methods that you can use throughout the entire unit or in various segments of it. Your determination of what instructional approach to use when is based on:

▶ the kind of knowledge—declarative knowledge (concepts and facts) may be best served by one approach, procedural knowledge (strategies and skills) by another

▶ your understanding of individual students' readiness to learn new concepts and their learning preferences

▶ your familiarity and comfort with the various instructional approaches

Implications for the Classroom

Complex interactions with content don't tend to happen while listening to lectures. In fact, simple retention of information, as measured by what students are able to recall 24 hours later, is lower for lectures than for any other instructional approach. Educational consultant and brain researcher David Sousa (2006) explains that this is because lectures leave students as passive consumers of the information, so rehearsal of that information is at a rote level as the student transfers the teacher's words to written notes. As mentioned above, retention of content increases when students are presented with information in both verbal and visual forms and when they are more actively involved in the learning.

"... be scrupulous in asking this question: Given the desired results and the targeted performances, what kind of instructional approaches, resources, and experiences are required to achieve these goals?"
—*Grant Wiggins and Jay McTighe*

"No one doubts that the lecture method allows a lot of information to be presented in a short period of time. But the question is not what is presented, but what is learned."
—*David Sousa*

The diagram shows the average percentage of retention of material after 24 hours for each of the instruction methods. Note that the percentages are not additive.

Source: Adapted from National Training Laboratories of Bethel and NTL Institute of Alexandria, VA, cited in David Sousa (2006), *How the Brain Learns*, 3rd ed. California: Corwin Press.

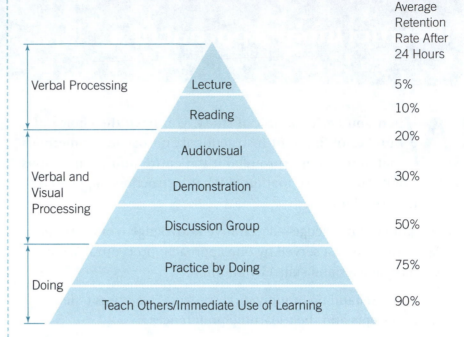

		Average Retention Rate After 24 Hours
Verbal Processing	Lecture	5%
	Reading	10%
Verbal and Visual Processing	Audiovisual	20%
	Demonstration	30%
	Discussion Group	50%
Doing	Practice by Doing	75%
	Teach Others/Immediate Use of Learning	90%

Even though the bottom section of the triangle, "Teach Others/Immediate Use of Learning," includes approaches such as cooperative learning and results in 90 percent retention of content after 24 hours, it would be a mistake to assume that doing everything in cooperative learning groups is the answer. Not only would that not address the learning preferences of all students, but many concepts and skills require different approaches. The basic message to be taken from all the information provided in this chapter is that effective teachers choose from a variety of instructional approaches, always keeping in mind that students are more likely to be successful learners when they are actively engaged in the learning, when the learning is made relevant to their lives and interests, and when new knowledge is presented in a variety of forms.

There are at least six effective and readily differentiated instructional approaches:

> ▶ *Project-based learning* occurs when students are assigned authentic, real-life tasks that they investigate over an extended period of time. This approach supports the developmental need for relevance and differentiation by students' interests. The challenge of project work is in making sure that all students are working at a level that challenges but doesn't frustrate them. (See Chapter 10 for suggestions.)

"Too often children are given answers to remember rather than problems to solve."
—*Robert Lewin*

▶ *Problem-based learning* was first developed in faculties of medicine. The intention is to provide students with a believable problem for which they must acquire new knowledge, declarative or procedural, in order to solve it. Some role-plays, simulations, and games qualify as forms of problem-based learning.

▶ *Inquiry learning* is an approach within the philosophy known as *constructivism*. In inquiry learning situations, students actively engage in the development of new knowledge through a combination of reading, writing, viewing, representing, discussing, experimenting, and discovering, often in response to essential questions.

▶ *Integrated learning* occurs when either a single teacher works with students on a concept through a variety of disciplines or several teachers team up to make connections across disciplines, often in response to one or more essential questions. Integrated learning enables students to make connections across the curriculum, improving relevance and supporting transfer of understanding across the disciplines.

▶ *Explicit instruction* takes place when the teacher models a strategy (see Chapter 9 for powerful instructional strategies), gradually releasing responsibility for the execution of the strategy to the learner. The intention is for students to learn to use effective strategies independently so that they become more efficient learners, but each student develops that independence at different times and will be supported by the teacher until that time. (See Chapter 10 for more information.) A related action is the *mini-lesson*, developed in the mid-1980s by Nancie Atwell and Lucy Calkins. The mini-lesson is a 15- to 30-minute session, which may be planned as explicit instruction in a new strategy or may be an impromptu response to an observed need.

> "You don't just learn knowledge; you have to create it. Get in the driver's seat, don't just be a passenger. You have to contribute to it or you don't understand it."
> —*W. Edwards Deming*

> "The mini-lesson is a forum for my authority—the things *I* know that will help writers and readers grow . . . . The mini-lesson is also a forum for students to share what *they* know and for us to figure out collaboratively what we know, to think and produce knowledge together and lay claim to it as a community."
> —*Nancie Atwell*

Explicit Instruction

Learn More About Explicit Instruction

Nancie Atwell (2002), *Lessons That Change Writers.* Portsmouth, New Hampshire: Heinemann.

In this book and companion binder, Atwell provides a year's worth of mini-lessons for writing workshops.

▶ *Cooperative learning* describes structured group activities built around five elements established by David and Roger Johnson (1999). The elements are:

- positive interdependence—No one individual can succeed alone; team members need each other in order to succeed.

- individual accountability—All members are responsible to the group and for the learning. Any member of the group may be required to respond on behalf of the group at any time.

- interactive skills—Team members know how to communicate effectively and how to manage conflict.

- face-to-face interaction—Members help each other learn and applaud each other's efforts and successes.

- group processing—Group members assess how well they work together and how to improve.

Cooperative learning is not synonymous with group work. Both are forms of collaborative learning where students are working together, but cooperative learning requires structured group activities. Cooperative learning has been found to enhance higher-order thinking skills (Shellard & Protheroe, 2000).

For Example

Kelly, Donna, and Shauna developed a media literacy unit for their grade 8 students. (See Blackline Master 8.4) (Shauna's class was a combined grade 7/8.) Video clips of Kelly's class show scenes of students engaged in quiet, productive group work. Kelly attributes this successful group work to several months of experimenting with various groupings. In the end, she settled on long-term heterogenous cooperative groups consisting of

two pairs of high and low students. Each group of four was also a mixture of students who had difficulty working in a group with students who were strong group leaders.

All three teachers attributed the successful group work as well to the individual accountability and group processing they made a part of each day's work. Depending on the centre they attended, students were required to complete either 3-2-1 Reflection (Blackline Master 8.5) or the "Say Something" Activity (Blackline Master 8.6) at the end of that day's work period. These sheets were filed in a group duotang for quick review by both teacher and student. (See pages 190 and 249 for more information about the media literacy unit.)

> "Learning has nothing to do with what the teacher *covers*. Learning has to do with what the student *accomplishes*."
>
> —*Harry and Rosemary Wong*

IN YOUR ROLE

Discuss this statement by David Sousa (2006, p. 95): "Lecture continues to be the most prevalent teaching method in secondary and higher education, despite evidence that it produces the lowest degree of retention for most learners." If you teach students in grades 6, 7, or 8, and you are lecturing in order to prepare them for a similar experience in high school, discuss whether or not you still consider that sound pedagogy in light of the information provided in this chapter.

Discuss the best instructional approach you ever experienced as a student. How did the approach support both your learning preferences and the type of knowledge being shared?

Is differentiated instruction an instructional approach, or is it a part of all instructional approaches? To help you determine your views on this, think about which of the above seven instructional approaches (including lecture) you already use. Graph the percentage of usage of various instructional approaches on a pie graph. Are you satisfied with the balance or imbalance of approaches you use? Do all approaches allow you to differentiate your instruction?

Considering your class learning profile (Blackline Master 4.2) or an individual student's profile (Blackline Master 4.1), what action could you take to enhance the effectiveness of any approach you already use by differentiating it for one or more of your students?

Lesson Design

I f unit design is the road map, instructional approach might be thought of as your decision about whether to take the four-lane highway or the scenic route. Lesson design is what you actually do during the hour or two you spend at your destination. Lesson design, therefore, always occurs after unit design and is influenced by both unit design and your choice of instructional approach.

The goal of lesson design is to sequence and organize a lesson, or series of lessons, in order to create learning experiences that will result in maximum student engagement and achievement. There is no universally accepted lesson design template, but the structure developed by Madeline Hunter back in the 1970s comes close. Although Hunter's design pre-dates most of what we now know about the human brain, educational consultant and brain researcher David Sousa asserts that it is "based on sound principles of brain-compatible learning while being flexible enough to use with a variety of instructional methods" (2006, p. 275). Hunter's design, expanded by Sousa to include some of the more recent brain-compatible strategies, includes the following components:

> ► The Anticipatory Set, "hook," or mental set captures and focuses students' attention.

> ► The Learning Objective or outcome identifies what students are expected to accomplish and is used again in assessment to determine whether learning has occurred.

> ► The Purpose states why students should accomplish the learning objective and how new learning relates to prior and future learning. The intent of the lesson is made clear.

> ► Input is the information, strategies, and skills students need to acquire and how these will be provided (i.e., the instructional approach and the available resources).

"By designing lessons we are referring to selecting and integrating instructional processes through the needs and inclinations of the learner."

—*Barrie Bennett and Carol Rolheiser*

Diamante Poem Lesson

Kathy Talks About the Poetry Lesson

- Modelling or demonstration of the new learning is provided by the teacher.

- Check for Understanding are the formative assessments used during the learning to determine whether students are accomplishing the objective and the next steps the teacher needs to take.

- Practice of new learning can be guided (teacher provides assistance and immediate feedback) or independent (student works alone, such as when doing homework). Practice is the place where students demonstrate their learning. Independent practice tends to be used when the new learning would benefit from the student's developing fluency, as in the case of a skill or strategy.

- Closure is an opportunity for students to mentally process what they have learned. Students link back to the learning objective and summarize the lesson, make connections to what they have already learned, et cetera. The teacher's responsibility in closure is to help students process their learning, not to provide a summary for them.

IN YOUR ROLE

Hunter's lesson design was widely adopted as *the* way to design every lesson in many jurisdictions. But, as Hunter herself protests, not every lesson requires every component. In fact, some instructional approaches will not use many of these lesson components at all. However, all the components are useful to students and may enhance understanding. For instance, I find Hunter's design especially useful when the instructional approach is explicit instruction—where modelling, checking for understanding, guided practice, and independent practice are sequential and essential elements of a good lesson.

When reviewing the instructional approaches considered earlier, and particularly the ones you are comfortable using, consider whether the approach would benefit from the inclusion of one or more of Hunter's lesson components. If so, experiment with it sufficiently to develop comfort in its use.

For some instructional approaches, and when designing a series of lessons, you may prefer to think in terms of WHERETO, Wiggins and McTighe's acronym of key considerations in the design of learning experiences (2005, pp. 197–198). Note that these elements are not necessarily implemented in sequence. Opportunities for differentiation are included in parentheses.

W—Ensure that students understand WHERE the unit is headed, and WHY. (Students may set individual goals, as well as working on class goals.)

H—HOOK students in the beginning and HOLD their attention throughout. (Think about making use of student interests when planning hooks.)

E—EQUIP students with necessary experiences, tools, knowledge, and know-how to meet performance goals. (Use a variety of entry points and allow students to create multiple representations of understanding.)

R—Provide students with numerous opportunities to RETHINK big ideas, REFLECT on progress, and REVISE their work.

E—Build in opportunities for students to EVALUATE progress and self-assess.

T—Be TAILORED to reflect individual talents, interests, styles, and needs. (Use flexible learning groups, a wide range of resources, and a variety of powerful instructional strategies.)

O—Be ORGANIZED to optimize deep understanding as opposed to superficial coverage.

Regardless of the design process chosen, there are five elements of design that either have not been discussed in detail in other chapters of this book or that need further attention: anticipatory set or hook, metacognition, grouping for learning, use of time, and resources.

Anticipatory Set, Mental Set, or Hook

The intention of the anticipatory set is to capture and focus student attention. This goal is enormously important to teachers of young adolescents, many of whom have had the experience of dealing with disengaged young adolescents and the behaviour issues, discontent, and sloppy, unfinished work that results. The anticipatory set or hook recognizes the relationship between student engagement and student achievement.

"Somewhere, something incredible is waiting to be known."
—*Carl Sagan*

The anticipatory set becomes even more important when you consider all that you are expected to accomplish through it:

▶ Set a positive emotional climate for the lesson to follow (Sousa).

▶ Connect new learning to past learning by activating prior knowledge and experiences.

▶ Focus students on what is important about the unit or lesson (Marzano).

▶ Involve students in active and early participation in the learning (Sousa).

Once you factor in that the brain tends to remember what we hear first and last in an instructional episode (Sousa), it becomes even more important that you craft your anticipatory set carefully to achieve your instructional goals. For example, if you begin a unit by asking students to talk about what they already know and misconceptions surface but are not addressed, the placement of those misconceptions at the beginning of the lesson will lead many students to remember the misconceptions and not the correct information. In this example, either address the misconceptions at the start of the lesson or address them throughout, making sure that you devote quality time to a closure activity where students will review and consolidate what they have just learned.

Implications for the Classroom

Marzano recommends that you focus student attention on what is most important about a unit rather than on what is unusual or novel, and that you use the precious minutes at the start of a unit or lesson to provide students with an organizing structure. This could be a graphic organizer that is completely or almost completely filled in so that students can see both the information they will cover in the unit and the relationships among the pieces of information. (Graphic organizers are discussed at length in Chapter 9.)

In contrast, Sousa argues for using humour and novelty to gain students' attention and to set a positive emotional climate: "If we like what we are learning, we are more likely to maintain attention and interest and move to

> "Children who are excited about what they are doing tend to acquire the skills they need to do it well, even if the process takes a while. When interest is lacking, however, learning tends to be less permanent, less deeply rooted, less successful. Performance, we might say, is a by-product of motivation."
> —*Alfie Kohn*

higher-level thinking. We tend to probe and ask those 'what if?' kinds of questions. When we dislike the learning, we usually spend the least amount of time with it and stay at minimal levels of processing" (2006, p. 245).

Harmin suggests leaping straight to helping students make personal connections to the topic, and says that the leap need not be "logical." For example, he begins a geometry lesson about circles by asking, "What circles of things or people or ideas are important to you? What feelings, if any, have you about circles? Have you any broken circles in your life? Are there any circles you could complete for others? Can you draw a silly circle?" (1994, p. 174). Alternatively, you can move immediately to students' values and beliefs. An example of how to do this is provided in the Anticipation Guide for the media unit. (See Blackline Master 8.7.)

And finally, Bennett and Rolheiser (2001, p. 128) say that the critical attributes of a mental set are: linking to the students' past experiences through questions or activities, having all or most students actively involved, and connecting student involvement to the learning objective.

IN YOUR ROLE

What do you think about the four different approaches to beginning a lesson or unit presented above? Which is most effective with your students in terms of their engagement? their academic achievement? How do you know? Is there anything in the individual or class profiles that will give you clues as to the kind of anticipatory set that works best for various students?

Maintain the anticipatory set for your next unit as you usually would, but try differentiating the set for a single lesson. For example, you might tell the entire class a humorous, interesting story that describes the important points of the upcoming lesson while your verbal-linguistic and logical-mathematical students have a fully or partially completed concept map in front of them to work on while you're talking, your bodily-kinesthetic students are involved in dramatizing the story (from the back of the room if it's too distracting for others), and your visual-spatial learners are drawing the elements of the story in a storyboard.

Nancy and Bob teach grade 7 and Kathy a combined grade 6/7. They worked together to write a unit about word choice in poetry that would deal with the big question, "What words work best for my audience?" (See pages 150, 188, and 200.)

Kathy's anticipatory set for the unit was so successful that her students were begging to be allowed to take the activity home to share with their parents. Here is how Kathy described what she did. (The transparency she talks about is available on Blackline Master 8.8.)

I asked my students if they thought slang words should be totally removed from our language. The hands flew up. Early in the conversation, most students thought they should be. They said that "only people in the 'hood" use slang and that these people use it with their gangs. Others said that homeless people use slang. All of this really surprised me.

With some probing questions, I found that the opinion suddenly changed and that students were quick to identify slang in our classroom and in their personal vocabulary. They recognized that the more they tried to omit the words they know I

target ("like," for example), the more frequent these words became. They could laugh at themselves, and it was joyful talk. There were so many students who wanted to contribute to this discussion. I called on several students who usually have nothing to say but who had their hands up and were just waiting to be called upon. What a great start.

Then I moved on to a transparency I had prepared. It was a formal-looking letter to parents to remind them to send in money for a fundraiser. Students quickly began to buzz because it was ridiculously full of MSN chat and blunt requests for the cash. Students worked in small groups to decode the letter. They understood that word choice is important when addressing different audiences. They were hooked.

Metacognition

Metacognition may be described as "the process of planning, assessing, and monitoring one's own thinking; the pinnacle of mental functioning" (Alvino, 1990, cited in Cotton, 1991). Findings from thinking skills research show that, while many people once believed that either we were born with the ability to be reflective or we were not, metacognition is both teachable and learn-able (Cotton, 1991). Further, when students receive instruction in metacognition, there is an increase in student achievement.

Metacognitive learners are able to (Foster et al., 2002, pp. 6–7):

▶ Describe their strengths as learners

▶ Analyze learning tasks to consider options

▶ Explain their choices in completing learning tasks

▶ Monitor the effectiveness of choices during and following the learning activity

▶ Regularly set goals for learning

Although students may be able to be successful in school without being particularly metacognitive, teaching metacognition supports learners in school and throughout their lives in a number of important ways, including (Foster et al., 2002):

▶ Helping them self-regulate their actions when dealing with challenging tasks; for example, if a student is conscious about how he approached a difficult text before, he can apply those same strategies to a new text, modifying as needed.

▶ Allowing them to take responsibility for their learning by helping them to discover the strategies that work best for them. This is, of course, critically important in a differentiated classroom where students are given choice in how they complete a task.

▶ Developing a stronger sense of classroom community and, later, of responsible citizenship because as students become more reflective, they also become more thoughtful and more considerate of varying perspectives.

► Encouraging the thinking that is valued in the workplace; for example, the abilities to explore and evaluate solutions to a problem and to set and achieve personal learning goals are referenced by the Conference Board of Canada as essential employability skills.

► Promoting self-understanding and a greater awareness of individual preferences, strengths, and goals.

Implications for the Classroom

To foster a metacognitive approach by your students:

- Model strategies through explicit instruction and mini-lessons.

- Model flexibility; talk about all the different ways a task can be approached and then give students choice in how they do the work.

- Encourage students to reflect by asking questions such as, "What was difficult in the work you did?," "How did you handle that challenging question?," and "If you did this activity again, what would you do differently?"

- Involve students in assessment *as* learning (see Chapter 10).

- Talk about metacognition. Give students a vocabulary for describing their thinking.

- Provide students with supports, such as checklists they can use to ensure they have met the requirements of an activity before handing it in.

Metacognition

Learn More About Metacognition

Graham Foster, Evelyn Sawicki, Hyacinth Schaeffer, and Victor Zelinski (2002), *I Think, Therefore I Learn!* Markham, ON: Pembroke Publishers.

Grouping for Learning

Regardless of the instructional approach you are using, if you want to be responsive to your diverse students, you need to make extensive use of short-term flexible groupings. These groupings are different from the random partners and small groups discussed in Chapter 5; random groupings are created to build a sense of community and reduce the development of cliques by ensuring that all students in the classroom have multiple opportunities to work with all other students. Short-term flexible learning groups are intended to optimize student learning, although they have the added benefit of building a sense of community based on the goal of learning.

Implications for the Classroom

The following are some helpful tips for creating short-term flexible learning groups:

→ Avoid groups of three, as one student tends to be left out.

→ The size of a group is not as important as the fact that each student has a job to do. Groups of four tend to work well for this reason.

→ Use homogeneous or ability groups sparingly. Students feel stigmatized if they are always in the low group (Friend et al., 1998), and their performance declines. If advanced students are grouped together, there is limited growth (Lou et al., 1996).

→ Homogeneous groups should be used only for short-term gap-filling with students who are missing critical information or skills.

→ If your goal is to tap into a student's strength, put them in an interest-based, heterogeneous (mixed ability) group.

→ If your goal is to have students support each other, partner high students with low. You can still establish groups of four; simply have two partnerships within the group. Remember that high and low are always relative to the activity. Low students will outperform high students if the activities play to their strengths.

→ When you partner high and low students, teach them to assist each other and have them take turns coaching each other. There is evidence that under these conditions both partners benefit and grow in the experience (Fuchs et al., 1997).

→ Consider creating groups that represent a range of learning strengths (e.g., a student strong in art working with students who have strengths in writing, mathematics, and technology). These groups are particularly effective when students are working on summative performance tasks.

→ Create short-term groups based on student responses on exit cards (see page 233).

IN YOUR ROLE

If you haven't done so, use your class profile (Blackline Master 4.2) to establish a number of heterogeneous groups based on interests and learning preferences. Use unit pre-assessments to create homogeneous groups based on need. And finally, make a list of high/low partners for an upcoming activity. It's when you become comfortable with putting students into small groups that you really understand that differentiated instruction is predominantly differentiation by groups, not by individuals.

Use of Time

Time has more impact on learning than simply dictating that what is heard first and last tends to be remembered. In a differentiated classroom, time is a flexible commodity. Instead of the old measure of "time on task," we strive for productive time on task—time engaged in the learning. David Sousa (2006) tells us that we stand a much better chance of engaging students in learning *and* retaining information when information lesson segments are 20 minutes long. Longer sessions tax students' working memory, making it difficult for them to attach meaning to new information. Large, uninterrupted blocks of time are many teachers' dream and they are certainly worthwhile, but it is important to give students brief down time after every 20-minute segment. This doesn't need to be a lengthy break; having students stand and move into a new phase of the activity will be a break, plus the movement is beneficial for your bodily-kinesthetic learners and for the young adolescent's need to be active. (See page 42.)

Use these suggestions to maximize productive time on task:

→ Get to know your students. Research shows that effective teachers spend more time getting to know their students from the very first day of school (Emmer et al., 1980). This tells students that they are important to you and that you want to build a relationship. That message alone will save you time in instruction.

→ Teach routines and procedures early in the year (Chapter 5) so that you don't have to review these every day. Highly effective teachers deal with a disruptive event once every two hours, compared with less effective teachers who have a disruptive event every 12 minutes (Stronge et al., 2004).

→ Make ample use of Think-Pair-Share, where you invite students to turn to a partner and share their opinion, summarize what they've just heard or read, and so on. This meets the need of young adolescents to talk and work with peers, as well as your need to keep all students actively engaged.

→ Vary the pacing and sequencing of content to match a student's knowledge and experience with that content (Whitener, 1989). This will require pre-assessing student knowledge and attitudes.

Resources

Differentiated classrooms need a wide variety of resources, but so do non-differentiated classrooms where teachers make use of varied instructional approaches. The only classrooms that don't need a variety of resources are those where the teacher lectures and all students, regardless of readiness, work from a single textbook.

Limited resources cannot be permitted to derail your efforts at increasing effectiveness through differentiated instruction. Fortunately, with access to public libraries, media libraries at your district office, the internet, your colleagues' classrooms, and your own ingenuity, there is no need to go without the resources that will best support individual learners.

"Technology does not necessarily improve education. Take a simple innovation like the pencil: One can use it to write a superlative essay, to drum away the time, or to poke out someone's eye."

—*Howard Gardner*

Locating and accessing necessary resources is, in some ways, easier in a differentiated classroom. Activities with flexible learning groups, for example, mean that you may need only four or eight copies of a particular novel, which are much easier to obtain than a class set. Young adult publishing has made enormous strides in responding to student interests, so it's easy now to find nonfiction books that address curriculum outcomes through student interests and at a variety of reading levels. And audio books are becoming less expensive, especially if you purchase cassette tapes rather than CDs.

Implications for the Classroom

Use the results of pre-assessments, your knowledge of student learning preferences and interests, and your lists of essential understandings and specific skills and knowledge to brainstorm needed resources. Think about:

Book access to computers if possible and if needed, but please note that, while computers enrich some possibilities of differentiation for some students, you are well able to differentiate effectively without them.

IN YOUR ROLE

Take your master list of needed resources to the next gathering of your book study group. Beyond the standard sharing of dictionaries, thesauruses, and atlases, can group members help you locate the other resources that you need?

Powerful Instructional Strategies

QUIZ

Which of the following powerful instructional strategies do you use on a regular basis? Take the quiz below and refer to the pages listed for any section score lower than seven.

Scoring one point for "never or rarely," two points for "infrequently," or three points for "always or frequently," how often do you:

1 ___ focus on the critical attributes of a concept?

___ have students create metaphors or analogies?

___ tier assignments for different levels of student readiness?

> **1** ❯ **Identifying Similarities & Differences, page 183**

3 ___ use graphic organizers specific to various text structures?

___ have students work at learning centres?

___ encourage students to draw, role-play, or work in a nonlinguistic form?

> **3** ❯ **Nonlinguistic Representations, page 197**

4 ___ require students to generate a hypothesis and explain their thinking?

___ use templates or checklists to structure work in problem solving, decision making, historical inquiry, or experimental inquiry?

___ use learning contracts with your students?

> **4** ❯ **Generating and Testing Hypotheses, page 203**

2 ___ have students summarize?

___ have students add information to completed notes?

___ model summarizing or note-taking in a variety of forms?

> **2** ❯ **Summarizing and Note Taking, page 191**

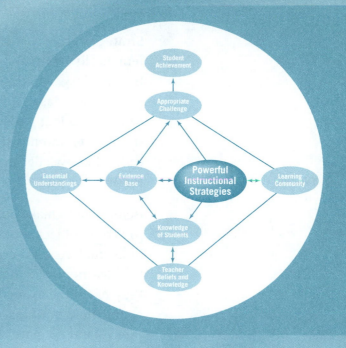

5 ___ ask higher-order questions?

___ expect students to generate their own questions?

___ wait at least five seconds after asking a question before accepting an answer?

5 ▶ **Questions, Cues, and Advance Organizers, page 206**

Look up the word *strategy* in the dictionary. Once you get past the definitions about the art of war and moving troops and ships into favourable positions, strategy is simply "a plan of action." When you teach your students various strategies, you are quite literally giving them new plans of action: ways to mentally process, organize, and work with information so that they can take charge of their own learning.

Strategies cross curriculum boundaries. The skills students use to systematically compare two texts in English class can be transferred to a history class, where they compare two perspectives on an event, or to a science class, where they compare two experimental conditions. When a student is able to independently transfer a strategy from one situation to another, the strategy has become part of the student's procedural knowledge—a skill or process that is automatic and does not require the student's full attention.

Being able to make automatic use of sophisticated processes and doing so across subject boundaries is a defining characteristic of an educated individual. As teachers, we want our students to be independent, life-long learners who are responsible for their own learning. This means they need to become metacognitive learners—individuals who think about their thinking and are in conscious control of their learning. (See Chapter 8, page 172, for more information about metacognition.) Metacognitive students become able to analyze tasks, determine which strategy will work best for a particular task, and monitor the effectiveness of their choice, relative to their own learning strengths and the task's demands, during and after the learning activity.

Our responsibility as effective teachers is to be deliberate and explicit in teaching the strategies that will help our students process important concepts in deep and meaningful ways. (See page 163.) Our responsibility as differentiating teachers is to encourage thoughtful and flexible work with these strategies by providing students with options and engaging them in reflection on what works, what does not work, and what they might do differently to better support their individual learning needs and preferences.

Differentiated instruction is a framework that applies to all students, kindergarten through grade 12, so the students in your grades may well be coming to you with several years of experience in differentiated classrooms. Some of your students may possess a finely honed sense of personal responsibility for their learning and a keen awareness of the instructional strategies that work especially well for them; others will resist taking responsibility for their own learning. Regardless of your students' backgrounds, you are teaching them at their developmental "prime time" for understanding themselves and how they learn (see Chapter 3, page 53). Grades 6–9 are ideal years for teaching metacognitive and instructional strategies, to achieve both the long-term goal of independent, responsible, and self-aware lifelong learners, and the more immediate goal of increasing student achievement in the subjects you teach. Fortunately, you don't need to abandon the important concepts of your discipline in order to teach strategies; you just need to determine which strategies are going to be the most useful in making sense of that content.

There are dozens of strategies, but a useful strategy is going to require time and repeated use in a variety of situations before students will be able to use it automatically in a single subject area, and then it will need revisiting for students to successfully transfer the strategy to another subject area. Deciding which strategies to teach in the limited time you have available is clearly important. How do you decide which strategies are most important to your students and your discipline?

This is where research really helps. After reviewing 35 years of educational research, and using a technique called *meta-analysis* in which the results of a number of studies are combined to determine the average effect of a given strategy, researchers have been able to delineate nine categories of instructional strategies that "have a high probability of enhancing student achievement for all students in all subject areas at all grade levels" (Marzano, Pickering, & Pollock, 2001, p. 7).

Categories of Instructional Strategies That Affect Student Achievement		
Category	**Percentile Gain**	**In This Book**
Identifying similarities and differences	45	Chapter 9
Summarizing and note taking	34	Chapter 9
Reinforcing effort and providing recognition	29	Chapter 10
Homework and practice	29	Chapter 10
Nonlinguistic representations	27	Chapter 9
Cooperative learning	27	Chapters 8 & 10
Setting objectives and providing feedback	23	Chapter 10
Generating and testing hypotheses	23	Chapter 9
Questions, cues, and advance organizers	22	Chapter 9

Source: Adapted from Marzano, Pickering, & Pollock, 2001, p. 7.

This chart should not be interpreted to suggest that identifying similarities and differences is twice as powerful as asking good questions and providing advance organizers. Marzano, Pickering, and Pollock (2001) are quick to stress that all strategies may not work equally well in all situations or with all students. Knowledge of your students is still the best litmus test for determining the strategies you teach in your classroom.

This chapter explains five of the nine categories of instructional strategies, offering practical examples and blackline masters as well as suggestions for how you might differentiate these strategies to meet the needs, interests, and preferences of your students.

Identifying Similarities
and Differences

I f I were teaching a lesson about figurative language, I might give you these two sentences:

▶ A Kris Kristofferson song is a dip into a deep warm pool under a star-filled sky.

▶ A Kris Kristofferson song is like a heart-stopping ride on a rollercoaster of emotion with a safe landing.

If you wanted to remember those sentences, the theory is that you would store them together in your mind because they were presented together and are similar (Sousa, 2006). However, although we store information in our brains according to similarity, we retrieve it according to critical attributes or differences (Sousa, 2006). You have probably already identified the critical attribute—the word *like*—that makes the second sentence a simile, while the first is a standard metaphor.

Critical attributes, the essential differences between one idea or object and another, can be thought of as the core of all learning. Discovering and discussing the similarities and differences between ideas is foundational to debate, persuasive writing, and the higher level thinking skill of analysis, and is central to the young adolescent's developmental need to view the world from a variety of perspectives (see Chapter 3). When using this powerful instructional strategy to teach and engage students, it is important to explore both similarities *and* differences to enhance storage and retrieval functions in the brain and to encourage recognition of multiple perspectives on a topic.

The different formats of teaching and working with similarities and differences that have proven to be highly effective are displayed in the following chart.

Identifying Similarities and Differences

Format	What's Key?	Teaching Points	Graphic Organizers
Compare and Contrast	Identifying characteristics to compare	Make sure students compare the important characteristics.	Venn Diagram (BLM 9.1) Comparison Matrix ABC Chart (BLM 9.2)
Classify	Sorting objects or concepts based on similarity and defining that similarity	If students classify the same object or concept in a number of different ways, they will notice different aspects of the information.	Data Chart It's Classified! (BLM 9.3) Probable Passage (BLM 9.4)
Metaphor	Realizing that two objects or concepts are connected by an abstract relationship	Make sure students focus on the abstract relationship.	Metaphor Images (BLM 9.5) Learn More About Teaching Metaphor Metaphor Bingo (BLM 9.6)
Analogy	Thinking about how dissimilar objects and concepts are related	This is the most difficult form as students are comparing two relationships.	Metaphor Bingo (BLM 9.6) or write the pattern A:B::C:D on the board and give an example (e.g., Winter is to Summer as Cool is to Warm)

Learn More About Teaching Metaphor

See Chapter 7 of Kelly Gallagher (2004), *Deeper Reading: Comprehending Challenging Texts, 4–12* (Portland, Maine: Stenhouse Publishers) for a dozen clever metaphorical image organizers.

Peanuts: © United Feature Syndicate, Inc.

Implications for the Classroom

If your goal is to stimulate students' divergent thinking, you should have them search for similarities and differences. However, if you want students to focus on the key difference or critical attribute, it's better to tell them the characteristic directly and then have them compare the items with regard to the given attribute.

Have students write summary statements explaining the similarities and especially the differences they have discovered to make sure they can identify them. Venn diagrams, for example, look deceptively easy to complete, but students (and adults) often have difficulty explaining what characteristic they have compared and the critical difference between two topics.

Provide frames for students to use when summarizing similarities and differences. For example, in writing a persuasive piece, students might be directed to provide a thesis statement—"Hip hop is better than reggae"—then list three similarities, three differences, and a concluding statement. The frame serves as a scaffold or support for students as they learn the organizational structure of compare and contrast writing.

Use data charts or comparison charts (McKenzie, 1979) to help students organize information from a variety of sources. List the sources down the left (e.g., textbook chapter, website, trade book) and the various aspects of the topic across the top. Students then have a structure for systematically compiling information from a number of sources.

Probable Passage is a prereading activity originally developed by Wood (1984) and modified recently by Kylene Beers (2003, pp. 87–94). To create this activity, choose key words from the selection students are going to read.

"School is like . . .

a toaster. You put something in and it comes out better than it was before.

a pool. You go in and have fun.

play-doh. You choose how to make it."

—Maddison
Grade 6 Student

Students then work in small groups to discuss what the words mean and arrange them in categories according to their probable function in the selection. If you want to offer maximum support, students can then use the words to fill in the blanks of a passage you've written about the selection. Beers's modification was to have students write a prediction statement that provides the gist of what the selection might be about.

Working with similarities and differences appeals to verbal-linguistic, logical-mathematical, and naturalist learners. Representing similarities and differences in graphic or symbolic form appeals to visual-spatial learners and enhances the understanding of all students. To better support bodily-kinesthetic learners, alter the activities in the above chart as follows:

- **Compare and Contrast**—Students can use string to form a Venn diagram on their desk or two hula hoops to create a large one on the floor. Have them write or draw the items on slips of paper or sticky notes. They can then arrange the items appropriately within the Venn diagram.

- **Classify**—Print the names of items on business card stock and have students sort the cards.

- **Metaphor**—Post the names or images of four metaphors in each corner of the room and have students go to the metaphor that best matches their thinking. Ask them to discuss their choice with the other students in their corner, and then report back to the class.

- **Analogy**—Obtain a set of loupes or magnifying glasses and use For Example on page 189.

Identifying similarities and differences is an instructional strategy that readily lends itself to a common differentiation structure called *tiering*. When you tier an activity, you are providing different levels of that activity to meet the different degrees of student readiness for the concept you're teaching. Note the reference to *readiness*, not overall ability. To start where students are and move them forward, it's important to recognize that *ability* is a generic, static, and unhelpful term, much like the term *intelligence* before Gardner added the "s." Readiness, on the other hand, is always specific to the concept being taught.

Since student readiness varies from one concept to the next, pre-assessments are essential to good tiering. (See Chapter 7 for examples of pre-assessments.) The other caveats of good tiering are that all the activities

- deal with the same objective or specific learning outcome

- are equally interesting
- take approximately the same amount of time

IN YOUR ROLE

To develop a tiered assignment, use the following steps:

1. Administer pre-assessment. (See Chapter 7.)

2. Sort students into three groups (struggling/striving, capable, or advanced) based on the pre-assessment results. You can sort into more or fewer groups if necessary. You may also find that you have several groups at the same level. You're starting where your students are, so your groupings need to be flexible responses to that reality.

3. Develop three activities by establishing the level of an existing activity and then modifying it to create two tiered versions, or, if constructing an entirely new activity, create the on-grade level first so that you're clearly targeting appropriate learning outcomes for your grade.

Some of the characteristics you might consider when constructing tiered activities are listed in this chart.

Considerations for Assignments Tiered by Student Need		
Level 1	**Level 2**	**Level 3**
Concrete	Mostly concrete, with some abstraction	Abstract
Minimal number of steps to complete the assignment	Can require more steps to complete the assignment	Can be more open-ended, leaving decisions about how the assignment is completed to the student
Reading level is appropriate to participants; may be below grade level	Reading level is at grade level	Reading level is above grade level
Activity may be partially completed to provide students with support via examples or by the teacher.	Activity is completed by students with some support provided by the teacher or in print.	Activity is more open-ended than levels 1 and 2. Support is provided by the teacher as needed.

Bob developed a three-tiered assignment on recognizing and creating similes. His pre-assessment is on page 150, and the activities he developed are on Blackline Masters 9.7, 9.8, and 9.9.

CLASS ROOM

Making Comparisons

Bob wanted to experiment with differentiating in a whole-class session. This was also the first time he had tried tiering, and so he was sensitive about his struggling students having their difficulties made public. Bob resolved this concern by organizing the activity sheets so that he was able to distribute the activities according to his class seating plan rather than grouping students according to their readiness.

IN YOUR ROLE

Bob's concern about drawing attention to his struggling students is an understandable and legitimate one, particularly in a classroom of young adolescents who are often intensely concerned about their peers' opinions. However, since students are always well aware of the differences among them, discuss the steps a teacher might take to ensure that his or her students will always be accepting of individual needs.

Share the tiered assignments you created from the previous In Your Role activity. There is no point in recreating the wheel!

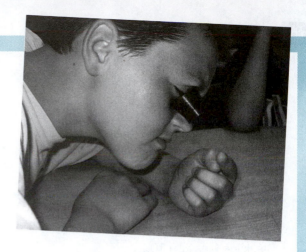

Looking through the wide part of a loupe at his finger a couple of centimetres away from the lens, Pierre modelled the analogy activity for his students. Following the suggestions in the book *The Private Eye*, he urged his students to ask the questions, "What else does it look like? What else does it remind me of?" 10 times and record their answer each time. Each student then chose the analogy that most interested them and used it as the basis for a poem.

Here is Zack's first draft. It may not be a great poem, but it is the first piece of writing Zack willingly laboured over in the first five months of the school year.

My Finger
My finger is a small Black Hole
It circles and spins…
Brings you in…
To more than just a finger.
It brings you into rivers and lakes
a whole different dimension.

I think every finger has its own world
That's where molecules live.
If you look down to each of your fingers
you think you're looking at some lines
but each finger you see is a world with
different species.

The lakes and rivers we see now are not
Mother Nature.

The trees and hills and everything . . .
Just another finger.

Learn More About Analogy Across the Curriculum

Kerry Ruef (1992), *The Private Eye: Looking/Thinking by Analogy*. Seattle, Washington: The Private Eye Project.

This book is a visual treat as well as a treasure trove of ideas to help develop higher order thinking skills, creativity, and literacy in science, writing, art, math, and the social sciences.

"The discoveries of science, the works of art are explorations— more, are explosions, of a hidden likeness."
—*Jacob Bronowski*

Donna, Shauna, and Kelly (see page 164) each began their grade 8 advertising unit with a class brainstorming session on the question, "What is media?" They then had groups of four students brainstorm types of media. To encourage maximum involvement, each student had to generate a list, recording it in their corner of a quadrant placemat. (See Blackline Master 9.10.)

Students then worked as a group to classify according to three purposes the media they brainstormed.

The teachers had hoped that students would deduce the three media purposes (information, entertainment, and persuasion) on their own, but found they needed to be directed. For further consolidation, as a homework assignment, students recorded the types of media they encountered over a 24-hour period on a three-circle Venn diagram, with the circles labelled Information, Entertainment, and Persuasion. (See Blackline Master 9.11.) Three-circle Venn diagrams can be quite challenging because something must be written about the ways the information items in the two or three circles are alike where any circles overlap. Afterward, Shauna commented, "My students had previous experience working with three-circle Venn diagrams; however, it would have been beneficial to review them previous to this activity. I realized students need help making the transfer from one subject to another."

Summarizing and Note Taking

Summarizing and note taking are grouped in the same instructional strategy category because "both require students to distill information into a parsimonious, synthesized form" (Marzano et al., 2001, p. 30). Both strategies are extremely important academic skills, especially in grades 6–9 where the content load increases substantially and students need to process information to a point where they will be able to both retrieve and apply it. Both, however, are strategies that students usually prefer to avoid. They cannot see the purpose, for example, of restating an author's words when they perceive the author's writing to be far superior to their own. Finally, it is assumed, often incorrectly, that students in grades 6–9 have long mastered both strategies.

> "There's no point to just retelling,' and our students are not parrots-in-training."
> —**Rick Wormeli**

Implications for the Classroom

A summary is different from a retelling. While both require the reader to work with important information, a retelling is a low-level skill that involves reviewing all important details in sequential order and a summary is a reconstruction of the essence of the text (Fountas & Pinnell, 2006). Help students see the difference by reminding them of the "bed-to-bed" stories they told when they were young (stories that began when they woke up and provided every detail of the day until they returned to bed in the evening).

Teach students the rule-based summarizing strategy (Brown, Campione, & Day, 1981) by using the think-aloud process as you work through a piece of text on an overhead. The steps in the rule-based strategy are:

1. Delete unnecessary or trivial material.

2. Delete repeated or redundant material.

3. Choose a single word to replace a list of items (e.g., use *dog* for *Saint Bernard*, *rottweiler*, *beagle*, and *terrier*).

4. Select a topic sentence or create one if it is missing.

The common expository text structures, words that signal or identify the structure, and some of the graphic organizers that can be used to support summarization are displayed in this chart.

Summarizing			
Structure	**Purpose**	**Key Words**	**Graphic Organizers and Other Formats**
Enumeration	Lists facts, characteristics, and/or features	First, second, third Then, next, finally Several, numerous For example, for instance To begin with Also, in addition, in fact, most important	Mind Maps It's Classified! (BLM 9.3) Main idea with supporting detail sections
Chronological Order	Sequences facts, events, and concepts in time or date order	After, before, now Gradually Since, when, while On [fill in date]	Timelines (BLM 9.12) Flow Charts Calendar (BLM 8.1) Clock Face (BLM 5.4)
Compare and Contrast	Explains similarities and differences	Although, as well as, both, but, conversely, either, however, not only, on the other hand, or, rather than, similarly, unless, unlike	Venn Diagram (BLM 9.1 & 9.11) Comparison Matrix ABC Chart (BLM 9.2)
Cause and Effect	Shows how one or more events can lead to others	Accordingly, as a result, because, consequently, nevertheless, so that, therefore, this led to, thus	Flow Chart Mind Map Effects Wheel (BLM 9.13)
Problem and Solution	Explains how a problem develops, then describes what can be done to solve it		

Source: Adapted from Wormeli, 2005.

If students understand the structure or organizational pattern of the text they're reading or viewing, they will find it easier to summarize because they know where to look for key information. Students will need your support in using these text structures in oral presentations and in written work. You can provide this support through the graphic organizers noted in the list or through summary frames. For example, a time order frame might look like "First, _____. Next, _____. Then, _____. Finally, _____." Note that texts can be a combination of several structures.

Summarizing is a cross-curricular activity that should not be limited to paper-and-pencil retells. The closure section of a lesson (see page 167), for example, is a place where students should routinely be encouraged to reflect on and summarize what they have learned in a variety of ways. See page 69 for an example of Summary Ball or Rick Wormeli's book for 50 summarization techniques sorted by learner preference and time.

Learn More About Teaching Summarizing

Rick Wormeli (2005), *Summarization in Any Subject: 50 Techniques to Improve Student Learning.* Viriginia: ASCD.

IN YOUR ROLE

Once you have taught your students a variety of summarizing techniques, using various text structures, differentiate the techniques using a ***choice board***. The sample Summarization Choice Board (see Blackline Master 9.14) is organized around the VAK (visual/auditory/kinesthetic) learning preferences that your students identified (see Chapter 4, page 67, and Blackline Master 4.5), but choice boards can easily be developed for a variety of purposes, from multiple intelligences (see Blackline Master 4.7) to Bloom's Taxonomy (page 208). See Blackline Master 5.3 for a blank grid and page 107 for more information.

Kylene Beers (2003) describes a summarizing technique developed by MacOn, Bewell, and Vogt (1991). Called "Somebody Wanted But So," it is a framework that students use to create a summary by deciding who the somebody is, what that person wanted, what happened to keep something from happening, and how everything was resolved.

Combine summarizing and identifying similarities and differences by having students summarize individually and then compare their summary to a partner's. How are the two summaries alike? How are they different? How does discussing similarities and differences impact students' understanding of summarizing?

Jacqueline, a high school math teacher, has developed an ingenious method for ensuring that her students process information multiple times, build knowledge through the duration of a course, and are well prepared for both unit tests and end-of-year examinations.

She begins by modelling how to write a unit summary at the end of the first unit in math.

Jacqueline continues the modelling for the second unit, but increases her requests for student input so that she can determine who is able to summarize and who is still having difficulty. At the end of the third unit, she asks all students to summarize the unit independently, but makes a point of providing specific feedback and support to students who struggled in the whole-class summarization of the second unit. (See Chapter 10.)

Jacqueline's students regularly assess their own summarizing skills, and Jacqueline assesses students' skills using the rubric glued into the front of each student's Survival Guide. Assessments provide valuable on-the-spot evidence of each student's understanding of the material taught in the unit.

Summaries include:

- definitions from the unit

- methods/procedures

- a worked-out example for each method/procedure

- an extension that demonstrates how the unit material is relevant to life

Students write the summary in their Survival Guide. Survival Guides can be notebooks cut in half horizontally, with each student receiving a half, or they can be created from large index cards attached with a key ring or from folded chart paper. Jacqueline finds the folded chart paper is appealing to her students, but if she doesn't give them explicit instructions in how to fold, the variations are often startling. (See Blackline Master 9.15 for folding instructions.)

Survival Guides can be developed in any subject and for any age of student. You might consider making one of your own for any courses you're taking. Jacqueline's students found their Math Survival Guides so useful that they were reluctant to give them to her to use as examples in her current work as a math consultant. Apparently, these Guides are proving to be invaluable consolidations and reminders of prior learning when students begin a new course.

Implications for the Classroom

Note taking provides students with the opportunity to process information. Requiring them to do so at a high level of analysis allows them to construct a useful synthesis. There is no educational value to copying notes: if you have students copy notes from the board or overhead screen, they're not processing, analyzing, or synthesizing. This does not mean that you should never give students notes you have prepared. Photocopies of prepared notes can be useful models of how to write notes and provide students with the information you deem important. If providing prepared notes, you will still want students to interact with the material, perhaps by highlighting or summarizing your work.

Consider giving students a photocopy of the notes you prepared when modelling each of these note-taking methods:

- Cornell notes—The page is divided into two columns; questions are in one column, answers in the other. Double-entry journals are a variation of this structure; headings are variations of "information" and "personal reflection" or "application."

- Informal outline—Key ideas are written at the left margin; details are indented under each key idea.

- Combination notes—The page is divided into three parts with a line down the middle for about two-thirds of the page, and then a line across the bottom. The left column is used for notes (see informal outline), the right column for images, and the bottom section for a summary. An advantage to this format is that it requires students to process information three times in three different ways (Marzano et al., 2001).

- Graphic organizers—These provide a visual way to take and organize notes, but they can be problematic if there is a lot of information to record and not a lot of writing space.

Encourage students to add examples and visual images to their notes as they deepen their understanding of a concept. Provide time for them to do this so that they begin to see their notes as working documents. The more students work with their notes, the more they're processing information, and the better they're preparing for upcoming tests.

> "Although we sometimes refer to summarizing and note-taking as mere 'study skills,' they are two of the most powerful skills students can cultivate."
>
> —*Robert Marzano, Debra Pickering, and Jane Pollock*

Invite students to work with you to develop tips for effective note taking. For example, students will want to pay attention to key words so that they know how to organize their notes, and they will need a symbol (e.g., a star or exclamation mark) to indicate important information you have stressed.

Teach your students all the different forms of note taking. You could devote a week or more to each so that students have plenty of time to try out each form in a variety of subjects. (If your students work with a number of teachers, get everyone on board.) Have an ongoing discussion about students' experiences. Which structure works for whom? Does it work in all subject areas? Has anyone thought of an improvement that makes a form of note taking more useful (e.g., use of symbols, highlighters, numbering to show connections among ideas)? At the end of the month, host a Gallery Walk to showcase individuals' preferred note-taking forms and the innovations they developed. Encourage students to experiment and to adopt others' note-taking techniques to see if they work.

Once students have learned the various note-taking forms and have reflected thoughtfully about which forms works best for them under which conditions, give them *free choice* in the note-taking form they use in your class. This is where differentiation happens at no cost to you in terms of time or effort. (Although you spent time teaching them various note-taking forms, you did so with content you were planning to deliver anyway.)

 Experiment with different note-taking techniques. Discuss your reactions to each technique with colleagues or with your students.

If you assess students' notes, review your rubric or checklist with your colleagues. What learning outcomes do your note-taking marks address? Does your assessment form consider relevance of information, organization of ideas, and elaboration of concepts as students work with new material, or is it focused on neatness and underlined dates and titles? If the latter, discuss how you can check for these specifics without negatively affecting the usefulness of the assessment in measuring student achievement of learning outcomes.

Nonlinguistic Representations

Having students create nonlinguistic representations:

▶ stimulates and increases
brain activity

▶ helps them visualize (one
of the most effective
strategies used by good
readers)

▶ maintains their focus on
the "big picture" by identifying larger concepts and
the connections between
them (graphic organizers
in particular)

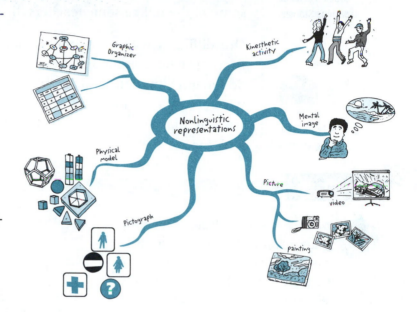

▶ supports the widest possible range of learning preferences
and strengths

▶ acknowledges the changing direction of career choices from
law and accountancy to arts, entertainment, and design
(a sign, according to Daniel Pink, that we are moving from the
information age to the conceptual age—see Learn More About
a Very Different Future on page 199)

▶ facilitates group work

▶ is particularly helpful to those with special needs (graphic
organizers in particular) (DiCecco & Gleason, 2002)

"Probably it's better to
put off using words as
long as possible and
get one's meaning as
one can through
pictures or
sensations."

—George Orwell

Although there are certainly exceptions, many teachers are not very comfortable modelling and encouraging the use of nonlinguistic representations. We tend to present most new knowledge by talking about it or by having our students read about it, even though we know that nonlinguistic representations would enhance student achievement. And many students seem quite happy with the linguistic emphasis; some of them, like some teachers, find it difficult to work visually.

Our difficulty with visual representations is a good reminder for us. Learners whose needs and preferences are routinely ignored in a predominantly linguistic and logical school system experience daily what we feel only occasionally: the sense of being at sea with an important strategy that everyone else seems to understand and thinking they look inept.

CLASS ROOM

Grade 9 Science Learning Stations

REFLECT

Janice Talks About Learning Stations

For Example

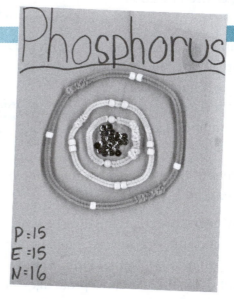

When Janice and Bill developed their grade 9 applied science unit on elements and compounds (see Blackline Master 8.2 and Blackline Master 8.3), they were careful to include an activity to support their students' learning preferences. Their first step was to administer a Multiple Intelligences Inventory (see Blackline Master 4.7).

The results confirmed their initial impression that many of the students in their applied-level classes preferred hands-on and visual activities.

Janice and Bill then developed a lesson that was set up at four learning stations. Students rotated through all four stations to describe the patterns in the electron arrangement of the first 20 elements of the periodic table. (See Blackline Master 9.16.) The four stations consisted of a computer simulation, an atomic structure demonstration kit, arts and crafts supplies, and textbooks, and provided students with the opportunity to draw and model Bohr-Rutherford diagrams for the elements using this variety of resources. Afterward, students debriefed the experience as a class, discussing which stations were most advantageous to the way they learn best.

Learn More About a Very Different Future

Daniel H. Pink (2005), *A Whole New Mind: Why Right-Brainers Will Rule the Future.* New York: Penguin Books.

IN YOUR ROLE

Learning stations or centres are an excellent differentiation structure as they can be differentiated according to need, interest, or learning preference and can be used with both tiering and choice boards. Janice and Bill had their students rotate through the stations to allow them to experience the same learning in a variety of forms and to begin recognizing their own preferences. This is a perfectly acceptable use of stations when your focus is on teaching students about themselves. However, once that self-knowledge about learning is established, true differentiated instruction means that there is variation in what stations students attend, the length of time they spend at a station, or what they do when at the station. Students might:

→ Attend only the station(s) they need

→ Spend differing amounts of time at a station

→ Choose how they do the work when at the station

→ Complete different amounts of work when at a station

Choices about who attends what station and what they do while there can be made by the teacher or the student, depending on the purpose of the activity.

If you have never used learning stations:

Look for a concept for which you have a variety of resources other than the textbook. Make sure your students possess the independent work skills, that all students know how to do the activities at the various stations, and that students know what to do if they finish work early (see page 102). Set up each station's tasks so that they take roughly an equal amount of time. Be organized—have the required materials available at the appropriate station and instructions printed on task cards.

If you have used learning stations before:

Incorporate a new nonlinguistic representation strategy into at least one of the stations, or set up learning stations where each station uses a different nonlinguistic strategy. Invite students to rotate through these stations, then discuss the usefulness of the various strategies and ways to incorporate them into future assignments or other subject areas.

Whether you are new to offering stations or are experienced, check the work at each station to make sure it focuses on important learning outcomes. If using graphic organizers at stations, make sure you have first modelled how to use the organizer and that you have demonstrated it several times before expecting independent use by your students.

Kathy introduced a lesson on diamante poems by having students using mental images to describe what they felt at a time when they were afraid. She then modelled the use of vivid language by describing her own mental images to express the fear she had felt concerning her first camping trip and the lightning storm she experienced on that trip, then showed students the poem she had written.

Weekend Getaway

Tent
dark, isolated
crashing, flashing, threatening
forest,   mud,   sand,   ocean
inviting, welcoming, nurturing
bright, cosy
cottage

Kathy then had her students use their descriptive words to write diamante poems. (See Blackline Master 9.17 for Kathy's lesson plan and tiered activity.)

IN YOUR ROLE

Read Kathy's lesson plan. (See Blackline Master 9.17.) Discuss what would happen in your class if you gave your students choice in a tiered assignment. How well do you think your students know their own needs? Would they make decisions based on need or for some other reason? How would you respond to the decisions they make? Would you require students to change assignment levels if they weren't challenged enough? if they were too challenged?

Then read Kathy's reflection on the next page. What are the differences from and similarities to your own viewpoint? What does this say about your beliefs about teachers? about students?

Consider Kathy's lesson plan and her reflection in relation to the points made in Chapter 5 about the development of an effective classroom learning community. What inferences can you make about Kathy's learning community as a result of this glimpse into her classroom?

Kathy's Reflection on Student Choice in Tiered Activities

In my diamante poem lesson (see Blackline Master 9.17), seven students selected the first two tiers, and fifteen selected the extension task, the third tier. I quietly redirected two students who clearly needed the basic tier. Two girls rejected my suggestion to rethink their tier selection and I watched them struggle to generate the three parts of speech required by the poem. I found myself feeling frustrated for a moment. But as I moved around the room helping those students who needed assistance, I realized they could write a poem; it just wasn't at a tier I would choose as ideal.

After reflecting on the lesson this evening, I've begun to see things differently. This differentiated activity allowed me to watch what students do when given an opportunity to make choices about content. This requires me to relinquish some power while students accept some additional responsibility for their progress. Although the majority of students are making the correct decision about which tier to select, it would be unrealistic to expect that all students would be sufficiently self-aware and self-confident to do this accurately after only a handful of opportunities to do so.

Opportunities to select from a menu of tiered tasks offer a powerful self-monitoring experience. To this end, my job is twofold. First, students who are not sufficiently self-aware need my intervention to redirect them to a task where they can be comfortable with the amount of risk taking demanded. Second, students who are not selecting the appropriate tiered task for their learning need to engage in meaningful dialogue afterward to begin to recognize their actual skill level and then come to appreciate that their decisions can affect their progress.

So now I see that even when students make an incorrect decision and enter into a task that might not be ideal, it is in the follow-up discussions that a powerful opportunity for growth lies. This incidental learning may, in fact, be more important than the answer to the essential question that is originally posed.

I certainly will not be providing student choice in all tiered tasks. I will continue to use my professional judgment to ensure that, most of the time, students are working at the ideal level of difficulty. There must be opportunity, however, for students to assume some of this responsibility in order to self-monitor their learning. Tiered tasks with student choice support this goal.

Finally, one recommendation I have for teachers who want to try tiered lessons is to avoid referring to the most difficult tier as a "challenge." I've discovered that this leads students to accept your "challenge" simply because you have "challenged" them. (Apparently some of us cannot resist a dare!) I will refer to the most difficult tier as an "extension" in the future. I believe this will help students to better differentiate between the mid-level and extended tiers.

Use a graphic organizer to plan your next unit. It helps you focus your attention on key concepts and make connections among them and across subjects. You can construct tests directly from the organizer with confidence that your test aligns with what you taught. You can also create questions that address links among concepts; such questions are automatically higher order.

To increase your use of nonlinguistic representations in your classroom, try any of the following:

→ Encourage students to stop partway through reading a text and describe the mental picture they are forming. Suggest they construct a mental map if it's an expository text or a video in their mind if it's a narrative text.

→ Have students give a Symbolic Book Talk (Robb, 2000, p. 163) instead of a written book report. Students take three to four minutes to summarize the book by demonstrating three symbols they feel are important to the book's theme. They explain each symbol, why they chose it,

and how it's significant to both the story and the theme of the book. Symbols can be actual objects, drawings, or images cut from magazines.

→ Create a group mind map as a form of review for a test. A mind map uses visuals and words and has the key idea in the centre of the map. This is different from a concept map, which uses words only and has the words placed on lines to illustrate relationships. In a concept map, the key idea is usually at the top (Bennett & Rolheiser, 2001).

→ Allow students to respond to an essential question through a Two-Minute Movie (Kajder, 2006). Students videotape and narrate the movie, but the movie is not to contain dramatized scenes. Rather, it is to consist of a series of images held up to the camera, with the narration recorded as a voice-over. Students can use digital photographs, original art of their own creation, or images from magazines or other media sources. Tell students to put the camera on "pause" as they switch images.

"In this [movie] business, you either sink or swim or you don't."

—*David Smith*

Learn More About Nonlinguistic Representations

Sara Kajder (2006), *Bringing the Outside In: Visual Ways to Engage Reluctant Readers*. Portland, Maine: Stenhouse Publishers.

Tony Buzan (1993), *The Mind Map Book*: *Radiant Thinking*. Woodlands, London: BBC Books.

Generating and Testing Hypotheses

We tend to think of hypotheses as belonging to experimental design in science, but a hypothesis is really just a supposition that acts as a starting point for further investigation. Hypotheses are used in:

▶ **Systems analysis**—analyzing government, ecosystems, or weather systems (If the June temperature plummets in Alberta, what will happen to summer in Ontario?). Begin by having students analyze familiar, contained systems, such as an aquarium.

▶ **Problem solving**—solving real problems that have multiple solutions (If I want to go to a party, but know my parents are going to say no, what should I do?). Problem solving involves looking for and finding the best solution.

▶ **Decision making**—identifying and weighing various criteria (I can't get the essay finished in time for tomorrow's deadline. I can buy one on the internet, or I can tell the teacher I didn't get it done. What should I do?). When you teach decision making, the focus is on having students use a systematic and defensible process, not just make a choice.

▶ **Historical investigation**—answering "What really happened?' or "Why did this happen?" (How could Hitler convince so many people that killing Jews was morally justifiable?). Historical investigation involves constructing a hypothesis about what happened and collecting evidence that will support or refute the hypothesis.

▶ **Invention**—testing multiple hypotheses to find the one that works

▶ **Experimental inquiry**—observing, explaining, predicting, and experimenting in various disciplines

> "The scientific theory I like best is that the rings of Saturn are composed entirely of lost airline luggage."
> —*Mark Russel*

It is an oversimplification that doesn't hold up terribly well in reality, but we like to speak of generating hypotheses either inductively (drawing conclusions or discovering principles based on looking for patterns in information) or deductively (using the principle to make a prediction about a future action or event). Marzano et al. (2001, p. 105) note that deductive hypothesis generation gives better results in schools, probably because it is difficult and time-consuming to ensure that students have all the experiences they need in order to work inductively. Working deductively, teachers present principles directly to students and then ask them to generate hypotheses based on those principles.

Learn More About Inductive Thinking

Barrie Bennett and Carol Rolheiser (2001), *Beyond Monet: The Artful Science of Instructional Integration*. Ajax, Ontario: VISUTronX.

This book provides helpful support if you would like to teach the inductive thinking strategies of concept attainment and concept formation.

Implications for the Classroom

The value of generating and testing hypotheses in an effective classroom is in deepening student understanding of key principles. Generating hypotheses, drawing conclusions, and explaining their thinking, preferably in writing, all require students to consolidate learning.

When students are first learning to think in terms of hypotheses, it can be helpful to give them a framework or template for reporting their thinking, with space provided where they're required to write explanations. Be sure, however, that the templates are supportive, not prescriptive. An example of the latter is the step-by-step template known as the scientific method:

1. State the problem to be solved.

2. Determine the variables.

3. Identify the hypothesis.

4. List the materials.

5. Provide a step-by-step procedure.

6. List observations.

7. State the conclusions based on the data.

"It seems to me that there is a good deal of ballyhoo about scientific method . . . science is what scientists do, and there are as many scientific methods as there are individual scientists."

P. W. Bridgman
Nobel Prize in Physics,
1946

Many of us were taught that the scientific method was *the only way* to conduct science experiments. The problem with this approach is that the focus for many students becomes filling in the blanks on the template rather than thinking about the concepts. Current thought in science is that students need to test and choose strategies in order to find the "best fit" for the problem. Starting with templates is helpful, but have students work toward turning the templates into checklists to encourage them to reflect on their scientific thinking processes.

Provide sentence stems, especially for struggling students, to help them structure and articulate their thinking.

Provide rubrics or develop rubrics with students (see Chapter 11) to clearly show that assessment is based on the quality of explanation offered, not the attractiveness of the final product.

IN YOUR ROLE

Hypothesis generation and testing works with any of the differentiation structures discussed in this chapter. It is central to inquiry learning. (See Chapter 7.) Regardless of what differentiation structure you use, hypothesis testing frameworks allow you to easily tier support by asking more or less complex questions, providing more or fewer prompts and explanations of the principles, and providing graphic organizers or other non-linguistic representations so that students have multiple ways to access and process information.

Once students know how to work with a framework and what you expect in terms of the depth and quality of their explanations, you can readily differentiate the topic they are studying by their interests. Develop **learning contracts,** agreed on by you and individual students, to outline exactly what students are going to study, the resources they will use, the way they will share their work, the criteria for quality and exactly how the work will be assessed, and all relevant dates in a timeline and/or a calendar—not only when the work will be due, but when they will check in with you so that you can do some formative assessment and support them in selecting appropriate next steps. (See Chapter 10.) Checkpoint dates are critically important in teaching your students time management techniques and helping them avoid the pitfalls of procrastination.

Contracts may be written so that each student has an individual contract with you, or you may create one contract for the class, with some required activities and some choice activities. In that case, you can save time by simply highlighting the appropriate required activities for each student.

Questions, Cues, and Advance Organizers

These three strategies all deal with ways to help students activate existing knowledge.

This book has already discussed advance organizers a number of times (see pages 142, 144, and 169). Cues are simply hints and reminders. This section will deal only with questions.

The questions we ask our students serve a number of important purposes. According to Cotton (2001), they help us to:

▶ Motivate students to become actively involved in a lesson

▶ Develop our students' critical thinking skills and inquiring attitudes

▶ Review and summarize previous lessons

▶ Assess achievement of instructional goals and objectives

▶ Stimulate students to pursue knowledge on their own

Given the multiple valuable purposes of questions, it is of little wonder that "questioning is second only to lecture in popularity as a teaching method" (Cotton, 2001, p. 1); we spend 35–50 percent of our time asking questions of our students.

Questioning is the most extensively studied of the instructional strategies. Research confirms its importance; we need to get better at asking questions that promote achievement, and our students need to be taught both how to answer questions and how to ask their own.

Simple counts of the kinds of questions teachers ask in classrooms confirm that, on average, 60 percent of our questions ask students to recall material that has been previously taught or read, 20 percent of our questions are procedural, and 20 percent of our questions ask students to mentally manipulate information in order to create an answer or to support an answer with logically reasoned evidence (Gall, 1984). Researchers (Cotton, 2001) urge that this last category, which in Bloom's Taxonomy terms would be higher-order questioning, be increased to 50 percent or more of our question-asking time because of the corresponding increases in:

- On-task behaviour

- Length of student responses

- Number of relevant contributions volunteered by students

- Number of student-to-student interactions

- Student use of complete sentences

- Speculative thinking on the part of students

- Relevant questions posed by students

Implications for the Classroom

The basic implication is, of course, self-evident: Ask more higher-order questions—ones that require inferences or analysis—and fewer basic recall or comprehension questions. Students do need to recall information, of course, but recall questions should be embedded within the larger purpose of the unit.

However, we have known about the importance of higher-order questions for some time; being told they're important doesn't make them easier to ask. Here are some suggestions for incorporating more higher-order questions into your classroom work.

→ Your questions help students focus on what is important. Prepare some questions as you plan lessons. This will allow you to consider your learning outcomes and ask questions that draw attention to those outcomes.

→ Teach students to make inferences and give them practice in doing so. This leads to higher-level responses from them and will make it easier for you to consistently ask higher-order questions.

→ Develop essential questions for a unit. These questions, by their very nature, are higher-order and lead to follow-up questions that are equally complex.

"All our knowledge results from questions, which is another way of saying that question-asking is our most important intellectual tool."
—*Neil Postman*

A new version of Bloom's Taxonomy was developed by, among others, Lorin Anderson, a former student of Benjamin Bloom. In the new taxonomy, nouns have been changed to verbs in consideration of thinking's being an active process, and evaluation and synthesis have been reordered based on the idea that we need to have thought critically before we can synthesize (Anderson & Krathwohl, 2001).

Old Bloom's	New Bloom's
Knowledge	Remember
Comprehension	Understand
Application	Apply
Analysis	Analyze
Evaluation	Design
Synthesis	Create

 The new Bloom's, as you will have noted, is much more student-friendly in its wording. A list of question starters and activity prompts for each level is provided in Blackline Master 9.18.

Note, however, that using these prompts does not guarantee that the question or activity is going to be at the correct level of response. For example, you will not get an analysis response if you ask the question "What caused the Ice Age?" and students need only recall the chart in their textbook titled "Causes of the Ice Age."

Feel free to ask questions before students have learned the information; this establishes an effective mental set for the learning to come (Marzano et al., 2001).

When asking questions, focus on what is important rather than what is unusual. The more students know about a topic, the more interest they have in learning more (Alexander et al., 1994).

Wait-time is hugely important to questioning, especially to asking higher-order questions. Research suggests that there is a three-second wait-time threshold for lower-order questions (shorter or longer times aren't helpful), but that there is no such threshold for higher-order cognitive questions. According to Cotton (2001), increasing the wait-time to five seconds before accepting an answer to a higher-order question results in increases in:

> "I roamed the countryside searching for answers to things I did not understand."
> —*Leonardo da Vinci*

- Length of student response
- Number of unsolicited student responses
- Amount and quality of evidence students offer to support their inferences
- Variety of student responses
- Number of questions posed by students
- Teachers listening more and engaging students in more discussions
- Teacher expectations regarding struggling students
- Variety of questions asked by teachers
- Number of higher-order questions being asked

If you then wait another five seconds after hearing the answer, you will find that students will give evidence and hypothesize.

To encourage more students to get involved in answering questions, ask that all students quickly jot their response to a question, and then call on several of them to read their answers.

IN YOUR ROLE

Replicate Susskind's question-asking study (1979) in your classroom. Estimate how many questions you ask in 30 minutes of whole-class lecture or discussion, and how many questions students ask. Record those numbers and, beside them, the numbers you think would be ideal. Then have a student tally the actual number of questions you ask and the number of questions students ask during a 30-minute session.

Bring your results back to the group at your next book study session and compare your estimates with the data.

Don't be alarmed if the actual results are far from your ideal. In Susskind's study, teachers estimated that they asked 15 questions and thought that was ideal. They actually asked an average of 50.6 questions. They estimated that students probably asked 10 questions and said that 15 would be ideal, while the students actually asked an average of only 1.8 questions.

In phase two of the experiment, determine the kinds of questions you ask and the kinds of questions your students ask. Involve your students by teaching them the new Bloom's Taxonomy and then, on a rotating basis, giving a few "classroom researchers" tally charts where they can check the types of questions asked during a class period. Discuss with your students what changes you and they will make based on the data that have been collected.

Effective teachers share responsibility for question asking with their students. Cris Tovani (2000, p. 86) reminds us that students who ask questions before, during, and after reading assume responsibility for their learning and improve comprehension in at least four ways:

▶ By interacting with the text—Readers who ask questions establish a purpose for reading and tend to be more focused.

▶ By motivating themselves to read—Readers are encouraged to stay with material when they're looking for answers to questions they have asked.

▶ By clarifying information in the text—Readers ask questions, the answers to which fill in missing information and allow the reader to enjoy and understand the text.

▶ By inferring beyond the literal meaning—Readers use questions to help them move beyond literal meaning and engage in inferential thinking.

Implications for the Classroom

Teach students the Question Answer Relationship (QAR) strategy (Raphael, 1986). QAR helps students identify the type of question they are being asked, making it easier for them to find answers quickly and accurately because they know what kind of thinking they need to engage in as they respond to the questions. The QAR strategy is helpful to students in daily classroom work and in responding to test questions.

There are four kinds of questions in QAR. The first two kinds have responses that are "in the book"; the last two have responses that are "in the mind."

Right There Questions In one spot in the text	**Here and There Questions** In several spots in the text
Author and Me Questions A combination of information in the text and the student's prior knowledge	**Just Me Questions** Inferential questions that do not require the text

To help students with "in the book" questions, have them highlight key nouns or verbs in the question and look for the same words or synonyms in the text.

Introduce the QAR strategy with a content example that allows you to clearly distinguish between the two types of questions.

Give students multiple opportunities to work in pairs or small groups classifying questions according to the four categories of QAR, because recognizing the question type is the first step toward deciding how to answer the question.

Use the differentiation structure called *cubing* (Neeld, 1986) to provide a novel twist on question asking and answering. As the name implies, cubing makes use of paper, plastic, or foam cubes with the questions written on each side of the cube. (A less time-consuming alternative is to use standard dice and write the corresponding questions on a piece of paper or on a set of index cards held together with a key ring.) Students work alone, with a partner, or in a small group to roll the cube and respond, in whatever form you wish, to the question. Cubes can be differentiated according to the level of the question. You can also use cubes for activities related to Gardner's entry points—a different cube for each entry point.

Make a cube using examples of some of the strategies listed in this chapter. For example, the six sides could have the headings Visualize, Compare, Question, Summarize, Create a Metaphor, and Mind Map It. Alternatively, create a cube activity for each individual strategy. For example, a cubing assignment about a novel that uses the strategy category of Identifying Similarities and Differences might have the following options:

→ How is the main character in this book similar to the main character of the last book you read?

→ Make a Venn diagram to compare and contrast two of your book's characters.

 → Close your eyes and point to the Metaphor Bingo board (Blackline Master 9.6). Use the image you pointed at to write a metaphor for the theme of your book.

 → Select 20 words at random from various chapters of your book. Use Blackline Master 9.3 to sort and classify your words.

→ Construct an analogy related to the main conflict in your book.

→ Your choice: Compare something about your book any way that you wish. Discuss at least three similarities and three differences.

Learn More About Questioning

Jackie A. Walsh and Beth D. Sattes (2005), *Quality Questioning: Research-Based Practice to Engage Every Learner*. California: Corwin Press.

Appropriate Challenge: Assessment *for* and *as* Learning

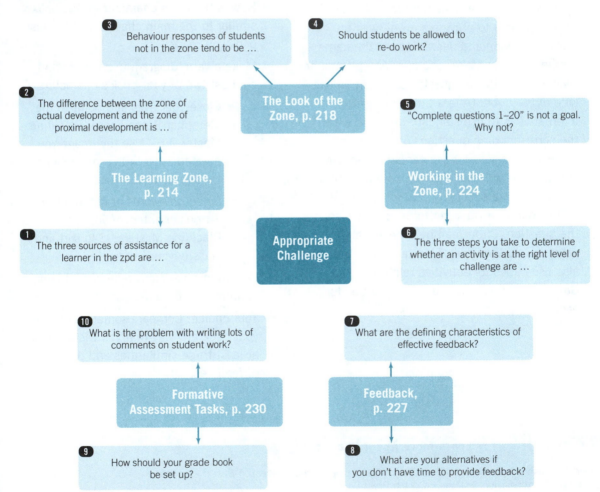

Appropriate Challenge

QUIZ

Refer to the appropriate sections for any part of this advance organizer that you have difficulty completing or answering, or for any idea you would like to explore further.

3 Behaviour responses of students not in the zone tend to be …

4 Should students be allowed to re-do work?

The Look of the Zone, p. 218

2 The difference between the zone of actual development and the zone of proximal development is …

5 "Complete questions 1–20" is not a goal. Why not?

The Learning Zone, p. 214

Working in the Zone, p. 224

1 The three sources of assistance for a learner in the zpd are …

Appropriate Challenge

6 The three steps you take to determine whether an activity is at the right level of challenge are …

10 What is the problem with writing lots of comments on student work?

7 What are the defining characteristics of effective feedback?

Formative Assessment Tasks, p. 230

Feedback, p. 227

9 How should your grade book be set up?

8 What are your alternatives if you don't have time to provide feedback?

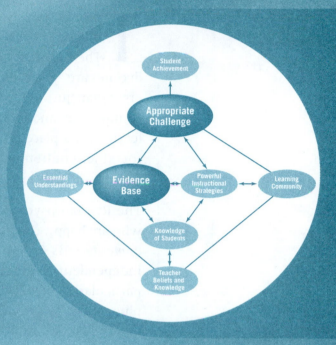

The Learning Zone

There is no way around it. To be a highly effective teacher, you must get your students into "the zone" and keep them there. The zone is something like the porridge and bed that Goldilocks declares are "just right." The difference between Goldilocks and learners is that "just right" for Goldilocks was a place where she felt happy, comfortable, and relaxed enough to fall asleep, whereas the zone for learners is a place where they are happy but just a little bit uncomfortable; challenged, not bored or frustrated; content, but not relaxed—in other words: a long way from falling asleep!

The Russian psychologist Lev Vygotsky (1978) states that students who are happy, comfortable, and relaxed are in the zone of *actual development*. This is the place where they can work capably and independently, where they hum along in their work and don't feel particularly taxed. Do you remember, as a good reader, enjoying zipping your way through a favourite series of books, whether in school as a child or last summer during your cottage or beach vacation? That's an example of being in the zone of actual development; it's a good place for independent work, a good place for practice, a good place for feeling confident about your abilities.

However, it is not a good place for learning. Learning happens in the zone of *proximal development*. In this zone, the work is just a bit tougher than students can handle without help. When they receive help and are then able to do something they could not do before, that skill becomes internalized and part of their new zone of actual development. They then independently practise and apply this new skill until nudged again into a new zone of proximal development.

"Children grow into the intellectual life around them."

Lev Vygotsky

Zone of Proximal Development

Zone of Actual Development

The fact that students need support to handle work in the zone of proximal development where learning occurs probably has many of you throwing your hands up in despair. Teachers already struggle with providing enough support for identified students with special needs or students for whom English is an additional language. How on earth can you provide help to all 30 students in your class or the 100 or more you might work with each day if you teach multiple classes?

Implications for the Classroom

Help does not come only from you and rarely takes the form of one-on-one intensive support. Help—what Vygotsky refers to as *scaffolding*—comes from three different sources and in a variety of forms already in play in an effective differentiated classroom.

Help Source 1—You

- You know your students because you have taken the time to get to know them (Chapters 4 and 7), so your planning (Chapter 8) and the differentiated structures you use, such as tiering (Chapter 9), mean you are better able to provide instruction at an optimal level.

- You have created a classroom community that supports open communication and mutual respect (Chapter 5), so students are more comfortable sharing their questions and struggles with you. You have to spend less time observing and speculating because students willingly tell you what they don't understand.

CLASS ROOM

Teacher and Student Interaction

- Your pre-assessments give you information that informs your planning of a unit so that work is not too easy or too difficult (Chapter 7).

- You have planned your unit around the essential understandings so that you know what knowledge and skills students need to acquire and what they should already be able to do in order to successfully acquire these (Chapter 8). In other words, you can sequence learning in an order that works for the individual.

- Your explicit teaching of instructional strategies (Chapters 8 and 9) means that students automatically receive modelling and guided practice, two valuable scaffolds for important work.

Help Source 2—More Capable Peers

- Your flexible grouping policy (centred on heterogenous groups most of the time) means that students who are more capable of a particular skill or strategy work alongside students who struggle with that skill or strategy (Chapter 8).

Formative Assessment

Melissa Talks About Formative Assessment

- Students working alongside capable students while talking about the work provides sufficient help much of the time, but you also have structured opportunities for students to deliberately assist each other (Chapter 8 and For Example in this chapter).

- You assign group tasks that are multi-faceted, authentic problems to allow all students to contribute their particular strengths to the work (Chapter 8). Your students know each other's strengths in addition to their own and recognize that different strengths are required for different tasks (Chapter 4). No one is the struggling student all the time.

Help Source 3—Artifacts

An artifact can be a typical classroom resource such as a textbook, math manipulative, test tube, or computer. It can be visual, for example, a photograph or work of art. It can also be a "symbolic meaning-making system" (Wells, 2001, p. 178), such as language or mathematics.

- You provide multiple entry points to learning (Chapter 4) for your students and opportunities for them to demonstrate understanding in multiple forms (Chapter 11). In other words, they can work with the artifacts that meet their particular learning needs and preferences.

- Your students create nonlinguistic representations (Chapter 9) in all subject areas.

- You teach your students text structures (Chapter 9) so they know how to make sense of the various ways texts are organized.

- Your students have strategies for accessing challenging texts (Chapters 8 and 9).

- You encourage a lot of dialogue in your classroom. It is understood that talk is learning (Chapters 5, 6, 8, and 10).

- Wherever possible, your students are engaged in meaningful, relevant, active learning—moving and doing rather than sitting and listening (Chapters 3, 4, 6, and 9).

- Your classroom is replete with a wide variety of resources at varying instructional levels, and with wall charts and other instructional aids (Chapter 8).

Learn More About Vygotsky in Real Classrooms

Gordon Wells, ed. (2001), *Action, Talk, and Text: Learning and Teaching Through Inquiry*. New York: Teachers College Press.

This book is a collection of action research pieces about the work of a research group exploring the role of talk in learning. (See pages 129–131.)

IN YOUR ROLE

Discuss with others what support you find most helpful when you're faced with difficult or challenging tasks.

What is the role of talk in solving problems? What is the role of talk in your classroom? After you've discussed this as a group, take a few minutes to observe in your classroom. Identify one place where you might increase the use of talk for learning.

The Look of the Zone

The zone of proximal development is the zone of instruction—where learning takes place. This is the point where the student combines existing knowledge and skill with the right amount and type of assistance to meet the achievable challenges of the lesson. Given the diversity of students in our classrooms, the right amount of assistance varies from one student to the next; so too does the right level of challenge in a lesson.

When a student is not "in the zone," their behaviours are usually manifestations of boredom or frustration. I was once told about a seven-year-old student whose actions mystified her teacher. This student handled every worksheet with ease and participated fully in classroom discussions. She had all the characteristics of a capable young student except one—on every worksheet she submitted, her name was printed upside down and backwards. Observation solved the mystery. It wasn't a strange new form of dyslexia; the worksheets, most of which required her to circle options and underline main ideas, were so easy that she was completing them upside down. Those worksheets were what teacher and brain researcher Kathie Nunley would call a spinal cord activity for that student—a routine task that can be performed with speed and accuracy while thinking about other things. The same worksheet might have been in the zone of proximal development for another student and at the frustration level of a third student.

Here is some of the language you might hear from your students if they are:

▶ bored (the work is too easy)—"I already know how to do this"; "I can coast"

▶ in the zone—"I get part of this"; "I have to work"

▶ frustrated (the work is too difficult)—"This makes no sense"; "I'm never going to get this"

Practise determining each student's zone by observing students as they complete a routine task, such as working on a spelling activity. Once you're used to interpreting what you see in routine tasks, you can easily switch to novel ones.

Jot down a note for each student as you observe. You can write your notes on mailing labels, index cards, or sticky notes, or you can record a note for each student on a class list. Write as fast as you can, and avoid recording any conclusions. For example, write "Rafi is tapping his pencil on the desk and looking around the room," not "Rafi is bored."

After you have completed this observation, and perhaps several others of the same

routine task, review your notes. What are the behavioural characteristics of students who are in the zone of actual development and are using the activity for practice? What are the characteristics of those who are bored? frustrated? Are any students in the zone of proximal development for this activity? How do you know?

Join with colleagues and share the findings from your observations. Review the flow chart below and discuss possible next steps for each student you observed. If you see too many next steps, focus on responding to the question, "What is the one thing the student can most benefit from at this point?"

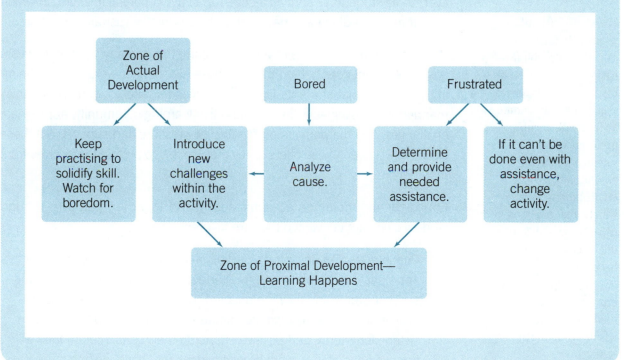

Panel 1: WHAT ARE YOU DOING?
Panel 2: BEING "COOL."
Panel 3: YOU LOOK MORE LIKE YOU'RE BEING BORED.
Panel 4: THE WORLD BORES YOU WHEN YOU'RE COOL.

> "Persistence is what makes the impossible possible, the possible likely, and the likely definite."
>
> —*Robert Half*

> "Combine curricular goals with our faith in our students' abilities to grow, throw in some instructional strategies that can accommodate a variety of learning preferences and intelligences in an emotionally safe environment, and watch what happens to achievement. Sure, it'll be easier to sit back and brag about our high expectations, but for the most part, they are, on their own, wishful thinking at best."
>
> —*Jane Bluestein*

Implications for the Classroom

Brain researchers tell us that the best learning state lies between boredom and anxiety. In the case of the young adolescent, boredom can be misleading. It may simply be the response a young adolescent assumes is required, or it may be legitimate. Boredom often manifests as disruptive behaviour; however, some students act out as a cover-up to avoid potential failure, in which case the correct diagnosis may be that the student is frustrated, not bored.

By the time students arrive in your classroom, they already have many years of school experiences behind them. If those experiences were so overwhelmingly negative that students view themselves as failures, you can offer all manner of engaging activities, a supportive learning community, appropriate challenges, and the perfect combination of pressure and support, but these students will reject these offers. They may do this to protect themselves from more failure.

Four actions, implemented consistently and together, can turn around students who are convinced they are failures:

1. Continue to offer engaging activities, a supportive learning community, appropriate challenges, and the perfect combination of pressure and support even when they are rejected. Remember that disengaged, disillusioned, and disappointed students may need you to make consistent, long-term, and positive efforts on their behalf before they will trust you and start to work. Specific ideas for challenge and support will be discussed more fully in the remainder of this chapter.

2. Believe that all students are capable of success. Jane Bluestein (2001) points out that there is a significant difference between believing and expecting. *Expecting* that all students will achieve high standards does not buy anyone's commitment, neither yours nor your students', nor does it teach students how to achieve those standards. *Believing* that all students are capable of achieving high standards and that you can help them get there results in your commitment, and will strongly and positively influence your students' beliefs and efforts. You can inspire and affirm them with your optimism.

3. If students attribute success or failure to their ability, luck, or other people, they're stuck in the circle of concern—a place where they can't control what happens to them. To help them move to the circle of influence, teach them about the relationship between effort and success. Studies have demonstrated that some students simply don't know that effort has an impact on achievement. Once they learn and experience this, it will change both their beliefs and their actions (Marzano et al., 2001). Note that it's critically important to your most disengaged and disheartened students that, if they take the risk and make an effort, their effort must result in success. A willingness to delay this gratification will not be present in early days. Make sure your most resistant students experience success on early assignments.

Recognize success through specific, personalized verbal praise. Studies have repeatedly shown that personalized acknowledgment is the best recognition that can be offered to an individual. If you feel you must give stickers, coupons, and treats, make sure the reward is tied to accomplishment of a specific goal, not just to showing up.

4. Give students the opportunity to redo or revise work to meet criteria. It is unrealistic to expect a student's best efforts the first time they complete every assignment. For most students, the opportunity to revise will be a confirmation of your conviction that effort leads to improved achievement and that you're supportive of their growth.

"That is the correct answer, Billy, but I'm afraid you don't win anything for it."

You may need to change your system if you encounter students who take advantage of the "do over" opportunity as a way to minimize effort the first time around. However, in your first response, be merciful. As Rick Wormeli suggests (2006, p. 132), "One of the signs of a great intellect is the inclination to extend mercy to others, and all successful teachers are intellectual."

Learn More About Redoing Work

Rick Wormeli (2006), *Fair Isn't Always Equal: Assessing and Grading in the Differentiated Classroom*. Maine: Stenhouse.

IN YOUR ROLE

Explicitly teach the importance of effort by telling students personal stories of when you succeeded at a task or achieved a dream because you persisted. Alternatively, read stories about people students admire. (One such collection is *If At First . . . How Great People Turned Setbacks Into Great Success* by Laura Fitzgerald. It includes short selections about individuals such as Oprah Winfrey, Michael Jordan, Lance Armstrong, and Walt Disney.) Students can put the biographical information into a simple timeline organizer and highlight the places where effort and persistence made a difference. (See Blackline Master 10.1 for an example with filmmaker Steven Spielberg and Blackline Master 9.12 for a blank organizer your students can use.)

Provide students with a simple form they can use to keep track of their effort and achievement. (See Blackline Master 10.2.) Work with students to develop meaningful descriptors for the effort and achievement levels, which should

range from *unacceptable* to *excellent*. (See Chapter 11, page 252, for a process for developing rubrics with students.) Have students verbalize what they learn about the relationship between effort and achievement.

Make some popcorn, grab a beverage of your choice, and watch any one of these or other feature films about effort and persistence:

Discuss the pros and cons of allowing students to redo work. Consider some of these questions:

- Should students be allowed to redo small assignments? large projects? tests?
- Should they be allowed to redo once a term? multiple times?

- Should redos be available for any reason or only for serious extenuating circumstances such as illness or a death in the family?
- If the redo is for a report card grade, what mark should the student receive? the new mark? a set mark such as 50 percent?

 If you or your group members don't believe in redos, claiming that redos are not allowed in the "real world," read and discuss the following quotation from Rick Wormeli (2006, p. 136):

Pilots can come around for a second attempt at landing. Surgeons can try again to fix something that went badly the first time. Farmers grow and regrow crops until they know all the factors to make them produce abundantly and at the right time of the year. People mark the wrong box on legal forms every day only to later scribble out their earlier mark, check the correct box, then record their initials to indicate approval of the change.

Our world is full of redos. Sure, most adults don't make as many mistakes requiring redos as students do, but that's just it— our students are not adults and as such, they can be afforded a merciful disposition from their teachers as we move them toward adult competency.

Assess yourself on each of the four actions that can turn around your disengaged and disheartened students:

1. Keep trying, even when your efforts are rejected.
2. Believe that all students are capable of high levels of achievement rather than expecting all students to achieve.
3. Teach students the relationship between effort and success, and make sure there is one!
4. Sometimes give students the opportunity to revise or redo work.

Which of these actions seem obvious to you? Which cause you to feel the most consternation or even anger? If you're already taking the actions that seem obvious, support a colleague who is having difficulty by describing what you do and the beliefs or thinking behind your actions. For any actions or beliefs that are problematic for you, return to the Concerns Based Adoption Model (see page 32), place your concern at the appropriate level(s) on the model, and determine a next step you can take to address the concern.

Working in the Zone

Effort results in success as long as the learning activity is in the zone of proximal development; in other words, at a reasonable level of challenge for the student. To determine whether a challenge is reasonable for an individual student *before* they attempt it, you must:

▶ Establish and share goals for the learning and the criteria for success

▶ Know what understandings or skills are necessary to achieve success (Chapter 8)

▶ Pre-assess the student's knowledge, skills, strategies, and attitudes, especially as they relate to necessary prior understandings and experiences, strategies, and skills (Chapter 7)

Once you know the right level of challenge, you need to group students effectively for instruction (Chapter 8) and create activities for different levels of readiness (Chapter 9).

Implications for the Classroom

Not only do *you* need to know the essential understandings (knowledge and skills) of a unit in order to plan and assess effectively, but *your students* need to know them, to be aware of the goal to work toward and the criteria that allow them to better reflect on and assess their own growth in relation to the goal. This is the meaning of "assessment *as* learning"—the student as thoughtful assessor of their own learning (Earl, 2003).

Before beginning the unit, provide students with the learning expectations or outcomes, worded in language that makes sense to them. For example, list them under a heading such as "You will know . . . " (knowledge) and "You will be able to . . . " (skills). Since lists of objectives, however "kid-friendly" the language, won't leave your students awestruck, consider also providing them with an advance organizer so that they understand the scope of the unit and begin to see connections among key concepts. Advance organizers can take a number of forms. The quizzes opening the chapters of this book have functioned as advance organizers for you.

Even with advance organizers and clear descriptions, goals need discussion and elaboration if they're going to make sense to your students. Have students analyze completed samples or exemplars of student work. The conversation you have about these samples allows your students to develop their understanding of the criteria used to assess work.

To develop criteria with students (Gregory, Cameron, & Davies, 1997):

1. Make a brainstormed list of important features, preferably from a review of a range of anonymous samples of student work.

2. Sort and categorize the list. Post the completed list of criteria.

3. Students and teacher refer to the posted criteria to give feedback and assess work.

Connect each day to the target learning outcomes or expectations and to the criteria as students work on assignments. Stating a goal in terms of what students will learn increases relevance, and being explicit about the criteria for success allows students to self-monitor and stay "in the zone." With a common language for discussing the work and common expectations of the results, both you and your students will also find it easier to pinpoint where the learning is a struggle or is too easy. Do the same when assigning homework: make sure students know the learning expectation and the need for review or practice of important concepts or skills in the assignment.

Encourage students to personalize goals as much as possible. (This is another reason lesson goals should not be of the "complete the assignment" variety.) Personalizing goals reinforces both student ownership of learning and the metacognition necessary for quality self-assessment.

When criteria are clear, you and your students will find it relatively easy to personalize goals because you'll be able to identify what criteria have been met and what criteria should be addressed as an appropriate next step. If work samples or exemplars are available, they add another important dimen-

"We, as teachers, make judgments about students all the time. Since these judgments are based on criteria, whether we can articulate them or not, we have only two choices: we can either make our criteria crystal clear to students or make them guess."

—*Judy Arter*

sion to your students' self-assessments because they provide tangible evidence against which students can compare their work. Students tend not to inflate their assessments if they're involved in the process from the beginning (Rolheiser & Ross, 2000). If, on occasion, self-assessments seem inaccurate, clear criteria provide objective evidence that will allow you to discuss any concerns with the student.

Self-assessment activities can be organized into three categories based on their complexity and the time they take to complete (Gregory, Cameron, & Davies, 2000). The categories are:

→ Pause and Think: Take a minute to reflect on learning, publicly or privately.

→ Look for Proof: Comment on an aspect of the work.

→ Connect to Criteria: Assess work in relation to criteria.

IN YOUR ROLE

Students can use either of the following *pause and think* activities to self-assess their achievement of learning goals (Wiliam, 2006). At the end of a lesson, review the learning goals and have students hold up a piece of coloured paper (green, yellow, or red) to indicate their success in meeting the goal. Work with the red students in a short-term homogeneous group to fill the gap in their learning. Green and yellow students can pair up to help each other.

You can do the same thing during a lesson by providing students with three coloured paper cups. Instruct them to put the green cup on their desk if they are following the lesson, yellow if they want you to slow down, and red if they are lost.

To help your students learn to *look for proof*, you can provide prompts such as those given on the "Say Something" activity sheet used in the grade 8 media unit (Blackline Master 10.3).

To help students *connect to criteria*, create and provide prepared self-checks and peer checklists based on the criteria you have negotiated with the class and posted on the wall.

Which of the three forms of self-assessment do you use most frequently? How do you think these assessments help the learner? How do they help you with your work? Do you tend to use self-assessments more in one subject area than another? What concerns do you have about teaching students to self-assess?

Feedback

Formative assessment is ongoing, happens during the learning, and provides you and your students with information about their understanding that can be used to determine what steps to take next. In other words, it allows learning to be advanced. Formative and diagnostic or pre-assessment are often referred to as "assessment *for* learning." Summative assessment, on the other hand, measures learning at the end of the lesson or unit, and is referred to as "assessment *of* learning."

Formative assessment may best be thought of as feedback for you or your students. Feedback is frequent, descriptive rather than evaluative, helpful, and sensitive to small learning gains. After reviewing 8000 research studies, John Hattie claimed, "The most powerful single modification that enhances achievement is feedback" (Marzano et al., 2001, p. 96).

> "Assessment is the ongoing redefinition of starting points."
> —*Janet Allen*

Implications for the Classroom

Feedback is helpful when it takes the following form (Marzano et al., 2001):

1. Tell the student what he or she is doing correctly as it relates to the learning expectation or outcome.

2. Tell the student what he or she is doing incorrectly, again as it relates to the learning expectation. Be specific and give new information or an explanation that helps promote new understanding.

3. Ask the student to keep working until he or she succeeds.

EGS102-TS

"Mr. Wickers called me 'gifted' in front of the whole class. I'm ruined."

Some feedback needs to be private.
Source: www.CartoonStock.com

If you're giving students feedback about their overall strengths and weaknesses, Mel Levine (2003) recommends a similar process that he calls "demystification":

1. Point out the student's strengths as specifically as possible. (For example, "Your book report showed me that you understand *Moby Dick*," rather than "You're a good reader.")

2. Demystify weaknesses by naming, explaining, and limiting them to the top three.

3. Build optimism and affiliation by being specific with the student about what he or she can do to succeed and reassuring the student that you're there for support.

Feedback can be written rather than oral, but it still needs to be specific. For example, achievement increases by 30% when homework has comments, but only 11% when just assigned (Marzano et al., 2001).

When it comes to providing feedback for homework, considering the homework's purpose may help you avoid grading and commenting on stacks of written work. If the purpose of the homework is to:

→ Practise a skill that students have learned, have students self-assess and graph their improvement.

→ Help students mentally prepare for and anticipate new learning, a class discussion of student connections and thoughts about the homework assignment may suffice.

→ Provide an extension or elaboration of class work, consider sometimes allowing students choice in how they communicate their learning. Not only will this differentiation make the homework more appealing to your students, but it will relieve you of the drudgery of commenting on 30 copies of the same assignment.

Practise giving either specific academic content or strength/need feedback to a student. If it's the latter and you're finding it a challenge to think of strengths, review your observational notes and the student's learning profile. (See Blackline Master 4.1.)

You might also find it helpful to refer to a list of strengths. (See Blackline Master 10.4.) The list provides language to use in feedback sessions, report-card writing, meetings with parents, and student-led conferences.

For Example

Students in Maya's music class loved the final term's big assignment: "Write an original composition on the theme of your choice. We should be able to tell how you feel about your theme by listening to your composition."

It was not an easy task. Maya expected her students to use everything they had learned throughout the year, and put different demands on different students so that all students would be able to meet the challenge. Maya wasn't able to listen to students' efforts as quickly or as frequently as needed. So Maya did the next best thing: she established a few key checkpoint meetings with each student. Students who needed a lot of assistance got more meetings, but everyone got at least two.

Prior to each checkpoint meeting, students were required to have a predetermined and differentiated number of peer assessments. All students had been trained in what criteria to look for and had an assessment form that gave

them the language they needed to provide specific feedback. The student brought the form to the meeting to verify that the assessment had been done and to discuss the actions the student had taken in response to the feedback given by peers.

Much to Maya's delight, the process worked flawlessly. Because students had been aware of their learning goals and criteria throughout the year, they had the language and the metacognitive skills to give meaningful feedback and the ability to make use of the feedback to shape their future actions.

Formative Assessment Tasks

The purpose of formative assessment is to use the results to put or keep students in the zone of proximal development. Formative assessments, or assessments *for* learning, "diagnose student needs, plan our next steps in instruction, provide students with feedback they can use to improve their work, and help students see and feel in control of their journey to success. Grading is laid aside" (Stiggins, Arter, Chappuis, & Chappuis, 2004).

There are a couple of important points in this quotation. The one that might have caught your eye is "Grading is laid aside." Assigning a grade to a formative task in the belief that the assessment serves the dual purpose of both formative and summative assessment does not work. Grades are what some call *terminal feedback;* students are rarely motivated to continue working on an assignment after the assignment has received a grade.

> "Using one assessment for a multitude of purposes is like using a hammer for everything from brain-surgery to pile driving."
>
> —*Walt Haney*

The second, and related, point is that if the formative assessment does not help you and your students identify a next step, it has little value.

Implications for the Classroom

One of the best actions you can take to use formative assessments for their intended purpose is to set up your grade book so that notations and scorings are by learning expectation or target learning outcome, not by assignment. If you enter results by assignment, you can't tell where students need to improve or the steps you need to take to help them achieve the expectation or learning outcome. If you enter results by learning expectations or outcome, you can give specific feedback and make next-step decisions. You can still list assignments under the appropriate expectation or outcome so that you can discuss patterns of response based on the type of assignment. For example, you might note that Lekeisha excelled at demonstrating understanding through art or that Jakob did his best work on assignments where he was able to satisfy his desire to work alone. (See Chapter 11, page 238, for more information.)

Written responses that you offer on a formative task need to provide direction—a vague comment such as "please revise" isn't helpful. If you note every place where a student needs to make a correction, you're doing too much of the work and the student will attend only to what you've marked. For example, instead of correcting each spelling, grammar, or punctuation error, indicate the line where an error occurs and tell the student to find and fix it. Instead of a checkmark beside each correct answer on a math assignment, tell strong students, "Seven of the ten answers are correct. Find the three incorrect answers and fix them." To get the struggling math student in the zone, you may need to say, "Three of the ten answers are correct. Notice the error you made on this question. (Explain the error.) Three other questions have the same pattern. Find the three questions and fix them."

In all formative assessments, whether written or oral, the goal is to provide you with an idea for a next step to advance the learner, and to provide the learner with information that will allow them to "make adjustments, adaptations, and even major changes in what they understand" (Earl, 2003, p. 25).

For Example

Partway through a unit on probability, Melissa gave her students a quiz as a formative assessment. She then set up learning stations for each of the three concepts she had taught in the unit, which were clearly delineated on the quiz: Listing Outcomes with a Tree Diagram, Experimental Probability, and Theoretical Probability. Students used the feedback Melissa provided on the quiz (marks and comments) to decide which station they should attend and for how long. After working at the learning stations of their choice, students were prepared for the end-of-unit test.

When activities are aligned to goals, goals and criteria are shared, and you know what understandings and skills students must have in order to achieve the goals, every classroom activity becomes an opportunity for formative assessment.

Consider one or more of the following suggestions for next steps. Note that the next steps are, of necessity, broadly painted as *struggling* and *excelling*. The steps you choose will be more refined because you have such a thorough and in-depth knowledge of your students.

When you're designing a formative assessment, make sure it measures an essential understanding of the unit. Then, having administered the assessment, sort the data into anywhere from one to three groups based on a single important difference related to the essential understanding, whether that difference is readiness to handle the concept, interest, reading ability, or learning preference. Use the assessment data to decide how you'll address that difference in order to provide each student with the appropriate degree of challenge.

In addition to the suggestions provided below, you can determine next steps by observing students while they work, conferencing with an individual student or a small group, or comparing a student's current work with earlier work.

Formative Task	If *Struggling...*	If *Excelling...*
Name or explain a concept from the unit and ask students to create a graphic organizer that elaborates on and provides examples of that concept.	Identify what the student doesn't understand about the concept. If it's a misconception, address it directly. If it's a gap in knowledge, try teaching through another entry point.	Go broader and deeper. Have the student extend the graphic organizer to show relationships among unit concepts. Give the student an opportunity to develop expertise in an area of interest and relate it to the concept.
Discuss the unit concepts with students.	Don't leave students with incorrect or incomplete answers. Probe further and follow up with activities that address gaps and misunderstandings.	Ask questions and provide activities that engage students at the highest levels of Bloom's Taxonomy (page 208), namely Evaluate and Create.

Formative Task	If *Struggling...*	If *Excelling...*
Assign blackline masters to students (e.g., Probable Passage, Blackline Master 9.4).	Students may put words in the wrong categories, revealing, for example, that they don't understand the meaning of "setting." Provide a mini-lesson to teach the terms.	In the next Probable Passage activity, provide the words but have students develop their own categories, or use as is but ask students to write a gist statement based on synonyms they determine for the given words.
Have students complete exit cards at the end of a lesson. (See Blackline Master 10.5.) This allows them to summarize their learning and gives you a quick glimpse into their understanding.	Group students with similar needs and develop an activity to address those needs.	Group students with similar needs and develop an activity to address those needs.
Have students find the answers to questions in their subject textbook.	Determine the source of the problem. Students may need the material presented at a lower reading level or on tape. They may just need a lesson in the organizational pattern of the textbook, question–answer relationships (see Chapter 9), or how to use text features to find information.	Depending on the learning outcome, you may want to provide students with multiple resources so that they can synthesize information, or give them a more challenging question–answer relationships assignment.
Give students a quiz.	Provide direct instruction to students, or use centres as Melissa did in the For Example above.	Allow students to choose centre activities as in the For Example above. Include extension activities at each centre.
Ask students to respond to a journal prompt about the concept.	Make sure the issue is one of lack of content knowledge rather than difficulty with the written format. You might need to help students make stronger connections to prior experiences.	Provide more challenging prompts, perhaps ones that ask students to create analogies or metaphors or discuss similarities and differences between this concept and another.

Evidence Shared

QUIZ

See the appropriate pages for any statements to which your answer is "no."

1 I prepare summative assessments before I begin teaching the unit.

> Making an Assessment Plan, page 237

2 My grade book is organized by learning outcomes, not by assignments.

> Making an Assessment Plan, page 237

3 I base grades on summative assessments.

> Summative Assessments, page 239

4 I assess only achievement of outcomes in an academic grade, not effort.

> Summative Assessments, page 239

5 I sometimes provide unit tests to students at the beginning of a unit.

Differentiating Tests, page 243

6 I sometimes give students opportunities to be tested through their preferred learning style.

Differentiating Tests, page 243

7 I frequently give students choice in the way they demonstrate their learning on a culminating task.

Authentic Assessments, page 246

8 I know about GRASPS for designing authentic performance tasks.

Authentic Assessments, page 246

9 I involve students in assessing their own work.

Developing Assessment Criteria, page 250

10 It is possible to differentiate assignments and still have a student's final grade be fair.

Sharing the Evidence, page 253

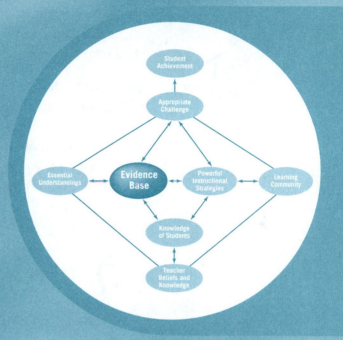

Sharing evidence—conducting summative assessments or assessments *of* learning, turning them into grades, and sending those grades home—truly is the elephant in the living room. It is the aspect of teaching many of us are most uncomfortable with, and it is certainly the show-stopper for many teachers who are contemplating changes in their classroom toward greater responsiveness to individual learners. It is difficult to talk about because, as Rick Wormeli (2006a) suggests, "The way you grade is very close to who you are as a teacher. And who you are as a teacher is very close to who you are as a person."

Grading matters; it would be foolish to say that it does not. Grades have an impact on what type of post-secondary education a student pursues—even whether there will *be* further education for that student. (Remember Steven Spielberg—Blackline Master 10.1.) If you're teaching students who are about to start secondary school, grades may determine what classes they will take and, in turn, what career options will be open to them.

What gets measured, gets attention.

Grading procedures have an impact on your relationship with your students' parents and on their assessment of your professional credibility, as is evident when you send home a justifiable grade of B to parents who expect and demand that their child be viewed unremittingly as an A student.

Grades also have an impact on your students; they may have been in school for only a decade, but every year of that decade they've been measured multiple times, and when those measurements have gone home, they have been made much of—positively or negatively.

Knowing that grades matter, and caring about our students beyond their time in our classroom, most of us are on a career-long quest to improve the precision and the helpfulness of our grading practices.

Making an Assessment Plan

Effectiveness before differentiation is as necessary in assessment as it is in any other aspect of our "Success for Every Student" model. Although it's simply not possible to achieve complete objectivity and precision in any human endeavour, we take huge strides when we thoughtfully plan our assessments as we plan our units.

Implications for the Classroom

Follow these steps to help ensure that your assessments are addressing the essential understandings of the unit or course of study:

1. Plan with the end in mind by determining the target learning outcomes or goals. These are the statements of what the student will be expected to understand, know, or do by the end of the unit, grading period, or year. See Chapters 6 and 8 for more information.

2. Plan and prepare the summative assessments that will tell you the degree to which students have achieved these goals or outcomes. This chapter will give you more information about how to construct good summative assessments, how to differentiate them, and how to arrive at meaningful report card grades for all when you have differentiated.

3. Plan and prepare the diagnostic or pre-assessments that will tell you students' knowledge, skills, and attitudes that will in turn allow you to "start where they are" in planning your instruction. See Chapter 7 for a variety of simple diagnostic instruments.

4. Plan and prepare the formative assessments you'll use to give students feedback on their learning as they develop and practise new understandings before being graded. These assessments also give you feedback so that you'll know how to alter instruction to enable all students' progress toward achievement of the goals or outcomes. Be prepared for this feedback to alter the format or structure of some of your assessments. See Chapter 10.

Set up your grade book so that the columns are for expectations or outcomes. You might want to word them in the form of the learning targets you share with students if it's easier to stay with one form of wording; cross-reference them to the number of the expectation or outcome so that you can retrieve the formal wording if necessary. Review the assessment activities you've developed and list the summative activities in columns underneath the expectation. Since robust assessment activities address more than one expectation, list the activity under each of the appropriate expectations.

See Blackline Master 11.1 for a blank copy of this form. Note the four columns under each expectation or outcome. Assessment experts disagree as to exactly how many pieces of data are necessary to arrive at a reliable conclusion about a student's achievement, but they all emphasize the importance of triangulating the data by having a number of pieces of evidence collected over time and from a range of different tasks (Davies, 2000). Most offer a number somewhere in the range of three to six (Cooper, 2007; Marzano, 2006; Pollock, 2007). I have settled on four in the example below; your school district or professional judgment may lead you to another number.

Expectations	7.1 Demonstrate an understanding of a variety of media texts				7.2 Identify some media forms and explain how the conventions and techniques associated with them are used to create meaning			
	1 Film review	2 Scene role play	3 Venn diagram	4 Unit test questions 6, 7	1 Film review	4 Unit test questions 3, 4, 5	5 Magazine and analysis	6 Techniques quiz
Student Names								

Summative Assessments

Pre-assessments or diagnostic assessments should never be entered in a grade book, except perhaps as evidence that you and your students can look back on to marvel at how far they've progressed in their understanding. Formative assessments shouldn't be entered in your grade book because their purpose is to give you and your students feedback during development in order to maximize progress in learning. Summative assessments come after students have had plenty of time to develop their learning, whether at the end of a unit or at a key point during the unit. These assessments are entered in the grade book because their intended purpose is to evaluate the student's achievement of essential understandings.

Implications for the Classroom

Put the majority of your energy and creativity into formative assessment tasks. Formal summative assessments tend to get most of the attention because they count for grades and because they're evidence that is shared, but informal formative measures are the place where your teaching will make a significant difference to the results students will eventually obtain on the summative assessments.

In a differentiated classroom, it is understood that the pace of learning varies with the student. If a summative assessment is anything other than a written test, consider administering it when students are ready for it. This may sound onerous, but it doesn't have to be. Why should all presentations happen one after another for two mind-numbing days in a row? You obviously want to set equitable parameters so that you're not assessing October's unit in May, but if some students are ready to give their presentation in the second week of October and some aren't ready until the third or fourth week, you're being responsive when you allow them that flexibility. In fact, there are advantages to the development of metacognitive skills when students have to think about whether they're ready for assessment. As well, struggling or disengaged students benefit when they see the bar set high through the work of more capable students who present early.

Tell students what the summative assessments are going to be *before* they begin the unit. Summative assessments are the bull's eye on the dartboard. When students know what they're aiming for and have lots of practice hitting components of the target through the various formative tasks of the unit, their likelihood of hitting the bull's eye soars.

No form of assessment is inherently superior to any other form. As long as everyone has an equal opportunity to succeed, the choice of form depends on what you want to measure and what would work best for your particular students. Some of the summative assessment options, divided into VAK learning preference categories, are as follows:

Visual	Auditory	Kinesthetic
• Completed graphic organizer • Essay/report • Portfolio • Learning log • Written questions on a test	• Oral testing • Debate • Oral defence • Verbal questions • Conference or interview	• WebQuest • Lab experiment • Manipulatives • Demonstration • Role play

A balanced assessment plan has students engaged in writing, saying, and doing their understanding and you engaged in the corresponding assessment actions of marking, listening, and observing (Cooper, 2007).

Summative assessments are an occasion where students should, whenever possible, be permitted to use their strengths rather than work on their areas of weakness. (See page 81.)

Measure what you want to know. We wouldn't think of factoring in what type of running shoe a student is wearing when assessing his or her ability to serve a volleyball, but we sometimes don't think twice when we give students a written test, ask them to explain the rules of volleyball, and then deduct marks because of spelling or grammatical errors. Literacy skills are important and should be assessed. But when the student is penalized four marks for spelling errors and receives a grade of three out of ten, he or she is no longer being assessed on an understanding of volleyball rules, but on spelling skills.

The same consideration must be given to assessments of effort. Effort has an enormous impact on success (page 221) and should be communicated to students and their parents so that they see the relationship between effort and success. If effort is not recorded on the report card alongside the academic mark, you'll need to find another way to talk to parents and students about effort because it cannot be embedded in the academic grade.

Taking it to an extreme in order to make the point, consider again the student who is demonstrating the ability to serve a volleyball. If the capable demonstration of a volleyball serve were worth one point and anything short of that capable serve were worth a zero, where would effort belong? Should we give one point to the student who tries really, really hard? We cannot, because, according to our marking scheme, that means the student is able to serve the ball. What we would likely do is change the marking scheme, making the successful serve of a volleyball worth two points so that we could acknowledge effort by giving students one point. We might want to do this in a formative assessment because students are still practising and we want them to stay in the game, but if that's the mark on a summative assessment, are we saying that they capably served the ball half of the time? That they couldn't serve at all but they were trying hard? Numbers become confusing and lose meaning when we require them to serve too many purposes.

All classroom assessments need to be criterion-referenced (evaluated relative to specific criteria), not norm-referenced (evaluated relative to other students' work). Comparisons of one student with another have no place in an effective or a differentiated classroom. This statement implies that there is no such thing as a cap on the number of A's and B's granted in your room, and

"Please tell me what one student's evaluation and assessment has to do with another student's. Either you have a certain level of understanding and mastery in a subject or you don't."

—*Eric Jensen*

that when explaining what the letter grade of C means, the word "average" is not part of that explanation.

Learn More About Assessment

Damian Cooper (2007), *Talk About Assessment: Strategies and Tools to Improve Learning.* Toronto: Thomson Professional Learning.

Anne Davies (2000), *Making Classroom Assessment Work.* Courtenay, B.C.: Connections Publishing.

IN YOUR ROLE

Our assessment practices were determined, in large part, by our experiences. As mentioned at the beginning of the chapter, they are part of who we are and are often highly resistant to change. Learning communities or study groups are one of the best ways to influence our assessment beliefs and practices (Wiliam, 2006). Through dialogue, collaborative development of assessment tools such as rubrics, and collaborative analysis of student work (Langer, Colton, & Goff, 2003), we respectfully challenge each other to ask and answer the tough questions, such as "Is this assessment measuring what I need to measure?" and "Does this assignment allow my students to demonstrate the full range of their knowledge and understanding?"

Begin the conversation by talking about the statements made in Implications for the Classroom. If each group member individually completes Blackline Master 11.2, it will be easier for the group to prioritize the items to be discussed. When completing the blackline master, decide which implications, if any, are problematic for you. Are they a problem because you don't agree or because you

don't know how to transfer the idea to a reality in your classroom? If it's the former, rewrite the statement so that it's true for you, then deconstruct it to reveal the beliefs that underpin it.

✗ *No form of assessment is inherently superior to any other form.*

✓ *Written tests are the all-round best option for valid assessments.*

These are my beliefs underlying this statement:
- *Students should be able to demonstrate any and all understandings through writing.*
- *It is possible for one form of assessment to be more valid than others.*
- *If students are given a consistent assessment format (i.e., tests), they will get better and better at using that format.*
- *I need to use tests because that's how my students will be assessed in high school, and my job is to prepare my students for high school.*

For example, if you agree with the statements in the implications list, but don't know how to make one or more of them a reality in your classroom, choose one statement you'd like to address, chunk it into a series of small, sequential actions, and take one action at a time, perhaps with the assistance of a supportive colleague (see Chapter 2).

Differentiating Tests

REFLECT

Unit Tests

Since written tests are common assessment measures used by teachers of young adolescents, let's examine a few simple ways you can make sure they are effective instruments *and* differentiated so that more students have an opportunity to succeed.

Implications for the Classroom

- Be clear about what you are assessing. Every question should correlate to one or more expectations or learning outcomes.

- Provide clarity for students by asking questions in a straightforward manner. Keep vocabulary simple, except for content terms. Highlight key words in the test questions so that students know to focus on them.

- Test under the same conditions as you teach and, if at all possible, in the same environment. For example, if students have had access to math manipulatives during class, put a set of manipulatives on each student's desk for use during the test.

- In a test where students are matching terms with definitions, put the definitions on the left and the terms on the right. Struggling readers will have an easier time finding the single word that matches the definition than reading through all the definitions to match the single word. Make sure that all the matching items are on the same page and keep the total number to eight or fewer (Wormeli, 2006b).

- Multiple-choice questions require that students be able to work with multiple complex sentences, often worded in such a way that the differences among them are negligible. Hence, they are a real challenge for struggling readers. Consider giving two versions of a test: one with multiple-choice questions, the other with short-answer questions for the same information.

- Rick Wormeli (2006b) suggests giving students the end-of-unit test at the beginning of the unit as a form of advance organizer. Students will be motivated to listen for answers throughout the unit; since those answers are the essential understandings of the unit, that's what you want. At test-taking time, give out clean copies of the same test or allow students to use their own still-clean copy. This, of course, works best with constructed responses (short-answer or essay questions). If your test is forced-choice (matching, true-false, or multiple-choice questions), Wormeli suggests rearranging the items so that students don't memorize answer patterns. For math tests, change the numerical values in the test but keep the same structure of problems. Having the test in hand from the beginning can make quite a difference to struggling or test-anxious students.

- Consider using the same test as both a pre-assessment and a summative assessment (see Chapter 7). Make sure students understand that the pre-assessment will have no impact on their grade and that you simply want to be able to show them the learning that took place as a result of their efforts (page 221). Have them reflect on their new understandings since the initial assessment.

- Make sure students have enough time to complete the test thoughtfully and carefully by taking the test yourself or, even better, giving it to an unsuspecting colleague or family member. Some students may require more time for completion.

- Make ample use of the powerful instructional strategies you've taught (see Chapter 9). Ask students to compare and contrast ideas, to develop metaphors or analogies, to summarize concepts, and to complete graphic organizers. Not only are your students well prepared for these achievement-enhancing strategies because you've spent time teaching them, but the strategies also allow students to provide responses in nontraditional formats. Students who can't construct coherent responses to short-answer questions may be perfectly capable of sharing all the necessary information and more if they're permitted to do so through a metaphor or a comparison matrix.

- Engage students in creating a bank of possible test questions as a study guide. Create your summative assessment using the questions students have prepared.

- Teach test-making strategies so that your students understand how effective tests are constructed.

- Teach test-taking strategies so that students understand how to study for and answer different types of test questions.

Analyze one of your unit tests in relation to the points above. What one change could you make that would enhance the overall effectiveness or the effective differentiation of this test?

As an alternative, think about a student who routinely has difficulty doing well on tests. Is there something in the tests' format you could change to enhance the student's opportunity to demonstrate understanding?

Make a list of the testing accommodations you make for students with special needs. Discuss the advantages and disadvantages of offering similar accommodations to all students, recording your points in a two column chart. Try to generate an equal number of points for both sides of this question. Individually decide where you stand on this issue, then take the opposite side in the group discussion. Argue persuasively for the position you do not support. After the discussion, reflect on whether the requirement to look at the question from a different perspective gave you any insight into how to influence your own mind.

 Have students get into groups according to dominant strengths on their learning profile (Blackline Master 4.1).

The VAK (visual-auditory-kinesthetic) profile is probably simplest for this activity. Give each group a copy of the test-preparation/test-taking template (Blackline Master 11.3) and ask them to complete it. This will be useful even if you have earlier provided students with Blackline Master 4.12. The completed templates can be shared with other groups so that all students see the impact of learning preferences in their work and perhaps be encouraged to try out each other's strategies. As a further metacognitive activity, students can complete the template or a journal or learning log entry after the next test to indicate what strategies they used, which ones worked, and why they were successful.

If you share students, take the time to coordinate schedules so that students aren't taking tests in every subject all at the same time. Look for or create commonalities among the tests so that you can teach students helpful test-taking strategies. For example, if several teachers use questions where students match definitions and terms, these questions should all be organized so that definitions are on the left and terms are on the right.

An authentic assessment is one that truly measures a student's understanding and ability to use the learning because it is authentic to how the student learned the material in the first place. If the student learned about a concept through inquiry into essential questions, for example, but was tested only for recall of factual details from a textbook, the assessment would not be authentic.

Authentic also refers to relevance to the student. Sometimes the skill or information is relevant to students because it's something they use in their lives or will use in the future. And sometimes the assessment is relevant simply because students perceive it as real (something for which they feel a sense of ownership) as opposed to fake (an assignment completed just because they're asked to do it). I like the way 11-year-old Clara expresses it in Alison McGhee's novel, *Shadow Baby* (2000, p. 13):

> *It hurts me to see a book report. It's painful to me. Book reports are to books what (a) brown sugar and water boiled together until thick are to true maple syrup from Adirondack sugar maples, (b) lukewarm reconstituted nonfat powdered milk is to whipped cream, and (c) a drawing of a roller coaster is to the roller-coaster ride. Give me a real assignment, I say.*

Test questions can be authentic, but we usually think of an authentic assessment as being a product, exhibit, demonstration, or performance task that demonstrates understanding, whether that understanding is of declarative or procedural knowledge. Inquiry-based learning, project-based learning, and problem-based learning (see Chapter 8, pages 162–163) lead naturally to a variety of authentic assessment tasks.

STUDENT TALK

Demonstrating Learning in Various Ways

"Let's not look at things through the filter of short-answer tests. Let's look directly at the performance that we value, whether it's a linguistic, logical, aesthetic or social performance . . . ."

—*Kathy Checkley*

Authentic tasks are the form of summative assessment in which teachers are most comfortable allowing student choice. While choice automatically signals differentiation, you need to be careful that the choices you offer are still authentic in terms of measuring achievement of the learning goals. For example, making a shoebox diorama of a scene from *The Outsiders* may be hours of fun for a kinesthetic learner, but if the expectation was to "identify the point of view in the text," the diorama may not be the best means of showing understanding of point of view. Further, if you offer students choices that require skills they do not have or that would take weeks of work by teams of people to complete, not only will your assessment be inauthentic, but you will become overwhelmed dashing from one student to the next, trying to teach the prerequisite skills that students need before they can address the expectation or outcome you're supposed to be assessing.

IN YOUR ROLE

At the beginning of the year, review your class profile of learner preferences (Blackline Master 4.2) and choose a few product/performance skills you're prepared to teach to the class. Choose skills you enjoy so that your enthusiasm will be evident in your teaching. For example, if you have a number of verbal-linguistic learners who really like to talk and you have an interest in storytelling, teach them the finer points of storytelling, create criteria for telling an exemplary story for the grade level, and make that a performance option throughout the year.

When you choose and teach a few specific product or performance skills, you'll be able to determine criteria for successful completion of the product that will be consistent over the course of the year. This will save you from having to constantly develop new assessments and will increase the likelihood of seeing improvements in the quality of work, since your students will have repeated opportunities to demonstrate their understanding through a limited range of product options.

Each time students choose how best to demonstrate their learning, engage them in assessment as learning by asking that they reflect on their responses to the questions on Blackline Master 11.4.

Decide together the product/performance skills to be taught at each grade level, who will teach each one, and how they are to be assessed.

> "Performance assessment is any assessment in which the teacher's role is to observe while students perform."
> —*Rick Stiggins*

You can use the acronym GRASPS (Wiggins & McTighe, 2005) to design authentic performance assessments. Each letter corresponds to a task element. Here's one about the Underground Railroad using that passion you have for storytelling.

Goal: Your task is to tell the story of the Underground Railroad.

Role: You are a person who travelled the Underground Railroad to freedom many years ago and who helped many people successfully travel it after you.

Audience: Your audience is your grandchildren.

Situation: Explain the need for the Underground Railroad to children who have never known slavery.

Product: You will tell your story, choosing either to have a live audience of your peers or to record it. Whatever your chosen presentation format, please give me an outline of the historically accurate and important factual information about the Railroad you have included in your story.

Standards: Your story needs to be factually accurate, to be told from the perspective of an older person passing along wisdom and advice to young people, and to meet the criteria of good storytelling we have established together.

You may have noticed that the GRASPS example required that student work meet the criteria of good storytelling. When you choose what production/performance skills you'll teach, or when you choose ones you're sure students can handle without instruction, be sure to match skills to curriculum outcomes and expectations and to note accomplishment under the appropriate objectives, for example, oral language and presentation expectations in the case of storytelling.

> "Rich performance tasks, in the form of culminating tasks, can bring closure to a unit of study by presenting students with the opportunity to synthesize and apply their learning."
> —*Damian Cooper*

When creating a rubric (see below) for a variety of performance tasks, remember that, since the majority of the objectives you're assessing are the same for all students, the rubric is also the same for all. If you're assessing criteria unique to the form of the product, that assessment can be on a separate form or added to the main rubric.

Larry Lewin and Betty Jean Shoemaker (1998), *Great Performances: Creating Classroom-Based Assessment Tasks.* Virginia: ASCD.

For Example

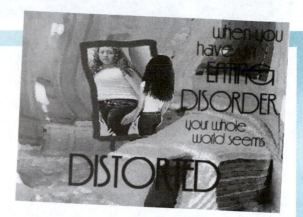

 Grade 8 teachers Kelly, Shauna, and Donna told their students about the media unit's culminating task on the first day of the unit (Blackline Master 11.5) and gave them the final assessment form (Blackline Master 11.6). Here are Shauna's observations:

After presenting the culminating activity to the students, I repeated several times the choice aspect of the assignment. I made it clear that if a group had another idea for presenting, I was open to hearing it.

I did this because I know that some students are quite computer literate (much more than I am!) or are otherwise technically savvy, and that they might be able to use their skill to showcase their knowledge. One group did ask if they could do a video commercial. After determining that they had the technical equipment and know-how to do this, I asked that they complete a storyboard for my approval prior to shooting. The final presentation was very well done. I think the real-life nature of the activity and the choice students were given made them very excited and motivated to complete the project and led to some very good results.

 CLASS ROOM

Working on a Culminating Task

 REFLECT

Shauna Talks About Culminating Tasks

 (See Blackline Masters 11.7–11.10 for peer and self-assessments.)

 Rewrite the culminating task from Blackline Master 11.5 or 11.11 using GRASPS.

 Refer to Blackline Master 8.4 (Grade 8 Media Unit Lesson Sequence) for the unit plan if needed.

Developing Assessment Criteria

Regardless of whether summative assessments take the form of tests, performance tasks, observations of student activity, questioning, or anything else, students should always know the criteria of performance and, where possible, be involved in establishing those criteria and assessing their own and their peers' achievement of the criteria.

Grading must focus on evidence of achievement of the learning outcomes, not on the medium through which the student demonstrates their mastery. If criteria are not established and discussed in advance, students will have difficulty understanding what is expected of them and you will have difficulty ensuring that your scoring of student work is reliable and unbiased. For example, feel free to comment on but do not mark the quality of the coat hanger sculpture if you don't have a learning outcome devoted to coat hanger sculptures!

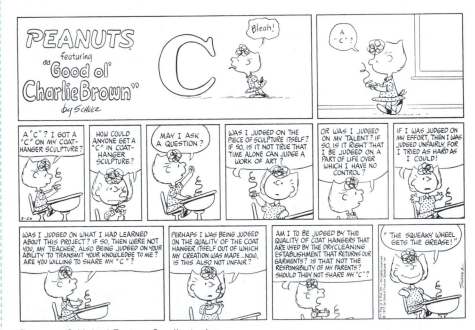

Peanuts: © United Feature Syndicate, Inc.

A few components of student work require quantitative marking. For example, knowledge of terms, mathematical formulas, and simple selected-response test items all can be assessed numerically (Cooper, 2007). However, if we want our students to know what is expected of them and how they can improve, and if we want to feel more confident that our assessments measure what they're supposed to measure and that our colleagues would measure the learning in the same way, we need to use rubrics.

A rubric is a set of guidelines for evaluating student work. It usually takes the form of a matrix with criteria listed on the left and ratings for each criterion described on the right. The rating scale is often in four levels. There is a description of performance for each level and measurable, discernable differences in the quality described for each level. When the rubric is well written, students not only have a clear, precise understanding of their current level, but they know exactly what they need to do to move to the next level.

The challenge, of course, is in making sure that the rubric is well written.

Implications for the Classroom

When creating a rubric, consider the following:

- ❏ Limit the criteria to four or five.

- ❏ Avoid generic adjectives like *good*, *poor*, or *excellent*. Descriptions need to be based on something that can be observed, not inferred.

- ❏ Make sure descriptors are clear, concise, and specific. Use straightforward, student-friendly language. Clarify vague words like *neat* and *important* (Pollock, 2007). Vagueness reduces the reliability of the rubric because other assessors might understand the term differently.

- ❏ Make sure descriptors are phrased as positive statements that invite high-quality work, not work that simply meets minimal expectations. For example, ask for "at least three examples," not "three examples."

- ❏ Make sure there are measurable, observable differences in the levels of quality.

- ❏ If possible, give students examples of work at each level so that they can see the range of responses.

> "A grade based on frequent use of rubrics with clear descriptors results in a more accurate rendering of students' mastery at the end of the grading period, while basing a grade primarily on mathematical averages often distorts its accuracy."
> —*Robert Marzano*

❐ Give students the rubric before they start to work so that they have the criteria for how the quality of their work will be judged. This makes it more likely that students will be able to plan their work (Jackson & Larkin, 2002) and to submit high-quality work (Andrade, 2000).

IN YOUR ROLE

Personalize rubric levels for students by asking them to define the levels of achievement in terms that are meaningful to them. My class came up with this one when we were talking about attractive but content-free performances and I told them about the commercial with the old woman who opens the packaging in a fast-food hamburger joint, lifts the bun, and demands, "Where's the beef?"

When I worked with staff in a First Nations school, their rubric levels were relevant to their experiences:

4	
3	
2	
1	

When you invite students to personalize the levels of achievement, you might hear them start to refer to their work as being of "whole cow" quality. That's a good sign that they've internalized the levels using their own terminology.

Decide what rubrics you'll be able to use repeatedly over the year, develop them collaboratively, and assess them against the suggestions provided in Implications for the Classroom.

Learn More About Creating Rubrics

Go to http://rubistar.4teachers.org for help in creating or locating rubrics for hundreds of outcomes.

Sharing the Evidence

Teachers who are new to differentiated instruction worry that the grades they share with parents will be meaningless because students have been doing different things and have been assessed in different ways. However, if the goals are the same, if the focus is on the common essential understandings, and if the criteria address the important aspects of those essential understandings, then it's only the path students took to the learning that was differentiated, not the evaluation of the learning. As we have seen in this chapter, summative assessments can offer students different ways of demonstrating their understanding while still being measured through a common assessment structure. One student might write an essay, another might give a presentation, and a third might create a WebQuest, but if they're all being assessed on criteria related to the outcome of explaining the suffrage movement in Canadian history, all can be assessed using the same rubric.

And, of course, some summative assessments are likely going to be common to all students, with perhaps slight alterations such as giving students more time to complete a test or requiring that every student create a storyboard of the defining moment in the novel of their choice.

When you have differentiated the tasks *and* are assessing based on different criteria, this is admittedly problematic for summative assessments. Use these tasks for formative assessments. In that situation, each assignment has clear evaluation criteria that reflect the nature of the task students are completing. In other words, a student in a group tiered for readiness can achieve an A on a complex task after meeting the criteria, while a student in another group can also achieve an A on a foundational task after meeting the criteria. This is fair and reasonable because the assessments are of different criteria and because the marks aren't counted in the student's final grade. Results of such assessments can still be shared with parents and students by explaining the

> "Grades are merely symbols and are only a part—probably a very small part—of our communication system."
>
> —*Ken O'Connor*

context and the nature of the entry behaviours so that class work starts where each student is and helps them progress. If your students are involved in assessment discussions from the beginning, and if you emphasize comments and descriptions of performance rather than letter grades (which aren't helpful in informing a student's next steps anyway), differentiated tasks with different criteria don't need to be a problem.

If you decide that some formative assessments are going to be counted in a student's final grade, it's still possible to differentiate the formative tasks. Record the grade under the appropriate outcomes and use a symbol to note that it was a differentiated task, how it was differentiated, and the level at which it was completed. When you calculate marks for final grades, you can weight the different assessments so that the differentiated formative tasks aren't overly represented in the student's final grade.

Finally, remember that you're teaching young adolescents at a time in their lives when they're most receptive to developing their metacognitive assessment *as* learning skills. If you've created a strong and effective classroom learning community based on mutual regard and understanding and have worked with your students to develop their knowledge of themselves as learners, they will be superb ambassadors and allies in explaining to their parents and others how the classroom works, what their grades mean, and what they need to do next in order to progress. Parents who witness this growth in their young adolescents are likely to view grades as what they are—your best professional judgment—and to view your willingness to differentiate for what it is—your responsiveness to their child as a unique individual.

Where Are You Now...

Human beings differ with their gifts and talents.
To teach them, you have to start where they are.

—*Yuezheng in 4th century B.C. Chinese Treatise, Xue J*

A common question in the minds of teachers when they first hear about differentiated instruction is some variation of "What does it look like? Am I already doing it?" The answer is, "It looks like many things when you're starting where individuals are, and you're undoubtedly doing some of it, but not all, never all." That answer isn't very satisfying for teachers who are looking for clear parameters and a formula to follow. Nor is it very reassuring for all of us who care so much, work so hard, and would really like to know that we're doing everything we possibly can for our students.

Effective differentiated teaching is a destination that is always a little or a lot out of reach because it's contingent on our ability to meet the needs and preferences of the young adolescents with whom we work. That group changes day by day, year after year, and so do we. So the answer to the question "Where are you now?" is going to be, and will always be, "Today, at this moment, I am at this point."

Our classrooms have become such complex places, filled with students who exhibit the widest possible range of academic and emotional needs. The fact that you picked up this book, that you are responsive to the individual in the midst of this often overwhelming complexity, speaks to your professionalism and integrity as a teacher. You, like the students you teach, need feedback, evidence, and acknowledgment of the vital work you do and the critically important, often life-altering, positive difference you make in the lives of your students.

> "Teaching is about honour and goodness and mercy. It really is. And no one will be watching you most of the time. You either live up to the calling of the profession or you don't, and most likely no one will ever know but you. But it matters because the kids are counting on you."
> —*Penny Kittle*

Scoring—Complete this inventory only when you're prepared to devote an hour to the work. It obviously won't take an hour for you to check all the boxes that are true for you at this moment in time, but it should take at least that long for you to reflect on, acknowledge, and celebrate your contribution to the most important work on the planet.

Knowledge of Students

Effective teachers of young adolescents:

❑ Recognize that diversity, not hormonal change, is the hallmark characteristic of this age group

❑ Highlight moral and ethical concepts embedded in curricular units

❑ Teach students about how they learn

❑ Provide experiences that are developmentally appropriate to support physical, emotional, social, moral, and intellectual growth

Effective *differentiating* teachers of young adolescents also:

❑ Help students develop deeper understandings of their own learning preferences

❑ Provide opportunities for "hands-on" learning and physical activity in response to both the developmental needs of the age group and the particular needs of students with a kinesthetic learning preference

❑ Believe and repeatedly demonstrate that people have different strengths, and that *struggling* and *advanced* are terms relative to specific situations

❑ Build learning experiences from students' knowledge and interests

Learning Community

Effective teachers of young adolescents:

❑ Build community focused on learning as a shared goal

❑ Model care and respect for all students and refuse to allow hurtful behaviour from others

❑ Are fully present or *withit* in the classroom

❑ Are emotionally objective in difficult situations

❑ Teach students to be responsible, in part by inviting their ownership of the classroom environment and procedures

❑ Ensure that all students have occasion to work with all other students in the class

❑ Debrief classroom issues with students

Effective *differentiating* teachers of young adolescents also:

❑ Connect with students as individuals based on knowledge of their personal interests and learning needs

❑ Personalize classrooms so that they're reflective of the interests, strengths, and intelligences of the people who inhabit them

❑ Give students choices so that they can learn to make decisions, select activities that are meaningful to them, build on strengths, and work at an appropriate level of challenge

Essential Understandings

Effective teachers of young adolescents:

❏ Plan and teach according to the *big ideas* of what students need to know and be able to do

❏ Make connections across subject boundaries to increase relevancy and meaning for students

❏ Use collaboratively created essential questions to engage students in inquiry

Effective *differentiating* teachers of young adolescents also:

❏ Recognize that success in the grade and in life requires that all students work with the same essential understandings of the discipline

❏ Provide a variety of entry points for students to work with important concepts

❏ Ensure a range of resources to support students' varying learning needs and interests

Evidence Base

Effective teachers of young adolescents:

❏ Pre-assess students' knowledge, skills, and attitudes in advance of a new unit and use this information for planning only, and not in students' grades

❏ Plan all assessments in advance of the unit and share summative assessments with students at the beginning of the unit

❏ Set criteria and create rubrics with students

❏ Set up their grade book according to learning goal, not assignment

❏ Value formative assessments not as marks for report cards but rather as opportunities for feedback to advance student learning and to inform instructional decision making

❏ Design assessments so that they measure student understanding and application of the learning

Effective *differentiating* teachers of young adolescents also:

❏ Allow students to work from their strengths, particularly when the stakes are high

❏ Delay beginning-of-year pre-assessments until all students are comfortable in the classroom

❏ Assess students (through pre-assessments, formative assessments, and summative assessments) in a variety of formats in order to get an accurate picture of understanding, skills, and attitudes

❏ Allow choice, particularly in large culminating tasks, whenever possible

❏ Teach students to personalize assessment structures (i.e., rubrics) so that they are meaningful

❏ Give specific feedback on an ongoing basis to their students, enumerating what a student is doing well before defining challenges, needs, or errors

Powerful Instructional Strategies

Effective teachers of young adolescents:

❑ Provide lots of opportunity for students to learn through talk—discussion, debate, role play, and story, in particular

❑ Explicitly teach research-based powerful instructional strategies

Effective *differentiating* teachers of young adolescents also:

❑ Vary the pacing and sequencing of content to match a student's knowledge and experience

❑ Use differentiation structures such as tiering, choice boards, cubing, contracts, learning stations, and a variety of short-term, flexible learning groups to meet the instructional needs and learning preferences of individuals and the developmental needs of this age group

Appropriate Challenge

Effective teachers of young adolescents:

❑ Make use of other students and resources as well as themselves to scaffold students

❑ Teach the relationship between effort and success

❑ Believe that all students are capable of success when given the right assistance

❑ Share learning goals with students at the beginning of the unit and on a daily basis, and encourage students to personalize these goals

❑ Sometimes allow students to redo or revise completed work

Effective *differentiating* teachers of young adolescents also:

❑ Build on students' strengths

❑ Group students heterogeneously far more frequently than homogeneously

❑ Provide multiple entry points to learning and opportunities for students to demonstrate understanding in multiple forms

❑ Provide specific and individualized feedback

❑ Provide respectful activities at the right level of complexity for the individual

Foster child Hollis Woods tells a school story in Patricia Reilly Giff's novel *Pictures of Hollis Woods* (2002, New York: Wendy Lamb Books):

> *The picture has a dollop of peanut butter on one edge, a smear of grape jelly on the other, and an X across the whole thing. I cut it out of a magazine for homework when I was six years old. "Look for words that begin with W," my teacher, Mrs. Evans, had said.*
>
> *She was the one who marked the X, spoiling my picture. She pointed. "This is a picture of family, Hollis. A mother, M, a father, F, a brother, B, a sister, S. They're standing in front of their house, H. I don't see a W word here."*
>
> *I opened my mouth to say: How about a W for wish, or a W for want, or W for "Wouldn't it be loverly," like the song the music teacher had taught us?*
>
> *But Mrs. Evans was at the next table by that time, shushing me over her shoulder.*

Differentiating teachers feel a little sorry for Mrs. Evans. She is quite likely a fine teacher, doing a good job, but in this situation at least, she has missed the opportunity to *know* Hollis—her experiences and her dreams. She has missed the opportunity to *enjoy* Hollis—her creativity and perhaps her humour. And, of course, she has missed the opportunity to *teach* Hollis. Mrs. Evans clearly has a misguided idea of Hollis's current understanding, making it impossible for her to help Hollis progress from that starting point.

When we are weary, overwhelmed, or both, trying to be more effective and more responsive in our work with young adolescents can seem an impossibility. Those are the times when we need to remember that implementing the components of the framework of effective differentiated instruction means that our professional lives are filled, not with missed opportunities, but with students whom we *know, enjoy,* and can therefore *teach*.

Words of Wisdom

Differentiated Instruction Is Rewarding

Glossary

Note: The terms printed in teal refer to structures that are frequently used by teachers who differentiate instruction.

A

Assessment as learning—students assess their own work and reflect on their growth as learners

Assessment for learning—assessments used to inform instruction (see diagnostic assessment, pre-assessment, and formative assessment)

Assessment of learning—end-of-lesson or end-of-unit assessment (see *summative assessment*)

Authentic assessment—assessment that is relevant to how the student learned the material

C

CBAM—Concerns Based Adoption Model (Hall and Hord, 1987); a model of the process of change for an individual

Choice board—a differentiation structure consisting of a grid with a different activity presented in each square

Constructivism—an instructional approach that says learners are actively engaged in constructing knowledge by beginning with experiences that have personal meaning

Cooperative learning—structured group activities built around five elements: positive interdependence, individual accountability, interactive skills, face-to-face interaction, and group processing

Critical attribute—a significant aspect of a concept that differentiates it from all others

Cubing—a differentiation structure consisting of a cube with a different question or activity presented on each face

D

Declarative knowledge—facts, information, concepts

Diagnostic assessment—assessment used before planning a unit to determine students' knowledge, understanding, and ability; also known as pre-assessment or assessment for learning

Differentiated instruction—a comprehensive framework of effective instruction that is responsive to the diverse learning needs and preferences of individual learners; also known as responsive instruction

E

Early adolescence—the stage of life between ages 10 and 15; the period between childhood and adolescence

Effective—having a powerful, impressive impact (in education, the impact is on student achievement)

Emotional objectivity—the ability to care without the expectation of a positive response in return

Entry points—ways in which a teacher can introduce new material to students and students can work with that material; multiple entry points give students multiple representations of the same core ideas

Essential questions—big questions based on big ideas/essential understandings. They have no single or obvious right answer, ignite curiosity, lend themselves to multidisciplinary study, are central to a discipline's big ideas, and are worded to engage student interest.

Essential understandings—big ideas essential for all students; they are not differentiated

Evaluation—a judgment or appraisal based on defined criteria

Evidence base—*all* the ways a teacher makes decisions, including reflection, knowledge of individual students, and observation, as well as the full range of formal and informal assessments

Exit cards—an assessment tool; students respond to a prompt on a card and hand it in at the end of a lesson; teachers use information on cards to design instructional activities and to group students for learning

Explicit instruction—teacher-provided intentional modelling or demonstration of a skill or strategy, followed by an opportunity for the student to practise and apply the new learning with teacher support, guidance, and feedback

F

Flexible grouping—temporary, short-term learning groups based on student interests, readiness, or learning preferences

Formative assessment—assessment during the learning; provides teacher and students with information about student understanding; also known as *assessment for learning*

Frontal lobes—the part of the brain in which moral reasoning takes place; may not be fully developed until well past the age of 20

H

Heterogeneous group—a group based on random selection rather than specific criteria such as academic achievement

Homogeneous group—a group based on specific criteria; an ability group is homogeneous

Hypothalamus—the part of the brain that controls hormones and is responsible for emotions such as fear, anger, and aggression; is most active during adolescence; the best way to calm it in educational settings is to provide choice in learning

I

Inquiry learning—students actively engaged in development of new knowledge through a combination of reading, writing, viewing, discussing, experimenting, and discovering; often the inquiry is in response to essential questions

Instructional approach—the teaching method used during part of or throughout an entire unit (see *inquiry learning*, *project-based learning*, *cooperative learning*)

Integrated learning—when students work on a concept through a variety of disciplines

Intelligences—formats in how the mind thinks; Sternberg says there are three; Gardner says eight or nine

Intelligences profile—a grouping of intelligences that interact with one another; there are three basic profiles (see *jagged profile*, *laser profile*, and *searchlight profile*)

J

Jagged profile—an intelligence profile where some intelligences are stronger than others

K

Knowledge of students—a teacher's understanding of each individual student's interests, learning preferences, and readiness to learn a particular concept

L

Laser profile—an intelligence profile where one or two intelligences are exceptionally strong and others are weak

Learning community—a group of people focused on the collective goal of learning

Learning contract—agreement between student and teacher to outline what choices a student may make in an assignment and what requirements the student must satisfy

Glossary

Learning preferences—individual differences based on a person's learning styles, intelligences, interests, gender, culture, etc.

Learning station—a place in the classroom where material is collected so that students can work on a specific topic or skill

Learning styles—often, although not always, four categories describing significant ways in which individuals differ in how they learn best and in how we prefer to acquire, process, and remember new information

Lesson design—the organization and sequence of a lesson or series of lessons in order to create learning experiences that result in maximum student engagement and achievement

M

Mental model—our beliefs and assumptions

Meta-analysis—a statistical research process whereby the results of a number of studies are combined to determine the average effect of a given strategy

Metacognition—reflecting on our own thinking and learning processes

Multiple intelligences—Howard Gardner's theory that we have nine intelligences, not just one

Multiple representations—a variety of ways in which students can demonstrate learning or you can provide new information; corresponds to *entry points*

P

Powerful instructional strategies—the research-based strategies proven to have a significant, positive, and demonstrable impact on student achievement

Pre-assessment—assessment used before planning a unit to determine students' knowledge, understanding, and readiness to learn a new concept; also known as *diagnostic assessment* or *assessment for learning*

Problem-based learning—students are provided with a believable problem for which they must acquire new knowledge in order to solve it

Procedural knowledge—processes, strategies, and skills

Procedure—way of doing something in the classroom

Project-based learning—students are assigned authentic, real-life tasks that they investigate over an extended period of time

R

RAFT—a differentiation structure where students choose the role, audience, format, and topic for an assignment

Readiness—a student's academic starting point; varies by concept

Reliability—consistency, stability, and dependability of results; a reliable result shows a similar performance at different times or under different conditions

Resiliency—the ability to bounce back after adversity, to regain functioning

Respectful task—all students are given tasks that are equally interesting, engaging, and important; tasks respect the learning needs of each student

Routine—a sequence of procedures

Rubric—an assessment tool with a multi-level measurement scale, descriptors for the characteristics of each level, and criteria based on the objectives of an assignment

S

Searchlight profile—an intelligence profile where differences among intelligences are not pronounced

Strategy—a plan of action for processing, organizing, and working with information

Strengths-based revolution—an approach in education and in business that advocates paying more attention to an individual's strengths than to their weaknesses

Summative assessment—assessment at the end of a lesson or unit; documents student performance, provides basis for assigning grades; also known as *assessment of learning;* see also *evaluation*

T

Teacher efficacy—the belief that teachers can influence how well students learn, even difficult or unmotivated students

Think-aloud—the verbalization of the thinking process when working through a piece of text or a concept

Tiering—providing different levels of an activity to meet the different levels of student readiness for the concept being taught

Triarchic Intelligences—Robert Sternberg's theory that we have varying combinations of three intelligences—analytical, practical, and creative

V

Validity—a measure of how well an assessment measures what it is intended to measure

W

Wait-time—the delay between asking a question and accepting a response; increases in wait-time result in increases in student achievement

Withitness—the quality of being fully present in the classroom, aware of all students, and able to manage a number of tasks simultaneously

Y

Young adolescents—individuals aged 10–15; also referred to as "tweens" because they are between childhood and adolescence

Z

Zone of actual development—where a student is able to work capably and independently, is not taxed, and feels confident about his or her abilities

Zone of proximal development—where a student feels the work is a bit tougher than he or she can handle without help; a term coined by Lev Vygotsky, and also known as the *zone of instruction*

References

Chapter 1

Lin-Eftekhar, J. (2002). UCLA Today: Creating an atlas of the human brain. Retrieved March 14, 2007, from www.today.ucla.edu/2002/021022brain_atlas.html.

Marzano, R. (2003). *What works in schools: Translating research into action*. Virginia: ASCD.

Salk Institute for Biological Studies. (2005). 'Jumping genes' contribute to the uniqueness of individual brains. Retrieved March 14, 2007, from http://genome.wellcome.ac.uk/doc_WTD020792.html.

Sylwester, R. (1995). *A celebration of neurons: An educator's guide to the human brain*. Alexandria, Virginia: ASCD.

Tomlinson, C. (1999). *The differentiated classroom: Responding to the needs of all learners*. Virginia: ASCD.

Chapter 2

Berman, P., & McLaughlin, M. W. (1978). *Federal programs supporting educational change*. Volume 8: Implementing and sustaining innovation. Santa Monica, CA: RAND.

Duffy, F. (2003). I think, therefore I am resistant to change. *Journal of Staff Development, 24*(1), 30–36. National Staff Development Council.

Gardner, H. (2006). *Changing minds: The art and science of changing our own and other people's minds*. Boston, MA: Harvard Business School Press.

Guskey, T. (2000). *Evaluating professional development*. Thousand Oaks, CA: Corwin Press.

Hall, G. E., & Hord, S. M. (1987). *Change in schools: Facilitating the process*. Albany, NY: State University of New York Press.

Hord, S., Rutherford, W., Huling-Austin, L., & Hall. G. (1987). *Taking charge of change*. Alexandria, Virginia: Association for Supervision and Curriculum Development.

Kise, J. A. G. (2006). *Differentiated coaching: A framework for helping teachers change*. California: Corwin Press.

Nash, O. (1959). Put back those whiskers, I know you. V*erses From 1929 On*. Boston: Little, Brown & Company.

Puckett, D. (2002). *Apple seeds: Reflections on the significance of the sowing*. Ohio: National Middle School Association.

Senge, P. M., Kleiner, A., Roberts, C., Ross, R. B., & Smith, B. J. (1994). *The fifth discipline fieldbook: Strategies and tools for building a learning organization*. New York: Currency Doubleday.

Spinelli, J. (2002). *Loser*. New York: HarperCollins Children's Books.

Tschannen-Moran, M., Hoy, A. W., & Hoy, W. K. (1998). Teacher efficacy: Its meaning and measure. *Review of Educational Research, 68*(2), 202–248.

Vogt, M. E. (2000). Content learning for students needing modifications: An issue of access. In M. McLaughlin & M. E. Vogt (eds.), *Creativity and innovation in content area teaching* (pp. 329–351). Norwood, MA: Christopher-Gordon.

Chapter 3

Alvermann, D. (1991). The discussion web: A graphic aid for learning across the curriculum. *The Reading Teacher*, October.

Association for Supervision and Curriculum Development. (2006). *Teaching the adolescent brain*. Four-part DVD. Alexandria, VA: ASCD.

Conlon, F., & Hudson, G., eds. (2005). *I wanna be sedated: 30 writers on parenting teenagers*. California: Seal Press.

Erlauer, L. (2003). *The brain-compatible classroom: Using what we know about learning to improve teaching*. Alexandria, VA: ASCD.

Gibbs, J. (2001). *Discovering gifts in middle school: Learning in a caring culture called TRIBES*. Windsor, CA: CenterSource Systems.

Jensen, E. (1998). *Teaching with the brain in mind*. Alexandria, VA: ASCD.

Johnson, D. W., & Johnson, R. T. (1992). *Creative controversy: Intellectual challenge in the classroom*. Edina, Minnesota: Interaction Book Company.

Manning, M. L. (1993). *Developmentally appropriate middle level schools*. Maryland: Association for Childhood Education International.

Nunley, K. (2003). *A student's brain: The parent/teacher manual*. New Hampshire: Morris Publishing.

Perlstein, L. (2003). *Not much, just chillin': The hidden lives of middle schoolers*. Toronto: Random House.

Puckett, D. (1999). "Adolescents" from *Reflections from a teacher's heart: The affective side of middle grades education*. Ohio: National Middle School Association.

Sousa, D. (2006). *How the brain learns*. 3rd ed. Thousand Oaks, CA: Corwin Press.

Strauch, B. (2003). *The primal teen: What the new discoveries about the teenage brain tell us about our kids*. New York: Anchor Books.

Thornburg, H. (1983) Can educational systems respond to the needs of early adolescents? *Journal of Early Adolescence*, 3, 32–36.

Wiggins, G., & McTighe, J. (2005). *Understanding by design.* Expanded 2nd ed. Alexandria, VA: Association for Supervision and Curriculum Development.

Willms, D. (2003). Personal communication—presentation at AERO conference, November 28, 2003.

Wolfe, P. (2001). *Brain matters: Translating research into classroom practice.* Alexandria, VA: ASCD.

Chapter 4

Applebome, P. (2005). The accidental boy scout, pp. 139–146 in *I wanna be sedated: 30 writers on parenting teenagers*, F. Conlon & G. Hudson (eds). Emeryville, CA: Seal Press.

Buckingham, M., & Coffman, C. (1999). *First, break all the rules: What the world's greatest managers do differently.* New York: Simon & Schuster.

Dunn, R., & Dunn, K. (1993). *Teaching secondary students through their individual learning styles: Practical approaches for grades 7–12.* Needham, Maine: Allyn & Bacon.

Gardner, H. (2006). *Changing minds: The art and science of changing our own and other people's minds.* Boston: Harvard Business School Press.

Gardner, H. (2006). *Multiple intelligences: New horizons.* New York: Basic Books.

Gardner, H. (1999). *Intelligence reframed: Multiple intelligences for the 21st century.* New York: Basic Books.

Gregorc, A. (1982). *Inside styles: Beyond the basics.* Columbia, CT: Gregorc Associates.

Hanson, J. R., & Dewing, T. (1990). *Research on the profiles of at-risk learners.* Research Monograph series. Moorestown, NJ: Institute for Studies in Analytic Psychology

Kise, J. (2006). *Differentiated coaching: A framework for helping teachers change.* Thousand Oaks, CA: Corwin Press.

Kolb, D. (1984). *Experiential learning: Experience as the source of learning and development.* Englewood Cliffs, NJ: Prentice Hall.

Liesveld, R., & Miller, J. (2005). *Teach with your strengths.* New York: Gallup Press.

McCarthy, B., & McCarthy, D. (2006). *Teaching around the 4MAT cycle: Designing instruction for diverse learners with diverse learning styles.* Thousand Oaks, CA: Corwin Press.

Moran, S., Kornhaber, M., & Gardner, H. (2006). Orchestrating multiple intelligences. *Educational Leadership* 64(1), 22–27.

Santa, C. M. (1988). *Content reading including study systems.* Dubuque, IA: Kendall-Hunt.

Silver, H., Strong, R., & Perini, M. (2000). *So each may learn: Integrating learning styles and multiple intelligences.* Alexandria, VA: ASCD.

Sternberg, R. (2006). Recognizing neglected strengths. *Educational Leadership*, 64(1), 30–35.

Sternberg, R. (1997). *Thinking styles.* New York: Cambridge University Press.

Sternberg, R. (1996). *Successful intelligence.* New York: Simon & Schuster.

Chapter 5

Allen, R. (2001). *Train smart: Perfect trainings every time.* San Diego: The Brain Store.

Barth, R. (1990). *Improving schools from within.* San Francisco: Jossey-Bass.

Benard, B. (2004). *Resiliency: What we have learned.* San Francisco: WestEd.

Bennis, W., & Biederman, P. W. (1997). *Organizing genius: The secrets of creative collaboration.* New York: Addison-Wesley.

Bluestein, J. (2001). *Creating emotionally safe schools: A guide for educators and parents.* Deerfield Beach, Florida: Health Communications Inc.

Kittle, P. (2005). *The greatest catch: A life in teaching.* Portsmouth, New Hampshire: Heinemann.

Kounin, J. (1970). *Discipline and group management in classrooms.* New York: Holt, Rinehart & Winston.

Marzano, R., Gaddy, B., Foseid, M., Foseid, M., & Marzano, J. (2005). *A handbook for classroom management that works.* Alexandria, VA: ASCD.

Marzano, R., Marzano, J., & Pickering, D. (2003). *Classroom management that works: Research-based strategies for every teacher.* Alexandria, Virginia: ASCD.

Mendler, A. N. (2001). *Connecting with students.* Virginia: ASCD.

Myers, C. B., & Simpson, D. J. (1998). *Re-creating schools: Places where everyone learns and likes it.* Thousand Oaks, CA: Corwin.

Palmer, P. (1998). *The courage to teach: Exploring the inner landscape of a teacher's life.* San Francisco: Jossey Bass.

Schaps, E. (1999). The child development project: In search of synergy. *Principal*, vol. 79, no. 1.

References

Sergiovanni, T. (1994). *Building community in schools.* San Francisco: Jossey-Bass.

Chapter 6

Brooks, J. G. (2002). *Schooling for life: Reclaiming the essence of learning.* Alexandria, Viriginia: ASCD.

Darling-Hammond, L. (1998). Teacher learning that supports student learning. *Educational Leadership* 55(5), 6–11. Alexandria, Virginia: ASCD.

Dweck, C., & Bempechat, J. (1983). Children's theories of intelligence: Consequences for learning. In S. Paris, G. Olson, & H. Stevenson (eds.), *Learning and motivation in the classroom.* New Jersey: Lawrence Erlbaum Associates.

Gabella, M. (1993). *The unsure thing: Ambiguity and uncertainty as a context for inquiry.* Paper presented to the Annual Meeting of the American Educational Research Association.

Hume, K. (2001). Seeing shades of gray: Developing a knowledge-building community through science. In G. Wells (ed.), *Action, talk and text: Learning and teaching through inquiry.* New York: Teachers College Press.

Little, J. (1986). *Hey world, here I am!* Toronto: Kids Can Press.

McNeil, L. (1986). *Contradictions of control: School structure and school knowledge.* New York: Routledge & Kegan Paul.

McTighe, J., & Wiggins, G. (2004). *Understanding by design professional development workbook.* Alexandria, Virginia: ASCD.

Michalko, M. (2001). *Cracking creativity: The secrets of creative genius.* Berkeley, California: Ten Speed Press.

National Middle School Association (NMSA). (2003). *This we believe: Successful schools for young adolescents.* Ohio: National Middle School Association.

Schenck, E. (2007). *The Houdini solution: Put creativity and innovation to work by thinking inside the box.* Toronto: McGraw Hill.

Stodolsky, S. (1988). *The subject matters: Classroom activity in math and social studies.* Chicago: University of Chicago Press.

Wiggins, G., & McTighe, J. (2005). *Understanding by design*, 2nd ed. Alexandria, Virginia: ASCD.

Chapter 7

Beers, K. (2003). *When kids can't read, what teachers can do: A guide for teachers 6–12.* New Hampshire: Heinemann.

Covey, S. (1989). *The seven habits of highly effective people.* New York: Simon & Schuster.

Elbow, P. (1973). *Writing without teachers.* London: Oxford University Press.

Levine, M. (2003). *The myth of laziness.* New York: Simon & Schuster.

Marzano, R., Pickering, D., & Pollock, J. (2001). *Classroom instruction that works: Research-based strategies for increasing student achievement.* Viriginia: ASCD.

Ogle, D. M. (1986). KWL: A teaching model that develops active reading of expository text. *The Reading Teacher, 39,* 564–570.

Popham, W. J. (2003). *Test better, teach better: The instructional role of assessment.* Virginia: ASCD.

Tompkins, G. (2004). *50 literacy strategies step by step*, 2nd ed. New Jersey: Pearson Education.

Van de Walle, J., & Lovin, L. (2006). *Teaching student-centered mathematics grades 5–8, volume 3.* Professional e-Book. Toronto: Pearson Education.

Chapter 8

Atwell, N. (2002). *Lessons that change writers.* Portsmouth, New Hampshire: Heinemann.

Bennett, B., & Rolheiser, C. (2001). *Beyond Monet: The artful science of instructional integration.* Ajax, Ontario: Bookation.

Cotton, K. (1991). *Close-up #11: Teaching thinking skills.* Retrieved July 31, 2007, from Northwest Regional Educational Laboratory's School Improvement Research Series website: http://www.nwrel.org/scpd/sirs/6/cu11.html.

Egan, K. (1992). *Imagination in teaching and learning: The middle school years.* Chicago: University of Chicago Press.

Emmer, E. T., Evertson, C. M., & Anderson. L. M. (1980). Effective classroom management at the beginning of the school year. *The Elementary School Journal,* 80(5), pp. 219–231.

Foster, G., Sawicki, E., Schaeffer, H., & Zelinski, V. (2002). *I think, therefore I learn!* Markham, Ontario: Pembroke Publishers.

Friend, M., Bursuck, W., & Hutchinson, N. L. (1998). *Including exceptional students: A practical guide for classroom teachers.* Scarborough, Ontario: Allyn & Bacon.

Fuchs, D., Fuchs, L. S., Mathes, P. G., & Simmons, D. C. (1997). Peer-assisted learning strategies: Making classrooms more responsive to diversity. *American Educational Research Journal, 34,* pp. 174–206.

Harmin, M. (1994). *Inspiring active learning: A handbook for teachers*. Virginia: ASCD.

Johnson, D., & Johnson, R. (1999) *Learning together and alone: Cooperative, competitive, and individualistic learning*. Boston: Allyn & Bacon.

Lou, Y., Abrami, P. C., Spence, J. C., Paulsen, C., Chamber, B., & d'Apollonio, S. (1996). Within-class grouping: A meta-analysis. *Journal of Educational Research, 75*, pp. 69–77.

Marsh, C. (2004). *Key concepts for understanding curriculum*. New York: RoutledgeFalmer.

Marzano, R. (2003). *What works in schools: Translating research into action*. Virginia: ASCD.

Nuthall, G. (1999). The way students learn: Acquiring knowledge from an integrated science and social studies unit. *The Elementary School Journal, 99*(4), pp. 303–341.

Shellard, E., & Protheroe, N. (2000). Effective teaching: How do we know it when we see it? *The Informed Educator Series*. Arlington, VA: Educational Research Services.

Sousa, D. (2006). *How the brain learns*, 3rd ed. California: Corwin Press.

Stronge, J., Tucker, P., & Hindman, J. (2004). *Handbook for qualities of effective teachers*. Virginia: ASCD.

Whitener, E. (1989). A meta-analytic review of the effect on learning of the interaction between prior achievement and instructional support. *Review of Educational Research, 59*(1), pp. 65–86.

Wiggins, G., & McTighe, J. (2005). *Understanding by design*, 2nd ed. Alexandria, Virginia: ASCD.

Chapter 9

Alexander, P. A., Kulikowich, J. M., & Schulze, S. K. (1994). How subject-matter knowledge affects recall and interest. *American Educational Research Journal, 31*(2), pp. 313–337.

Anderson, L., & Kathwohl, D. A. (2001). *Taxonomy for learning, teaching, and assessing: A revision of Bloom's taxonomy of educational objectives*. New York: Longman.

Beers, K. (2003). *When kids can't read, what teachers can do: A guide for teachers, 6–12*. New Hampshire: Heinemann.

Bennett, B., & Rolheiser, C. (2001). *Beyond Monet: The artful science of instructional integration*. Ajax, Ontario: VISUTronX.

Brown, A., Campione, J., & Day, J. (1981). Learning to learn: On training students to learn from texts. *Educational Researcher, 10*, 14–24.

Buzan, T. (1993). *The mind map book: Radiant thinking*. Woodlands, London: BBC Books.

Cotton, K. (2001). Close-up #5: Classroom questioning. Retrieved August 4, 2007, from Northwest Regional Educational Laboratory's School Improvement Series website http://www.nwrel.org/scpd/sirs/3/cu5.html.

DiCecco, V. M., & Gleason, M. M. (2002). Using graphic organizers to attain relational knowledge from expository text. *Journal of Learning Disabilities, 35*, 306–320.

Fountas, I., & Pinnell, G. (2006) *Teaching for comprehending and fluency: Thinking, talking, and writing about reading, K–8*. Portsmouth, New Hampshire: Heinemann.

Gall, M. (1984). Synthesis of research on teachers' questioning. *Educational Leadership, 42*(3), 40–47.

Gallagher, K. (2004). *Deeper reading: Comprehending challenging texts, 4–12*. Portland, Maine: Stenhouse Publishers.

Kajder, S. (2006). *Bringing the outside in: Visual ways to engage reluctant readers*. Portland, Maine: Stenhouse Publishers.

MacOn, J., Bewell, D., & Vogt, M. (1991). *Responses to literature*. Newark, Delaware: International Reading Association.

Marzano, R., Norford, J., Paynter, D., Pickering, D., & Gaddy, B. (2001). *A handbook for classroom instruction that works*. Virginia: ASCD.

Marzano, R., Pickering, D., & Pollock, J. (2001). *Classroom instruction that works*. Virginia: ASCD.

McKenzie, G. R. (1979). Data charts: A crutch for helping pupils organize reports. *Language Arts, 56*, 784–788.

Neeld, E. C. (1986). *Writing*, 2nd ed. Glenview, Illinois: Scott Foresman.

Pink, D. H. (2005). *A whole new mind: Why right-brainers will rule the future*. New York: Penguin Books.

Raphael, T. (1986). Teaching question answer relationships, revisited. *The Reading Teacher, 39*, 516–522.

Robb, L. (2000). *Teaching reading in middle school*. Toronto: Scholastic Professional Books.

Ruef, K. (1992). *The private eye: Looking/thinking by analogy*. Seattle, Washington: The Private Eye Project.

Sousa, D. (2006). *How the brain learns*. Thousand Oaks, CA: Corwin.

Susskind, E. (1979). Encouraging teachers to encourage children's curiosity: A pivotal competence. *Journal of Clinical Child Psychology, 8*, 101–106.

Tovani, C. (2000). *I read it, but I don't get it: Comprehension strategies for adolescent readers*. Portland, Maine: Stenhouse.

Walsh, J., & Sattes, B. (2005). *Quality questioning: Research-based practice to engage every learner*. Thousand Oaks, CA: Corwin.

Wood, K. (1984). Probable passages: A writing strategy. *The Reading Teacher*, 37, 496–499.

Wormeli, R. (2005). *Summarization in any subject: 50 techniques to improve student learning*. Virginia: ASCD.

Chapter 10

Bluestein, J. (2001). *Creating emotionally safe schools: A guide for educators and parents*. Deerfield Beach, Florida: Health Communications.

Earl, L. (2003). *Assessment as learning: Using classroom assessment to maximize student learning*. Thousand Oaks, CA: Corwin Press.

Fitzgerald, L. (2004). *If at first … how great people turned setbacks into great success*. Kansas City, Missouri: Andrews & McMeel Publishing.

Gregory, K., Cameron, C., & Davies, A. (2000). *Knowing what counts: Self-assessment and goal-setting*. Merville, B.C.: Connections Publishing.

Gregory, K., Cameron, C., & Davies, A. (1997). *Knowing what counts: Setting and using criteria*. Merville, B.C.: Connections Publishing.

Levine, M. (2003). *The myth of laziness*. Toronto: Simon & Schuster.

Marzano, R., Pickering, D., & Pollock, J. (2001). *Classroom instruction that works: Research-based strategies for increasing student achievement*. Virginia: ASCD.

Rolheiser, C., & Ross, J. (2000). Student self-evaluation—What do we know? *Orbit*, Classroom Assessment Issue, Vol. 30, No. 4, 33–36. Toronto: OISE/UT.

Stiggins, R., Arter, J., Chappuis, J., & Chappuis, S. (2004). *Classroom assessment for student learning: Doing it right—using it well*. Portland, Oregon: Assessment Training Institute.

Vygotsky, L. S. (1978). *Mind in society*. M. Cole, V. John-Steiner, S. Scribner, & E. Souberman (eds). Cambridge, MA: Harvard University Press.

Wells, G., ed. (2001). *Action, talk and text: Learning and teaching through inquiry*. New York: Teachers College Press.

Wiliam, D. (2006). Assessment: Learning communities can use it to engineer a bridge connecting teaching and learning. *Journal of the National Staff Development Association (JSD) Assessment*. Vol. 27, No. 1, Winter 2006, 16–20.

Wormeli, R. (2006). *Fair isn't always equal: Assessing and grading in the differentiated classroom*. Portland, Maine: Stenhouse Publishers.

Chapter 11

Andrade, H. G. (2000). Using rubrics to promote thinking and learning. *Educational Assessment*, 57, 13–18.

Cooper, D. (2007). *Talk about assessment: Strategies and tools to improve learning*. Toronto: Thomson Professional Learning.

Davies, A. (2000). *Making classroom assessment work*. Courtenay, B.C.: Connections Publishing.

Jackson, C., & Larkin, M. (2002). RUBRIC: Teaching students to use grading rubrics. *Teaching Exceptional Children*, 35, 40–45.

Langer, G. M., Colton, A. B., & Goff, L. S. (2003). *Collaborative analysis of student work: Improving teaching and learning*. Alexandria, Virginia: ASCD.

Lewin, L., & Shoemaker, B. J. (1998). *Great performances: Creating classroom-based assessment tasks*. Virginia: ASCD.

Marzano, R. (2006). *Classroom assessment and grading that work*. Virginia: ASCD.

McGhee, A. (2000). *Shadow baby*. New York: Picador.

Pollock, J. (2007). *Improving student learning one teacher at a time*. Virginia: ASCD.

Stroud, B. (2005). *The patchwork path: A quilt map to freedom*. Cambridge, Massachusetts: Candlewick Press.

Wiggins, G., & McTighe, J. (2005). *Understanding by design*, 2nd ed. Virginia: ASCD.

Wiliam, D. (2006). Assessment: Learning communities can use it to engineer a bridge connecting teaching and learning. *Journal of Staff Development* 27, 1, 16–20. National Staff Development Council.

Wormeli, R. (2006a). Differentiated grading. Presentation at National Middle School Association Conference, November 2006, Nashville, Tennessee.

Wormeli, R. (2006b). *Fair isn't always equal: Assessing and grading in the differentiated classroom*. Portland, Maine: Stenhouse Publishers.

Index

Index

Index

Index